AF580764

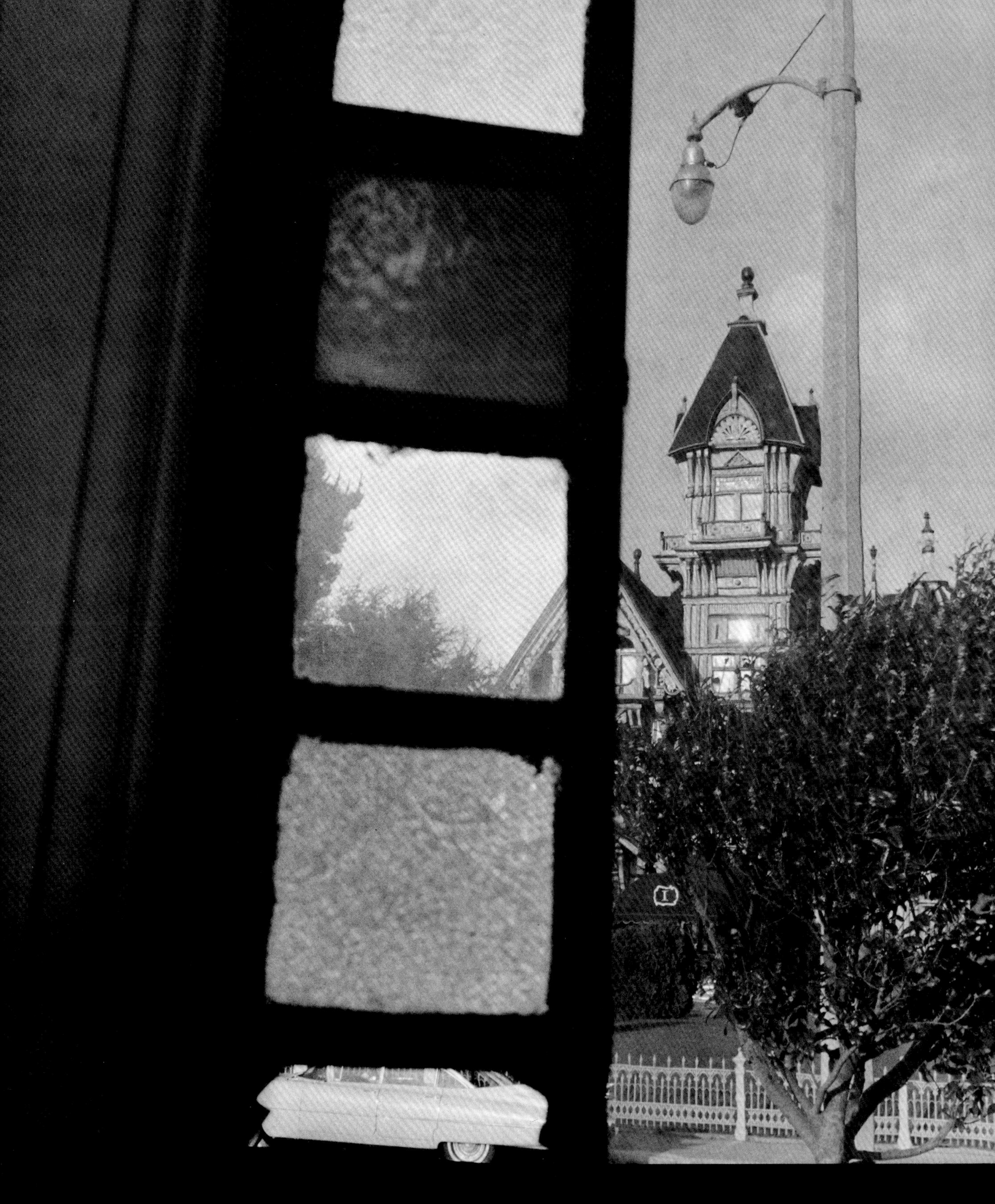

Frontispiece:

116 *Carson Mansion with Parked Automobile Seen through Cross-barred Window.*
Eureka, California, 1960.

GUTMANN

August 24 – October 20, 1985

Art Gallery of Ontario
Musée des beaux-arts de l'Ontario
Toronto, Canada

Canadian Cataloguing in Publication Data

Sutnik, Maia-Mari.
Gutmann

Catalogue to accompany an exhibition held at the Art Gallery of Ontario, Aug. 24-Oct. 20, 1985.
Bibliography: p.
ISBN 0-919777-18-X

1. Gutmann, John – Exhibitions. I. Gutmann, John. II. Art Gallery of Ontario. III. Title.
TR647.G87 1985   770'.92'4   C85-099440-3

ISBN 0-919777-18-X

The Art Gallery of Ontario is generously funded by the Ministry of Citizenship and Culture, Province of Ontario; the Municipality of Metropolitan Toronto; and the Government of Canada through the Museum Assistance Programmes of the National Museums of Canada, and the Department of Communication (Cultural Property Export and Import Act); and the Canada Council.

Design: Ivan Holmes
Separations: Rodney Spencer Graphics Inc.
Typesetting: Canadian Composition Limited
Printing: Cliff and Walters

Cover:
20 *Turning to Look*. 1935.

CONTENTS

PREFACE

The exhibition of John Gutmann's photographs is one in a continuing series of exhibitions by leading figures in modern photography. The Art Gallery of Ontario has shown retrospective surveys of the work of Robert Frank (1980), Bill Brandt (1982), and Harry Callahan (1983), among many other exhibitions that have investigated the history and nature of photography.

This exhibition focusses on the long and distinctive photographic career of John Gutmann, whose vision has been pervasive, yet he has remained by choice an elusive figure. Since 1933 he has worked outside the mainstream of twentieth-century American photography, taking no part in the prevailing conventions and esthetic debates in photographic practice. Instead he has engaged in many endeavours, distinguishing himself as an accomplished painter, professor of art at San Francisco State University, a noted collector of primitive art, and a documentary filmmaker. It is as a photographer, however, that his creative vision becomes most accessible and revealing. Gutmann has not been overtly concerned with the process of making art in photography, the art has been coincidental. Central to his perception as an image maker is that the medium provided an opportunity to view the world and to imagine it at the same time. His vision responded to subject content and materialized into particular thematic ideas that established an "archive" of categories. Gutmann's attitude and methodology of working, and its underpinning, is discussed in the essay provided by Maia-Mari Sutnik, who organized the exhibition. Michael Mitchell, photographer and writer, has also contributed an essay – a lively account of Gutmann in the "new world" of America and photography.

We are thankful to Jeffrey Fraenkel, Fraenkel Gallery, San Francisco, for making Gutmann's prints available, and of course to John Gutmann for lending the vintage prints from his personal holdings. It is our good fortune to have benefited from John Gutmann's collaboration. We are greatly indebted to him for his advice and assistance which has guided this important exhibition of his work, which we are extremely pleased to host.

William J. Withrow,
Director

ACKNOWLEDGEMENTS

With due recognition of the San Francisco Museum of Modern Art's large retrospective of John Gutmann's photographs in 1976, this exhibition is the most comprehensive survey of his work to date. Although this claim must be seen as an attempt to assemble a cross-representation of Gutmann's *oeuvre* from a very large archive of negatives and vintage prints, it makes no claim to be a definitive statement on Gutmann. Since the Center for Creative Photography, University of Arizona, will eventually become the custodian of Gutmann's negatives, it is hoped that they will pursue research and study to present his work in the broader context of photography as a whole.

Gutmann over his long career has exhibited his photographs in more than sixty exhibitions. Prior to 1945 he also exhibited paintings and drawings extensively, after which his attention focussed predominantly on photography as a form of creative expression. The extensive bibliography in this catalogue summarizes the vast appearance in print of his photographic work. It should be noted that all sources for magazine illustrations, particularly the European and early American, could not be published with complete information. Every effort has been made to make this first bibliography as comprehensive as possible.

It has been an enormous privilege to become familiar with Gutmann's extraordinary vision. He has held himself at a distance from the centres of photographic activity; yet, at the same time, he has stayed fully abreast of artistic activity in all the visual arts. He applied his extraordinary commitment equally to his position as professor of art, and his own critical standards and methodology in his photographic work. I am deeply indebted to his advice, insight, and willingness to reveal and reconstruct his exciting and productive careers in painting, teaching, film, and photography.

Many persons have assisted with the exhibition and catalogue in various capacities. I am first and foremost grateful to Dr. Katharine Lochnan, Curator of Prints and Drawings, whose interest in and support for the continuous development of an exhibition program of photography, has made this exhibition possible. I am also thankful to Dr. Roald Nasgaard, Chief Curator, for his critical comments regarding the manuscript. Other members of the Art Gallery of Ontario staff have collaborated in many capacities. Barry Simpson, Registrar; Cynthia Ross, Traffic Manager; Akira Yoshikawa, Art Storage Coordinator; Anthony Jones, Deputy Chief Curator/Administration; Ralph Ingleton, Practitioner/Conservation; Bernie Oldcorn, Head/Technical Services and his staff; Alan Terakawa, Production Coordinator; Catherine Van Baren, Editor; and Ivan Holmes who expertly designed this catalogue. Special acknowledgement is due to Nina Levitt who undertook the task of structuring and verifying the exhaustive bibliographic references, and who also coordinated the numerous tasks of preparatory work for the catalogue and the exhibition. With her assistance the tasks of assembling the research was made infinitely less difficult.

I am most appreciative of the assistance of Tess Taconis, for generously undertaking research; David Harris, Lecturer in the history of photography, Concordia University, for his valuable suggestions regarding the essays; and Kathryn Dean as editor of the manuscript. The assistance of Carol Lindsay, Chief Librarian, the *Toronto Star*, and Larry Nelson, Hamilton Central Library, is also acknowledged for supplying illustrations for reproduction. I am extremely thankful to Michael Mitchell for contributing a sprightly personal view of Gutmann's entry into photography, for his photograph of Gutmann reproduced in this catalogue, and mostly for sharing my enthusiasm for Gutmann's work.

Jeffrey Fraenkel and Alain Dupuy of Fraenkel Gallery have been most helpful with the loans to the exhibition.

Finally, a deep measure of gratitude is due to Lew Thomas for bringing Gutmann's photography to my attention, first in the book *Photography and Language*, edited by Thomas in 1977, and later for introducing me to Gutmann. His enthusiasm and understanding of the significance of Gutmann's work was an early inspiration for this exhibition. Throughout, Thomas' insight has been most valuable, as has the dialogue about our somewhat divergent approaches to Gutmann's work. I am also thankful to him and his family, Natalie and Kesa Thomas, for accommodating my visits in San Francisco.

MMS

THE PHOTOGRAPHY OF JOHN GUTMANN

John Gutmann's photography is a synthesis of both social and esthetic concerns; it springs from his impulse to respond clearly, to capture an immediate impression, and to define its visual possibilities. His remarkable vision is offset by a spontaneous expression of imagery that fuses reality with the illusory and the allusive. These expressive polarities of his photography have been examined in their co-existence in Gutmann's collection of images in *The Restless Decade*,[1] his view of America during the 1930s. The importance of this dualism and Gutmann's methodology of organizing and cross-referencing content has been noted by Lew Thomas: "Far from undermining the coherency...the density of visual information and complexity of focus prevalent in Gutmann's photographs serve to create a system of resonance between the images and their designated categories."[2] Gutmann's categorical spectrum originates as cognizant responses: first, to the requirements of photojournalism and, second, to personal choices of themes suited to the tenor of his experiences and the general times. These categories and sustained themes: Documents of the Street, Automobile Culture, The Depression, Foreign Cultures, Women, Death, Graffiti, Structured Vision, and an enigmatic category, Beyond Reality, are explored as different modes of expression. While emphasis is on subject matter, Gutmann's expression of it appears stylistically diversified. Some images reflect distinct categories, others signal cross-referentially, and in others, form and content transpose and fuse. "The content to me is very important," states Gutmann,

but I like it when [*the photograph*] *is also enigmatic. If you don't know what it is, you begin to speculate, and that is what I want. I want people to be interested in my pictures, to say: "What does it mean? Is there anything else?" And I don't feel there are any absolutes in life.... In my philosophy in life, everything is related to something else. Every experience is relative...which I find very exciting, because of the contrasts.*[3]

The origin of Gutmann's attitude and approach have not yet been fully explored. This survey of his work will examine the diversity of his expression, and the roots of that diversity, introducing interpretive possibilities. Central to his attitude is that photography provides us with the opportunity to view the world and to imagine it at the same time beyond its immediate representation.

The photograph of Berkeley's 1936 *Leap-Year Parade* (no. 31) is an example of cross-referentiality. It is at once a Document of the Street and an image in the realm of Beyond Reality. The narrative point of view is evident in the concentration on representational information: a crowd gazing at a fraternity parade. It captures students in frolic and conveys the spirit of the socio-political forces besetting the nation in the midst of the Depression. But the fraternity's cynicism toward Karl Marx brings to life a larger drama, a parody of the communism that inspired mass action and militancy, and sought to correct America's social ills. The impact of this central narrative is blurred, however, as are the categorical demarcations of the image. The scene can also be viewed as an ambivalent event, with suggestions that go beyond reality. The consequences of the event are unknown. It alludes to the diabolical; the ritualistic devil figure standing on the hearse gives an intimation of the spiritual corruption that many Americans associated with Marxist ideology. The picture's absurd elements also legitimize and reinforce the symbolic and metaphorical aspects of the encounter. Is Marx and his "Red Hots" out of step for America; is "on to Moscow" bon voyage or good riddance? Gutmann creates a new climate for the image by providing a caption that is partially external to its visual substance. The "Leap-Year" – the year with a day out of step – is ironically a contrived calendrical revolution. Gutmann's title sums up the metaphoric and the objective character of the picture. It is as dependent on the reality of its content as it is on Gutmann's form of thought and mode of imagination. The unifying ground is the photographer and his preoccupation with *this* moment. Gutmann seizes a complex set of circumstances with a clear personal vision of interaction between assigned categories.

From the outset, Gutmann's photographic vision has been clear. It has not been hindered by any overriding need to define the nature of the medium, or to use the medium to define spiritual needs, as is exemplified in the work of Alfred Stieglitz and Edward Weston. Nor did he use the medium to describe the political views of a Paul Strand, or to express collective purposes, as in the case of The Photo League and the Farm Security Administration photographers. On the contrary, the substance in Gutmann's vision is of a wide categorical nature. Gutmann's principle of psychology of "man and his world," and his visual intensity, speed, and response to it change not only with the subject matter at hand, but also with the permutations of the possibilities within the subject. The objective and the subjective merge, and form and structure change radically from picture to picture. Gutmann states his attitude:

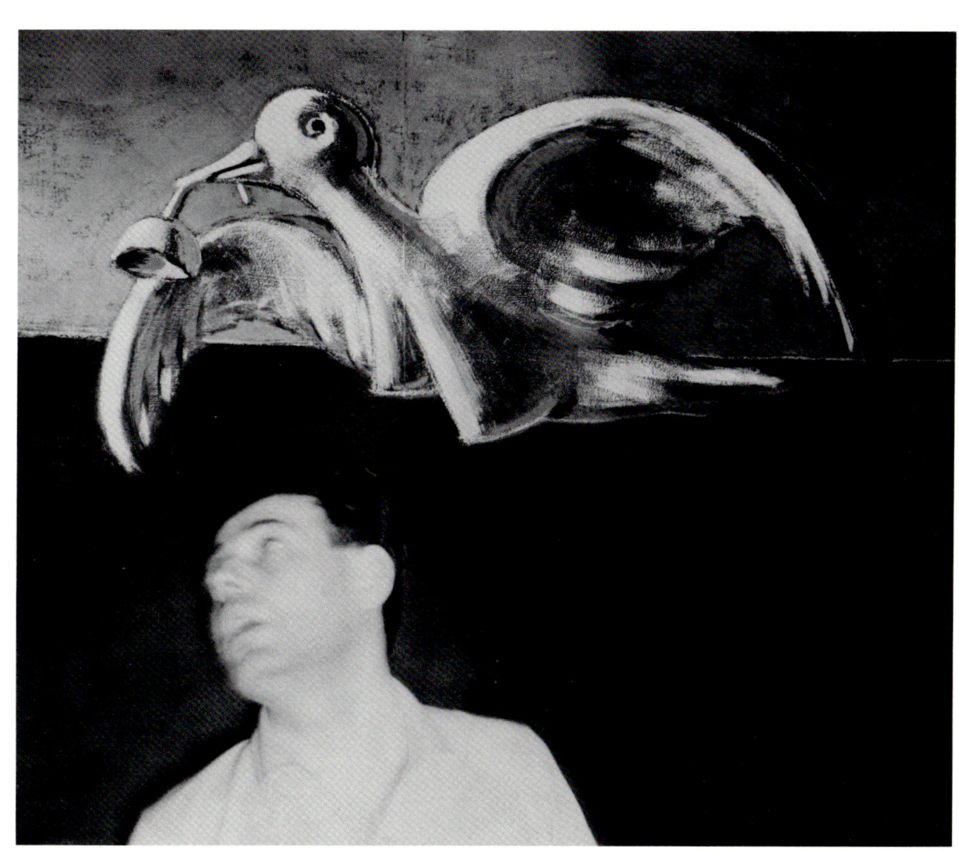

John Gutmann, *Self-portrait with Lovebird*. 1934.

My philosophy is – this is my photograph. I can do anything I want. I don't feel so driven by the idea that I must make the ideal, final version. Sometimes I experiment. I look at the subject from different view points. Sometimes I pair images. I think in life, there are different kinds of interpretations possible for any of us. People associate differently and the effect is sometimes completely different psychologically.[4]

Gutmann's view rests on the acceptance of a reality rendered by the camera's mechanical precision, appearing once as objective reality, but in which the subjective may equally dominate. It is then not a question of veracity – how true or real the world of Gutmann's pictures is – but as he has declared, it is "as I saw it" and selected emphatically "by my choice".[5]

In Gutmann's first experimental roll of film, exposed in Berlin, characteristics emerge of the visual energy and ideas that, later, he would enlarge upon and assimilate into the dazzling spectrum of his vision of American culture. *Autumn in Charlottenburg*, 1933 (no. 1), the earliest Document of the Street, introduces Gutmann's interest in content and the structure of the image. The scene at first appears tranquil. A geometric composition divided by verticals, it also suggests a back and forth motion through its treatment of space: the verticals shift from tree to tree to lamppost, while the perspective of the street and roofs of houses leads to a misty infinity. At the same time, street life – cars, casual strollers, a dog – move forward, and the eye is pulled to an SA.SS flag and banners, the presentiments of fatal veneration. It is a thought-provoking and compelling view of the city. In *Goodbye Berlin*, 1933 (no. 3), Gutmann demonstrates by stressing angularity and tilted framing, his immediate ability to see cogently through the lens.

I felt my new camera was an extension of my eyes. I sometimes look at things this way – up and down. Why not do the same with photography? Of course I'm not the only photographer to get away from the conventional idea of the verticals in buildings.... It was a normal thing an intelligent person using a new medium like this would try to explore.[6]

This early experiment in framing the image transcends mere exploration to become an evocative personal farewell, internalizing Gutmann's melancholy – a poetic metaphor for the city he was soon to leave behind.

October, 1933 (no. 2), part of Gutmann's first experiment, exposes the allusive quality that was to recur more forcefully in later images. Yet, the presence of the dark-clad young woman looking into a shop window is not merely allusive. It is the strongly felt reality of the shrouded reflection in the window. The interior of the window is shadowy and mysterious. An ominous dagger-shaped view of Berlin houses splits the figure from her reflection. An image of strange geometry – broken, folded, and multidimensional – it suggests a dramatic forecast of the enormity that would descend upon the nation. The fusion of observed reality with irrational elements is exploited not for mere visual effect. At the time Gutmann experimented, there was no reason for him to photograph except to learn about the camera. Yet, instinctively he felt that photography in one sense was not only a process for recording representation, but also conveyed the unstated, the invisible, or even truth before the actual moment. Now, under a different set of circumstances than 1933, we

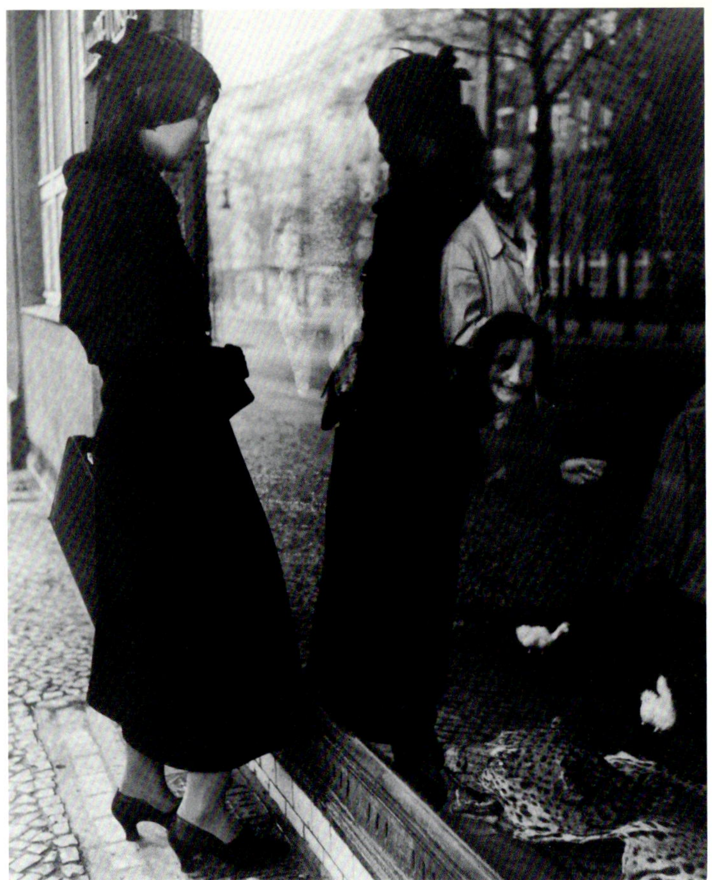

2 *October*. Berlin, 1933.

can return to experimental images time and time again and perceive a greater statement, a wider understanding. While such conclusions may strike one as convenient, photographs imprint our memory. They force us to recall our past and challenge the limits of our consciousness. Through an early trial period Gutmann's perception of a hidden world is made visible.

Women as subjects have attracted Gutmann. *Memory of Friedel*, 1933 (no. 4) is a prelude to his most sustained theme. With admiration for his subjects, he has revealed not only his most sensual but also his most self-reflexive images. As a group, they reveal a relationship that combines the totality of his vision to variegated relationships in his personal life, on which Gutmann's discreetness is as judicious as his subjects are mysterious. They tell no secrets: the nude, aloof *Wanda*, 1935 (no. 22) with white shoes; the sensuously reposed *Nude on Couch*, 1937 (no. 49); the compassionate silence of *The Sisters*, 1960 (no. 113); the clear beauty of the nurses of *All-Black Flint-Goodridge Hospital*, 1937 (no. 41); and *Cup of Coffee and Cigarette*, 1950 (no. 103), a portrait of Gutmann's beautiful late wife, artist Gerrie von Pribosic. In the composition of these works, he has extracted elements from his training in painting and drawing, which recall precedents in those Expressionist works in which line and form are essential resolutions. At the same time, these subjects define a different set of concerns. The allusion is clearly to "woman," transformed into a new subject, conceived by Gutmann's own internalizing responses. No longer is their image a reproduceable facsimile or a transcription; it is linked with a realm that fuses the universal "woman" myth and Gutmann's consciousness, a private realm where seductive expression resides. Gutmann's women are not dissimilar to Man Ray's women. In André Breton's response to Ray's portraits in his "*THE visage of THE woman*," he also describes the essence of the theme of women in Gutmann's work: "It needed the eye of a great hunter, the patience, the sense of movement pathetically right when a balance, transient besides, occurred in the expression of a face, between dream and action."[7]

When considering Gutmann's photography, his relationship to the visual arts must not be isolated from the sum of ideas that evolved during the complex Weimar culture before 1933. The sense of self as creator may be attributed to Gutmann's vigorous studies in art during the 1920s at the Künst Academie of Breslau. There he distinguished himself to qualify for the master student program with Otto Mueller (1874–1930). Mueller's broad, simplified, unidealized figures in nature partly inspired the expressive spontaneity that characterizes much of Gutmann's own paintings. By 1928, Gutmann had earned his master's degree and already found teaching jobs in art. He also held a one-man exhibition (1931) of paintings and drawings at the historic Gurlitt Gallery in Berlin where Mueller and members of Die Brücke had exhibited their forceful paintings sixteen years earlier. It is also through his association with the Expressionists that Gutmann discovered his lifelong passion for African and indigenous folk art forms, which he has over the years collected significantly. The Berlin in which Gutmann found himself was one in which the creative expression of the avant-garde artists, writers, and filmmakers was closely interwoven with socio-political ideologies. They aspired to a view of a hopeful new world, and to take the modern movement into previously unknown areas. Experimental ideas prospered with cultural links: the continuance of Constructivism, the new Soviet cinema, and Vladimir Mayakovsky's magazine *LEF*. All played a role in uniting the problems, shared by many Germans, of a functional, technologically conscious, and socially oriented mid-European culture.[8] Germany's fascination with the "picturesque myth of the skyscraper-cum-cowboy civilization,"[9] and with the perceived industrial efficiency of American cities, as projected by the media, provided new sources for the arts. "Amerikanismus" emerged during the mid-1920s and was reflected in titles such as *Die Stadt: Bilder der Grossstadt* (drawings and woodcuts by Frans Masereel), *The Big City* (ballet by Kurt Jooss), *The Street* (film by Karl Grune), and *Amerika: Bilderbuch eines Architekten* (Erich Mendelsohn photographs). This book also inspired Bertold Brecht's play *In the Jungle of Cities*. Cities of New York, Chicago, Detroit, played a part in strengthening the role of the city theme. The potency of American cinema, jazz, and sports, became new sources of artistic forms, which were explored by painters and photographers alike. It is not surprising that Gutmann chose to photograph the metropolitan milieu of America, where he responded with excitement and acute observation to characterize the popular emblems of America.

The Weimar was an era dominated by technology: reconstruction and the mechanization of industry motivated artists to concern themselves with design and architecture. The experimental in photography found widespread practice in Paris and in the Soviet Union, but it was in Germany that the advances were made, and the power of the camera fully exploited. Photography gained its strength as the result of two things. "First there was the productivist ethic of self-subordination to the 'social command' of a new industrial world, now strengthened by the awareness that photography was essentially a democratic medium which all classes were beginning to use. Second there was the rapid advance of photographic technology...."[10] It was, however, the photography in the illustrated magazines and in photoreportage that was the greatest source of fascination for Gutmann. He recalls:

...my girlfriend and I, we would sit in café houses for four or five hours reading journals...foreign papers and many magazines. I would see a lot of photographs, but I never analyzed them. I think Salomon was perhaps the only name familiar to me. Layouts by Umbo, Citroën, and others, because of the content. I payed little attention to names, but Salomon's pictures I found at first probably quite interesting because of their political subjects... but I was exposed to so much.... It [Berlin] was the greatest city in the world at the time I lived there.[11]

In 1931 Gutmann exhibited in the ambitious Berliner Secession. He felt a promising career ahead. Working on further post-graduate studies in art, painting and making contacts with artists and intellectuals, he was becoming part of the climate: the rational, the irrational, the theoretical, and the fascinating creative ferment. Gutmann registered his experiences and believes that his impressions were preserved: "One cannot avoid the subconscious to form a visual foundation."[12] But after a brief job as art editor of Berlin's *Neue Revue* magazine, Gutmann knew by the late summer of 1933 that there were no options. Due to Hitler's regime he had to leave Germany.

Gutmann's entry into photography that year is now almost legendary.[13] For him photography became the expedient solution to gain political safety and to make a living in America:

...When I came to this country I tried to find a job as a teacher which because of the Depression was impossible.... As an artist it was ridiculous to hope to be able to make money...all American artists were starving. I really went to photography out of a need to try to make some money in this country.... That was the main reason I took up photography. And then I discovered right away I was fascinated with this new medium of seeing. It was a new medium! It was making its own rules for me. I experimented with that machine and tried to find out what it and I could do. It was completely different than working with a brush.... I found out very easily and very fast that this medium has its own characteristics.... I taught myself and the camera taught me. I had never had a camera, never was *interested to be a photographer, until the necessity arose. I had absolutely no insecurity at all that I could make good photographs. From the beginning I felt I was well equipped visually because I was very secure as a painter.*[14]

On the boat to America Gutmann's experiments with the camera led to confidence in intuitive play that merged his subject matter with his imagination. *The Initiation*, 1933 (no. 6) is an early picture of an absurd performance with sharp and linear exaggeration. The precise event eludes definition, is removed from its actual context as an element of irrationality shines through it. Gutmann's recognition of the medium's capacity to project images of a surrealist appearance appealed to his investigations.

It's the element of luck and chance which makes really photography more the surrealistic medium than any other medium. Because of the chance element in photography it is more present than in painting, which is really more deliberate, more planned... but photography takes advantage of chance and then ends up with something surprising.[15]

Gutmann never considered himself a Surrealist, but has a clear understanding of its aims and Breton's enterprise of the "purely inner model," *automatism*, the subconscious, and dreams. In Breton's view, an artistic creation away from conventional vision becomes "a recreation of the world in terms of inner necessity experienced by the artist."[16] This idea is evident in Gutmann's astonishing *Portrait of a Marriage*, 1935 (no. 21), in which the results were quite unanticipated. This image of Gutmann's friends was the outcome of a casual visit that he made to deliver a drawing they had purchased from him. As they were also interested in his photography, he responded by taking their picture.

I said to her why don't you lean over and get a little sunshine, and she just took a strange position. I told him to go somewhere but not to be standing right next to her. Later when I saw the picture it was unrealistic, completely surreal to me. When I showed it to them, they acted like in shock. He said: "I would appreciate if you would forget about it." So, I respected him and did not exhibit it until 1976 in San Francisco. He was dead. She was dead. Ten years after the picture was taken, I found the reason for the reaction; he was a homosexual and while this marriage on the surface was good, it was a great struggle, which I never knew when I took the picture. I only had the desire to make a picture of them, not knowing the results or the effect. What they were so upset about was that it really was a picture of their marriage.[17]

Images unforeseen and acceding to the marvellous, to a new order of things, through quite an ordinary subject of everyday life, often appear in Gutmann's work. There is often a suggestion of hidden meanings – a dream-like state that asserts itself, a quasi-hallucinatory character that infiltrates reality. *Cavalcade of the West*, 1939 (no. 58), *Ultimate Rehearsal*, 1938 (no. 55), *Horseback Rider Passing by Snowed-in Cars on a Manhattan Street*, 1947 (no. 93), and *Father Doll*, 1951 (no. 105) all manifest the absurd, the fantastic, the spontaneous, and the sense of opposition and ambiguity that arises from the illogical relationships between objects and their setting. They approach pictorial analogues of "automatism." In the midst of real encounters, they bypass the rational and accede to a realm Beyond Reality that is both poetic and documentary.

In his photography, Gutmann has not restricted himself to the creation of the recondite. From the beginning, he also turned to subject matter that would record an aspect of reality, the momentum of the event. None of Gutmann's photography was part of the mainstream concerns in California. His extraordinary viewpoint exemplified an essentially independent approach: self-reliance, a passion for observation, a fresh perception of a new world, imagination and intelligence. Not unmindful of his need for rudimentary skills in darkroom technique, he joined the California Camera Club in 1934. Bemused, he recalls,

I didn't know about processing.... There was no possibility of me to get my own darkroom, so for a few dollars I joined the club. The artistic ambitiousness of some of these old-timers, who were really pretty corny Pictorialists didn't disturb me at all, because they had lots of information... how to develop, how to print, different formulas... how to get more contrast... less contrast... stuff like that. But, when they saw my pictures, they didn't like them. Some of my pictures were in two halves, I had two compositions in one picture, and they had rules! L-shaped or symmetrical, a centre of interest... but I remained a member, until I went into the war I paid my dues.[18]

Over time, Gutmann's stylistic development demonstrated variance in resolution. Notwithstanding the demands of making a living and the press's demand for pictures of harmonious structure, Gutmann established a visual vocabulary, a continuous referential system of categories with distinguishing marks and attitudes. Certain subjects necessitated certain methods of production, as both spontaneity and prejudgement played a role in the creative process. He would exploit the characteristics of the medium to purvey the unanticipated and give ascendancy to multiple possibilities. From one of his very first assignments on photographing divers, he realized *Out of the Pool* (no. 7) was an untimely picture for 1934.

No editor at the time would have published it. They would have thought I was a photographer who did not know his business. Because it was too much out of focus and cut off in subject matter. But, later, I printed it. And maybe eight, ten years later I printed Towards the Pool *(no. 8) taken the same day. I realized only then what a great relationship there was – there were women and there were men – one group coming out of the pool with water dripping, the other group dry going into the pool.*[19]

Similar images are models of Gutmann's acceptance of the potentials of the camera: its disposition toward fragmentary framing and its relative tension, description of seductive surface, vantage point, and segmentation of time. The out-of-focus foreground subjects are often blunt and snappish. Framing in bold spatial crops and the angular configurations already seen in his first Berlin pictures, and patterning light and dark all convey visual spontaneity in the treatment of his subject matter. At his most brilliant, Gutmann's quick wit and the camera's slow shutter speed merge in *The Jump*, 1939 (no. 64). In this enigmatic moment, there is a hand pointing to a painted white spot on the ground, a full-length curving shadow of a man, and a blurred amorphous form springing from some concealed force, expelled over the spot. The jumping frog suggests free association with some previously experienced moment more than a transcript of current fact.

In such approaches to his subject matter, Gutmann forecast tendencies and motifs that were to be explored by subsequent photographers. The images of Robert Frank, Diane Arbus, Lee Friedlander, Bruce Davidson, Garry Winogrand, have become so familiar now that Gutmann's precursory photographs do not seem startling until one is alerted to their date.

The Gutmann image archives grew as editors failed to be venturesome – the ambiguous, the ambivalent, the tentative, and the personally expressive did not meet their standards. By 1940, the more enlightened *Coronet* published Gutmann's *Jitterbug* (fig. 1) of 1937, from the New Orleans Mardi Gras. In this series of photographs,

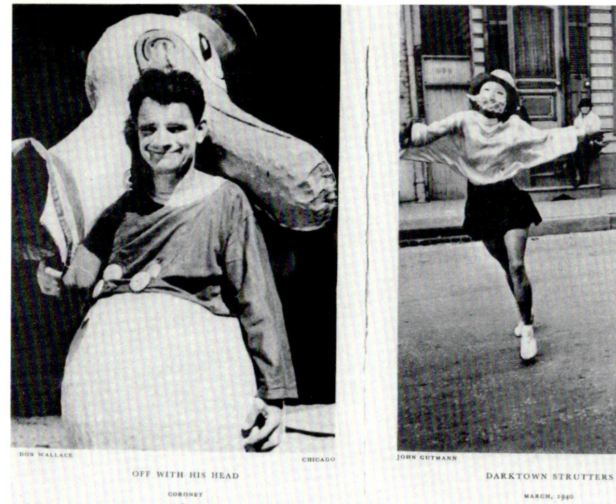

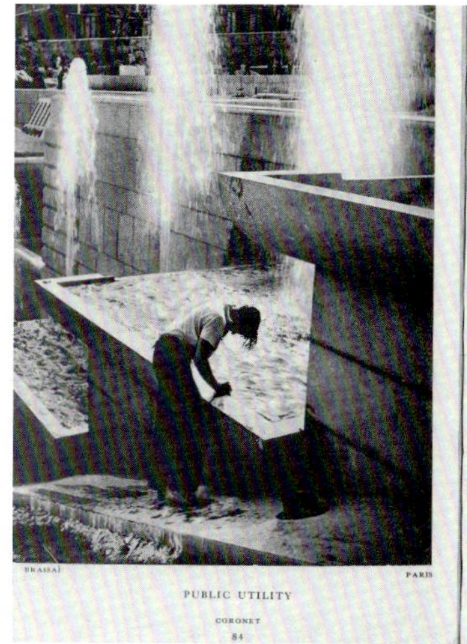

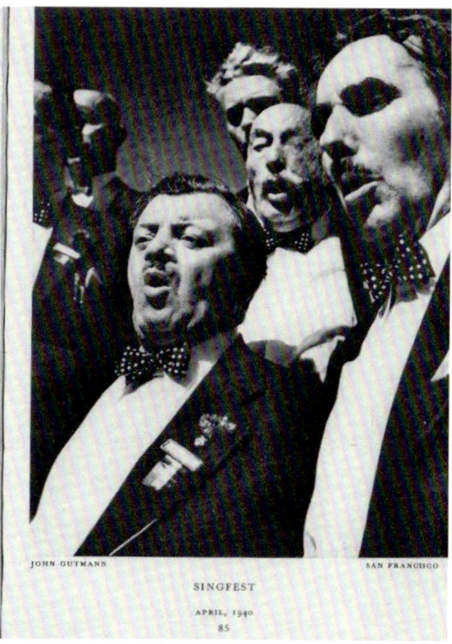

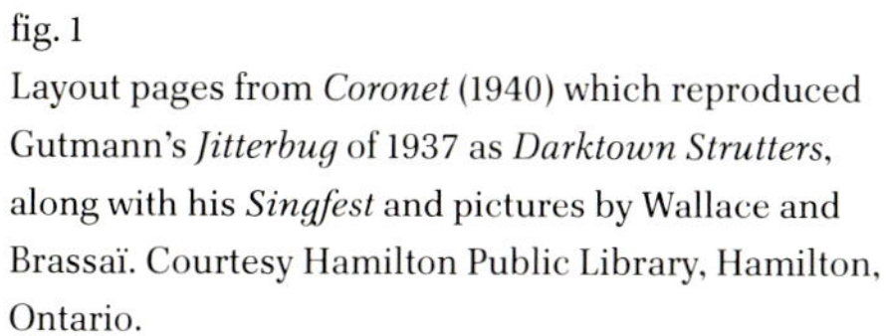

fig. 1
Layout pages from *Coronet* (1940) which reproduced Gutmann's *Jitterbug* of 1937 as *Darktown Strutters*, along with his *Singfest* and pictures by Wallace and Brassaï. Courtesy Hamilton Public Library, Hamilton, Ontario.

figures dance and parade, masks conceal and flaunt, crowds liberate and congeal – matter, space, time, and energy coalesce, forming one extemporaneous experience.

As Gutmann saw it, photography provided the opportunity to respond to individual moments – moments in which Gutmann the sensualist and Gutmann the intellectual could recreate the environment in expressive forms. Moments of intuition and chance were of equal significance. *Guns for Sale*, 1936 (fig. 2) prefigures the thrust found in Frank's images of America in the late fifties – partly blurred, moving, and precarious, broken shadows and filtered light. To this extent there are similarities, but the intent differs. To Gutmann, the inherent aspects of time, direction, a sense of place, and language were the terms of reality that supported a construct, that made him conscious of the visual possibilities. In describing the process of this image, Gutmann says,

...guns! It was unusual. You wouldn't find in Europe a display like this of guns. It was incredible. Sometimes I would take something like this very close-up by itself, but my whole attitude as a photographer interested in life – is very *important, more important than making art. So when I saw something like this, I would feel a close-up was not enough. I wanted to show more of what was going on. I knew there was a train that would come by. And also there were people walking by. And I was lucky for at the same time when the train came I selected the right moment. In photography luck is important too. I waited for maybe 50–60 people to pass and I didn't take the picture until I knew it was right, I knew there was a crop, what would be out of focus, and it was the shot I wanted.*[20]

Gutmann's requirement as a photojournalist, however, was to cull images perceptible to the magazine audience in Europe. His pictorial link to this demand was to define the new society he encountered through signs, language, the newsworthy, and caption text. The pictures of the monumental California *First Drive-In Theatre*, 1935 (fig. 3) and *Inside the First Drive-In Theatre*, (no. 19) represent both the socially unique and the newsworthy. In one view, words disseminate to verify the subjects; the other view becomes a counter-image, compelling for its lack of overt drama and for its subtle irony. Empty, it has an ironic invisibility in an arena that functioned solely to reinforce visibly America's inviolable values and dreams. Such icons of America gave Gutmann the focus of fresh discoveries, of the uncanny and the remarkable. In his visual inauguration, Gutmann found primary source material that would be explored by succeeding photographers. Gutmann's 1935 fascination with the Drive-In was later shared by Dorothea Lange (1954), Robert Frank (1956), Bruce Davidson (1965), and Robert Adams (1968), but his is the more intransmutable. Their images of the big screen, while individualistic in vision, share a foreboding and the bleak strain of marked

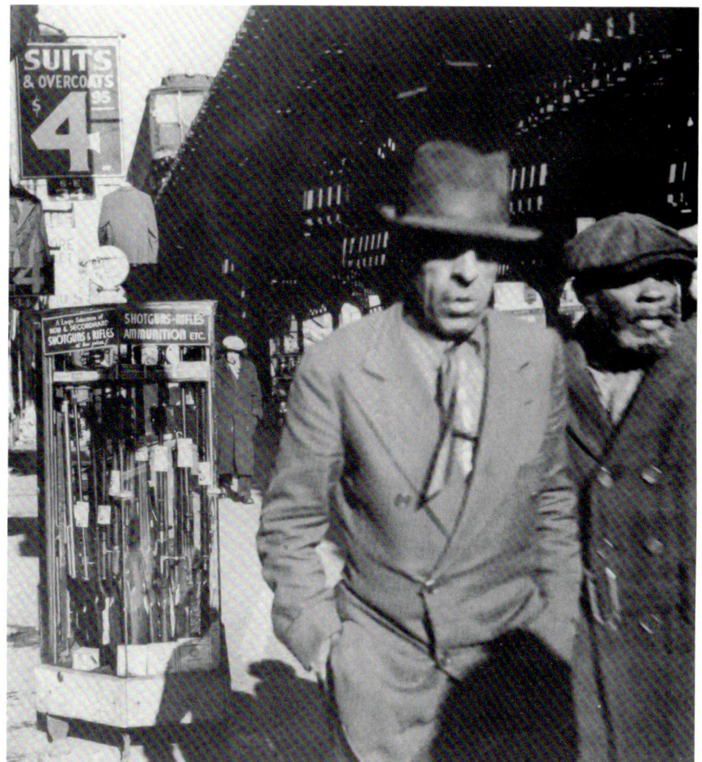

fig. 2
Guns for Sale. New York, 1936.

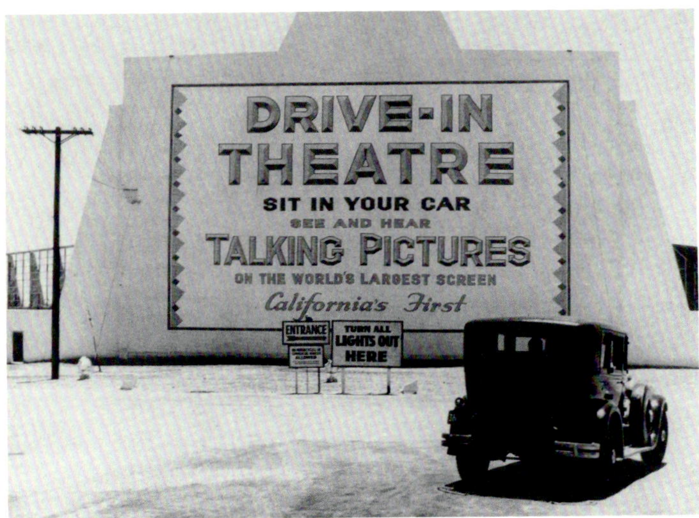

fig. 3
First Drive-In Theatre. Los Angeles, 1935.

time. Gutmann's optimistic approach, on the other hand, describes the landmark from two points of view: the external facade is the narrative – words and details of content inform the image; the vast internal tract is the formal concept of equivalency. The two images are united by linguistic and structural logic. The device of pairing images and introducing two points of view is sustained in Gutmann's work wherever it prevails logically.

Future tendencies in photography were also forecast in his approach to the 1948 series of landscapes, empty terrains, and new urban developments. In *A Tree at Hunter's Point* (no. 94), and *Three Crossings* (no. 98), which predicted the cool topographical work seen almost thirty years later in Lewis Baltz' *Nevada* (fig. 4), Robert Adams' Oregon, and Joe Deal's Riverside photographic projects that addressed concerns for establishing a measured and detached vision of landscape. Gutmann, however, does not presume to be a stylistic harbinger.

My work has a very contemporary look, many young photographers like it. And it has anticipated certain photographic practices, but I don't want to take particular great credit for it. It's probably the sensibilities of a sophisticated European responding to all the amazing and new experiences. And I have not been afraid of trying anything crazy.... I discovered most things by playing with my little machine, exploring the medium itself and really seeing what I could do with it.[21]

In his relatively few landscape images, Gutmann resisted conventions of landscape photography. They were not concerned with pictorial moods; nor were they idealized celebrations of nature as in the work of an Ansel Adams, or tributes to the sheer descriptive images of nineteenth-century topographical photographers. Instead, his observation accepted the objectivity of the field of vision as subject matter. Gutmann draws a clear link with the environment, to allow it to exist for itself and to suggest its own order. In this resolution he demonstrated how the medium suggested a visual approach to the subject matter.

The Depression for Gutmann represented not an era of social distress and unrest, but one to which he responded with astonishment. He explored aspects of the bizarre, the exotic, and the marvellous, and at the same time he found moments of compassion and sensitivity. But Gutmann was always at the centre of gravity, absorbing a vision of time, matter, energy, and space. Capturing the substance of *Jitterbug*, 1937 (no. 40) Gutmann's eye is caught with the exhilarating sensuousness of the masked dancer. Her presence in spellbound tension contrasts with the rhythmic sobriety of her partner. This fragmentary moment from his segregated Mardi Gras document reinforces an inescapable existentialism: one in fact creates one's own values for a fully active existence. Gutmann's perception of this is conveyed by the gesture between him and his subjects, one which is more beautiful and more open than that of any photographer of the era. A similar approach is apparent in *Cord in Harlem*, 1936 (no. 24). An automobile glistens brightly with chrome details, mirroring an elastic abstraction of the street – an abstract microcosm which contrasts with the firm voluptuous form of the car. It is a symbol dominating and pushing itself out of the picture frame. The flanking figures simultaneously open the doors. Whether they are entering or exiting is not nearly as meaningful as their endowed extravagance of power and their grace in the current of national gloom. For Gutmann, the image was not mere illusion; it represented a phenomenon that he saw as a reality and a visual truth throughout events during the Depression.

The social comments reflected in Gutmann's pictures of marks, scrawls, graffiti, messages, and props demonstrate his attentiveness to the transcription of the "primitive," the untutored. As photographs, *Longshoreman's Poem*, 1938 (no. 51) and *The Landlady Graffiti*, 1937 (no. 33) are poetic containers that hold the visual and the verbal. The universal syntax and elemental truth of graffiti are equally powerful and poignant as the announcements in *Ben's Barber Shop Window*, 1946 (no. 86). The plurality of signs and pictures on Calcutta's Bowbazaar Street (no. 83) and the naïveté of Calcutta's Sex Specialist's advertising (no. 84), both from 1945, have an irresolute purpose and fragile irony. They reflect Gutmann's interest in an art that is timeless in spirit and both ancient and modern:

I am much more moved and interested in things which were not

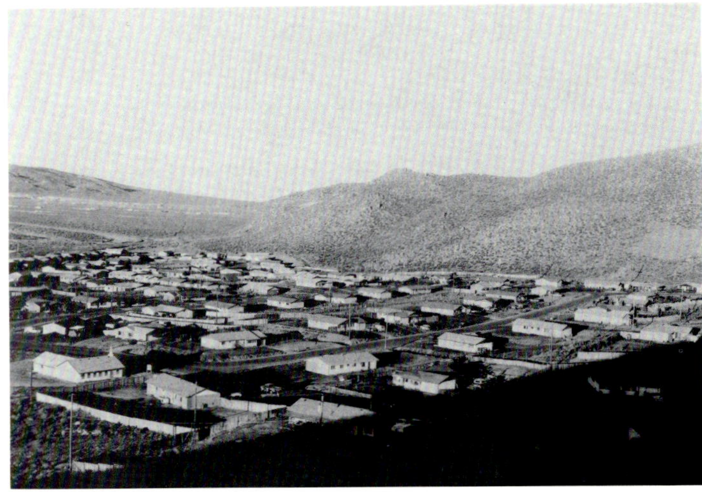

fig. 4
Lewis Baltz, *Lemmon Valley, Looking North* from the portfolio *Nevada*, 1977.

created primarily to make art, but have really some meaning in life of people. That is why I collect primitive art, which is a false name for what these objects are. What I find is a certain honesty and truth, I feel these objects really play a part in the life of the people. The marvellous thing is that I can also respond to their great beauty with my life experience in art.[22]

The psychological response to a "direct" transparent art has a kind of emotional truth. But in its facelessness and anonymity, it can also be perceived as disquieting. The punning title, *The Artist Lives Dangerously*, 1938 (no. 52) at first seems merely witty. Gutmann's title, however, is no disclaimer. Unaware of any cause for alarm, the boy works at his vigorous representation on the street as cars zoom by. For all the metaphoric danger implied, it is also a spontaneous categorical synthesis for Gutmann. It denotes four categorical electives: graffiti-art, a street document, a connotative caption that enlarges the content, and for European eyes the presence of the ubiquitous automobile. The potential of signs and language served Gutmann as valuable manifestations of popular culture. As subject matter, language declared its multifarious idiomatic relationships.

No subject proved as limitless as the celebrated automobile, and America's obsession with it was fertile territory. Gutmann saw it as the quintessential American icon. It was ever present, dominating streets, parking lots, garages, beaches, drive-ins, dumps, student campuses, and it was seemingly omnipotent. It symbolized power, wealth, glamour, and a wondrous inventiveness. Gutmann observed its every facet: fenders, headlights, adornments, decals, its relationship to life and its surroundings. Transformed, the automobile stood as a reminder of God's Love (no. 57), a transport for ideological proclamation and aggression (no. 56 and fig. 5), a billboard for commerce (no. 16), and an homage to itself, for its own aggrandizement (no. 28). In contrast, Gutmann's European experience had been limited to his family automobile and those of the wealthy. From the beginning, Gutmann has sustained an incomparable breadth and bite in this subject. A parked convertible Volkswagen in New York's Soho district in 1981 (no. 137) recalls a composition taken some forty-three years earlier of an automobile parked on the slope of San Francisco's Nob Hill (no. 53). While the eccentric and bombastic disposition of the pre-World War II automobile has changed to that of a more tepid visual symbol, Gutmann has continued to discover it in irrational and provocative situations. A charred, garbage-strewn street in New York of 1978, dense with uncleanliness, is juxtaposed with a Rolls Royce discreetly edging its way into the picture (no. 124).

Gutmann's travels in the mid-forties took him to China, Burma, and India. There he remained stimulated by the challenge of finding subject matter that would reveal the new and reflect the themes he had developed in America. He focussed on his established categories, and yet his overall approach was more classical, more proportioned, and for him more appropriate for the subject. They detail vignettes: what people do, how they live, their environment; the pictures are also supported by lengthy captions that transcribe direct information. The image of *Oiled Hair to Make it Shine*, 1944 (no. 75) transcends its more obvious didactic intent. The textural resonance of extreme contrasts in the play of light and dark reveal a subject fully considered. The sense of the woman's self-absorption, her unawareness, nearly conceals her "presence." One is left to speculate about her visage and to absorb the rich tangible nature of her cultural esthetic.

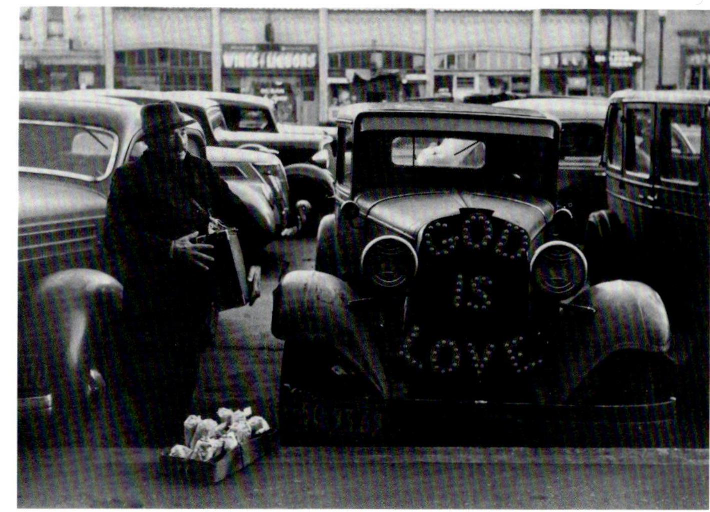

57 *"God is Love"*. San Francisco, 1939.

The densely packed *Country Market at Cheng-Kiang*, 1944 (no. 72) adheres to Gutmann's subthematic interest in crowds: on streets, in fields, or wherever humanity amassed. However, the overall shapes and rhythmic patterns of the crowds are antithetical to Gutmann's usual visual esthetic. But for him, the challenge in this mode of seeing, from a greater distance, was the compression of more visual data. The crowd also defies the notion of specific subject interest. While Gutmann's vision was stimulated by such scenes, he also explains another motivation:

...[The] one motive was you didn't have a centre of interest; again, the Pictorialists always would say you have to have a centre, they criticize a picture with too many things going on. It was just the thing that would intrigue me – to make a picture with many, many things going on.... In the peasant markets of China I discovered all sorts of activities. I like people to read my pictures, to come close to see what is really going on. Of course, I am not the only photographer.... Weegee and others, for example, have done these crowd negatives, but I share the idea.[23]

Gutmann's "bird's-eye" views are flexible organisms. They yield both to an evocation of power and to a certain neutrality. The collective personality of *Mardi Gras Crowd on Canal Street*, 1937 (no. 34) is one of festive responsiveness. *Holy Week Crowd in Prayer*, 1957 (no. 109) and *European-Trained Troops of the Chinese Nationalist Army at Parade*, 1944 (no. 77) display a collective purpose, but function more as topographical maps in which the individual is diminished. Gutmann's oblique observation of the photographer in *The News Photographer*, 1935 (no. 18) in the midst of an assembled crowd surrounded by tributory flags, including the Nazi flag, must have been not only unsettling for Gutmann; it must have created a metaphor for his own role as "news photographer" of American events for Germany.

In contrast to the open planimetry of an unstructured picture field of crowds, are a number of formal investigations that recall Constructivist concepts. Gutmann's interest was not in exploring

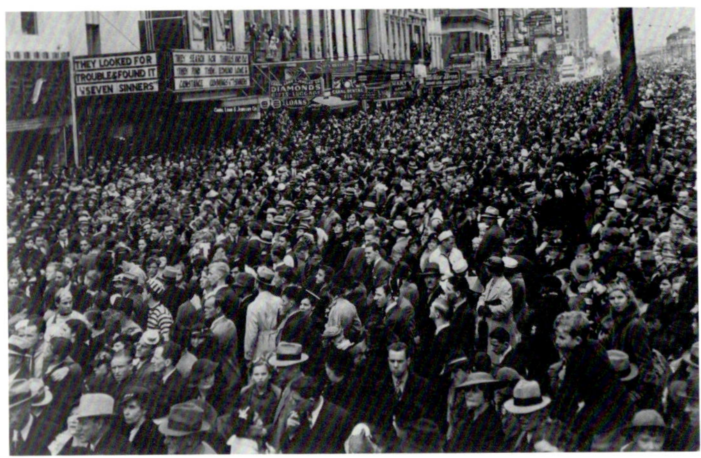

34 *Mardi Gras Crowd on Canal Street.* New Orleans, 1937.

the uses of abstract geometric forms in space inspired by the modern machine esthetic and espoused by the movement in Russia. Neither did he subscribe to the "socialism of vision" declared by László Moholy-Nagy. Gutmann's interest was in formulating a dialogue with space that would humanize the austere geometry which was the essence of technology. Gutmann's meeting with Moholy-Nagy in 1939 had relatively little bearing on Gutmann's ideas of a "structured vision," although they shared pedagogical ideas of common interest. (Gutmann was by this time teaching the history of modern art at San Francisco State College.) However, Gutmann does not dismiss his interest in Constructivism, the Bauhaus, or the periodic evidence of their ideas in his work. *The Open Window*, 1939 (no. 61) is essentially an exploration of the spatial field in which naturalistic space is invaded by the strong lines of the window components. The visual tension of *From the North Tower of the Golden Gate Bridge*, 1947 (no. 91) and *Maintenance Worker Moving Down on Main Cable of the Golden Gate Bridge*, 1947 (no. 90) has an independent dramatic power in which the force of the diagonals cutting through space transfer Gutmann's vantage point to the spectator. In later works of similar concept, Gutmann considers irregular grid structures, surface texture, split composition, and compartmentalization. These characteristics are effectively described in *Carson Mansion with Parked Automobile Seen through Cross-barred Window*, 1960 (no. 116) and in *Dagger from the Door*, 1961 (no. 118). Gutmann's concept of "structured vision" is an expression of space as an "inner movement" and an orchestration of visual properties.

The prominence of symbols appears systematically in Gutmann's work. Nowhere is this as transparently reflected than in his admitted obsession with the life-death principle, not as representation of "an end," or as a dissolution, but as a transformation. The elusive nature of this obsession is also evident in the role photography plays in its own enterprise. With its allusion to the past – a sense of loss – and through its possible revival in the print, a tentative immortality is assured. However, the moment that remains as a surviving record can only be described as the present. Gutmann in his death imagery adopts different attitudes. In a photograph such as *Child's Grave*, 1937 (no. 46) the Mexican cemetery is straightforward observation, but in *Dead Hindu Girl*, 1945 (no. 82), the presence of death in daily life is strongly felt and emphasized by his caption reference to the culture of India, "Awaiting Burning at the Pyres of the Nimtolla Ghat, Calcutta." A sense of irony, on the other hand, is present in his view of the store window in which skeletons and reflections form in Gutmann's mind a *Dance Macabre*, 1979 (no. 134). A disquieting image suggestive of death can also be read into the graffiti-laden *The Landlady Graffiti*, 1937 (no. 33), in which a cast-away battered doll appears "lifeless" in contrast to the optimistic message "flats to let." Equally disquieting is Gutmann's record of *The Victims*, 1960 (no. 114) where extinction of life is an horrific absolute in the dried stacked corpses. Gutmann relates his idiosyncratic view:

I had this fascination with death already in the thirties when I got interested in Surrealism; my obsession has been skeletons and pictures of death ... and lately I have come to the conclusion that while I am getting officially older every day (though I don't feel any older), probably instinctively I use these symbols as a kind of protection, to make myself familiar with death that to me it's nothing special. The Mexicans have a similar attitude which I like very much. Death as more an adventure and even funny ... comical as seen in the skeleton figures which I collect.[24]

Gutmann does not treat death as raw subject matter. It is embodied in the metaphysical and must transcend itself. Ultimately, the symbolic will survive as the subject of his life and death images.

Gutmann's fertile vision has existed in distinct spheres: in the sphere of expressive documentary observation drawing from reality, in the formal, and in the sensual and the poetic. Within each sphere, the complexity of expression, be it gestural or subtle, has expanded

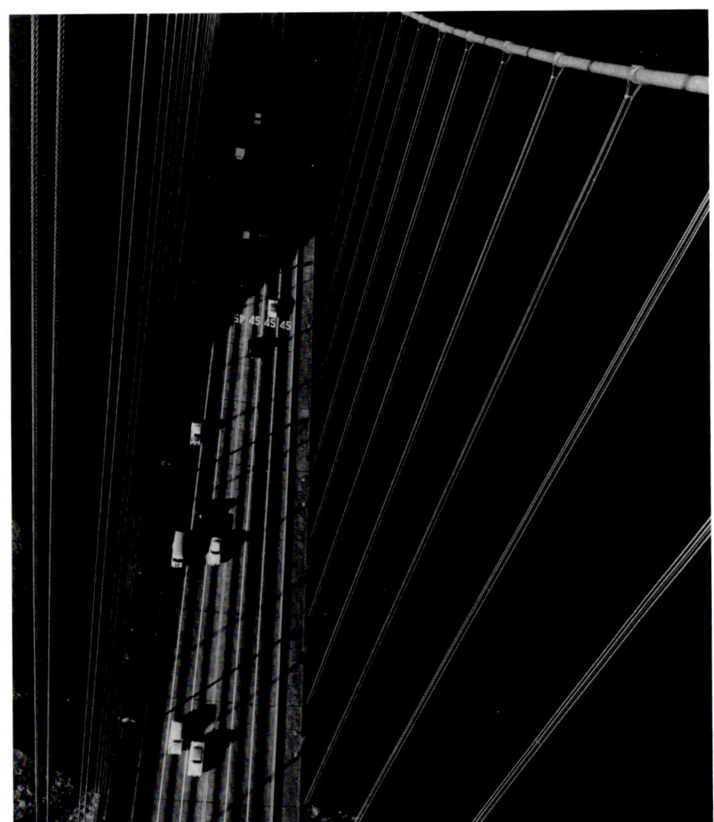

91 *From the North Tower of the Golden Gate Bridge.* San Francisco, 1947.

his artistic invention to suit subject matter and content. Inspired both by pre-existing resources and by his own profound originality, through his extraordinary diversity he has used varied pictorial means to serve his medium, and to project different realms of his experience. To stress his belief in the importance of subject matter is not to overlook the possibilities of also discovering content in form. While Gutmann found his subject matter in recurring human themes and events, it was feeling for the irrational and the rational that polarized his vision. At the heart of Gutmann's genius is surefootedness and a positive view of the multiplicity life offers. His response has been to synthesize his creative vision, one that produces, assembles, alternates, and is individualistically coherent. Photographic history has found no name-tag for Gutmann – he himself prefers to be linked with the "unclassifiables."

Maia-Mari Sutnik

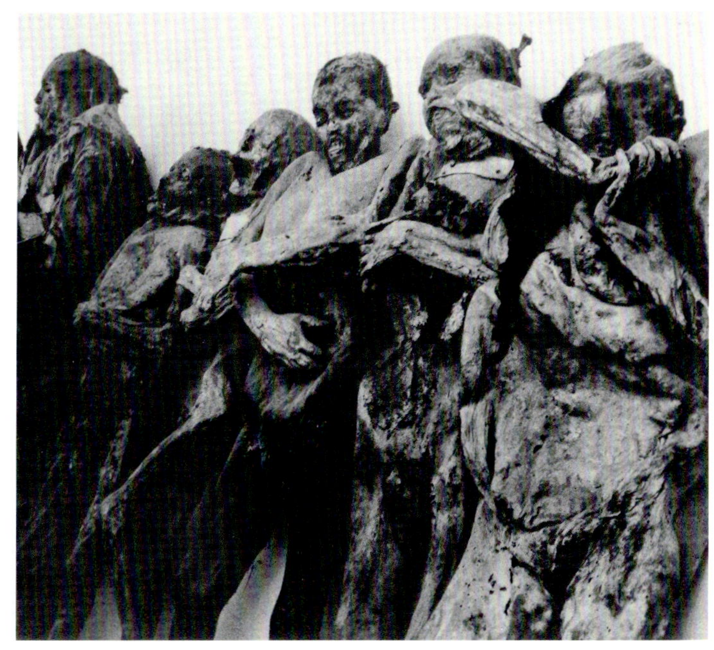

114 *The Victims.* Guanajuato, Mexico, 1960.

Notes

1 Lew Thomas, ed., *The Restless Decade, John Gutmann's Photographs of the Thirties*, (New York: Harry N. Abrams, Inc., Publishers, 1984).

2 Ibid., p. 5.

3 John Gutmann in taped interview with M-M Sutnik, San Francisco, October 19–20, 1983.

4 Gutmann in interview with Sutnik.

5 References are to exhibition titles assigned by Gutmann in 1976 and 1985. (See Exhibition List, p. 93.)

6 Gutmann in interview with Sutnik.

7 André Breton, "THE visage of THE woman," in *Photographs of Man Ray: 105 works, 1920–1934* (New York: Dover Publications Inc., reprint of 1934 original), p. 44.

8 John Willett, *Art and Politics in the Weimar Period: The New Sobriety, 1917–1933* (New York: Pantheon Books, 1979), p. 98.

9 Ibid., p. 98.

10 Ibid., p. 140.

11 Gutmann in interview with Sutnik. Photoreportage and illustrated magazines were developed in Germany by Stefan Lorant in *Münchner Illustriete Presse*, a forerunner of *Berliner Illustriete Zeitung*, and succeeding picture magazines, including *The Weekly Illustrated, Life, Look, Picture Post*, and many other picture magazines that dominated during the 1930s to 1960.

Erich Salomon (1886–1944) was one of the first photographers to use small handheld cameras and available light to photograph high-level political and cultural events during the late 1920s and early 1930s. Paul Citroën (b. 1896) and Umbo (Otto Umbehr) (b. 1902) were intellectuals who were actively engaged in photography during the same period as Salomon.

12 Gutmann in interview with Sutnik.

13 Gutmann's entry into photography is extensively treated by Max Kozloff in his seminal essay "The Extravagant Depression" in *The Restless Decade*, and by Michael Mitchell in this catalogue. Most articles published on Gutmann have cited the circumstances of his departure from Germany and his motive for taking up photography.

14 Gutmann in interview with Sutnik.

15 Ibid.

16 André Breton quoted in J.H. Matthews, *The Imagery of Surrealism* (New York: Syracuse University Press, 1977), p. 51.

17 Gutmann in interview with Sutnik.

18 Ibid.

19 Ibid.

20 Ibid.

21 Ibid.

22 Ibid.

23 Ibid.

24 Ibid.

IN THE NEW WORLD: JOHN GUTMANN AND AMERICAN PHOTOGRAPHY

Ever since Paul Delaroche responded to the public debut of photography in 1839 with the words, "From today painting is dead," photographers and painters have never been easy bedfellows. The former see painters as practitioners of an anachronistic craft – messy and imprecise – that appeals to only a tiny elite. The painter regarding the photographer, on the other hand, suspects the presence of a mass media hack – an appropriator who invents nothing. The medium is mere mechanics, at best a prodigious generator of raw material that the painter may deign to transform. By synthesis the artist creates anew, while the photographer merely eats the world.

What, then, are we to make of John Gutmann, a painter nurtured on Die Brücke Expressionism, who, upon ejection from the fading cultural riches of Weimar Germany in 1933, landed on both feet in America with a camera in his hand? How could art jump into bed with commerce with such equanimity? If Gutmann had an answer (and he did) the California arts culture into which he had landed did not.

Gutmann arrived in San Francisco on New Year's Eve, 1933. It was barely a year since the newly formed f/64 Group – Ansel Adams, Imogen Cunningham, Willard Van Dyke and Edward Weston – had staged their first exhibition at the city's M.H. de Young Museum. California photography was just emerging from a period of the artistic "fuzzy wuzzies" and the f/64 photographers formed the vanguard. They were the purists. Although Gutmann remained unaware of the fact, for much of his first year in San Francisco, Adams was waging war in the pages of *Camera Craft* for the kind of photographic practice that Gutmann was innocently indulging in. The enemy was William Mortensen, self-appointed defender of the Pictorialists.

To their way of thinking, the Pictorialists had handily cleared up the antithesis of painting and photography. They had done it by obscuring photography. Their procedures had an impeccable lineage; the bible of the movement – Henry Peach Robinson's *Pictorial Effect in Photography* – having been published in Britain in 1869, prompted attitudes and procedures parallel to those of painters. The works exhibited in the salons of the *Camera Pictorialists of Los Angeles* (founded 1914), were the typical derivatives of Robinson's movement. Their romantic glow resulted from lenses designed to abjure sharp focus and from a host of hybrid printing technologies – gum bichromate, bromoil, fresson, and soft platinum – that nicely removed photographics from photography. The Pictorialists loved rain, fog, and darkness. Their favoured subjects were the sea – not the Pacific Ocean – and nymphs, naiads, and shepherdesses – never the girl next door. The Pictorialists despised the hoards of amateurs with their No. 1 Kodak and Bull's Eye cameras, who were quite content to leave the lab work to George Eastman in Rochester. If Eastman was going to spoil photography by making it easy, the Pictorialists were going to hoist it back into art by making it hard again. A good Pictorialist print was all process. The photographer entered the darkroom, worked his smelly alchemy, and two days later an artist emerged carrying a dark print into the light. What you could see of it was all beauty.

In the late twenties, the apprentice Pictorialist Ansel Adams climbed up into the Sierra with a lens that worked. He came down and carefully printed the image on the kind of shiny paper that newsmen used. Then he showed it to his friends. Mortensen saw it and could see that it was all wrong: too much detail and too much light. Mortensen and his 3,000 students down at Laguna Beach all knew that an artful photograph should look like an "Italian Renaissance painting." By contrast, Adams and his San Francisco circle were promoting the radical notion that a photograph could look like a photograph and still be art.

Accordingly, Adams and Mortensen began a debate that lasted for most of 1934. They missed the arrival of the Expressionist John Gutmann just as he, with fresh memories of the Nazi fanaticism still at his back, missed their teapot tempest. In fact, Adams and Mortensen's positions were not too dissimilar. Both wanted to delete the ampersand from "art & photography" and both turned away from the urban twentieth century, Mortensen to his masquerades and Adams to the mountains. He made sure that art photography required a camera bigger than a picnic basket and, when he came down the mountain, he gave the people the ten-step zone system which was sure to keep them all in the darkroom. If he'd known that Gutmann's ship was arriving he might well have joined forces with Mortensen and pulled the gangplank back up.

By their standards, John Gutmann did everything wrong. His "automatic" Rollei, the latest product of German engineering (1932), was unknown in America, and just as well, for it was too small. His entire photographic background consisted of reading through a camera manual twice and the exposure of several rolls in Germany to make sure he'd got it all right. Moreover, he was a painter who was going to survive in Depression America by taking pictures for the German agency Presse-Foto. As a photographer, he wasn't even think-

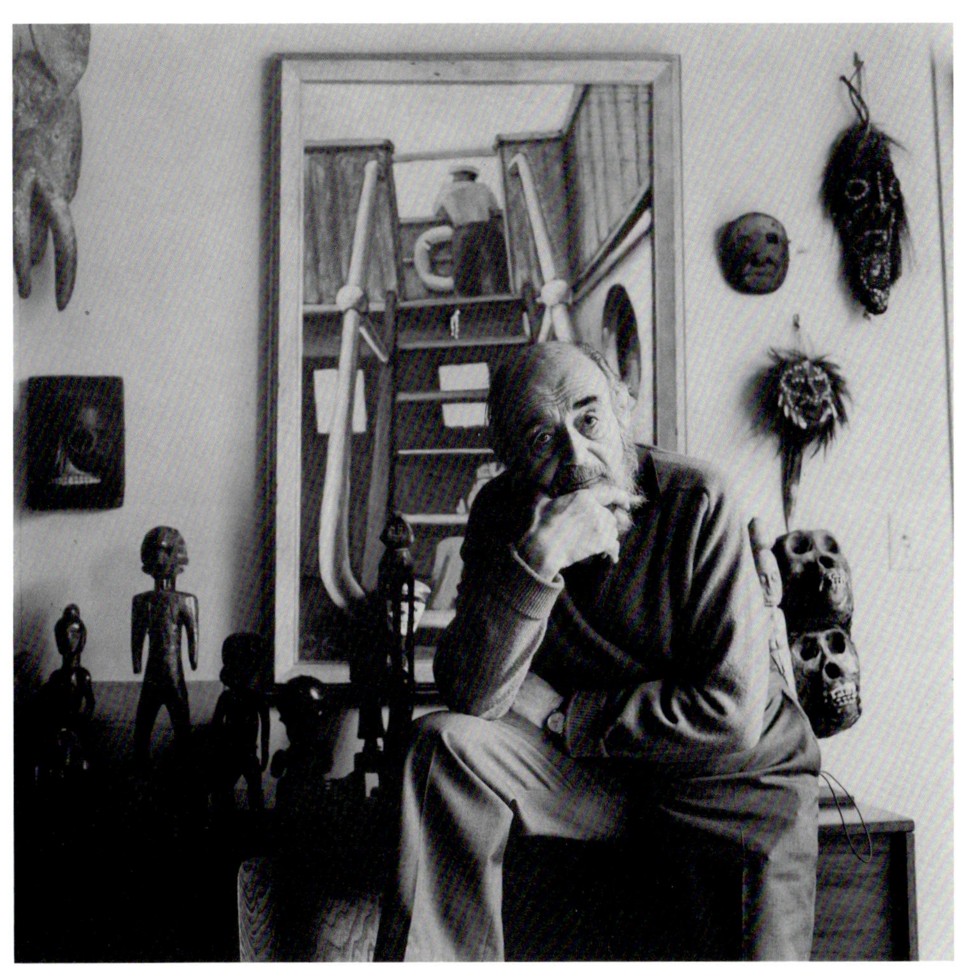

John Gutmann. San Francisco, 1985.
Photograph by Michael Mitchell

ing about art and certainly not about process. At first, when he needed prints, he went to the drug store like everyone else.

Gutmann's entry into photography was purely pragmatic. As a master student of the Die Brücke Expressionist Otto Mueller, he had received a sophisticated visual training. He knew that the German illustrated weeklies he had read in Berlin cafés were hungry for pictures on that perennially fascinating subject, American culture. Although his first-hand acquaintance with photography was limited to having served as a one-shot model in front of Helmar Lerski's enormous camera when the latter was photographing for his masterpiece, the book *Köpfe Des Alltags* (1931), Gutmann felt he could quickly master the basics required for magazine work. Between assignments, he would do his real work as a painter.

However, photography is a seductive medium. It can be surprisingly generous to the tyro and then a tease to those who stay with it. The more one works, the harder it seems to make the transcendent image. As Gutmann worked over the next decade, his photography became progressively more important to him. By the time he returned in 1945 from two years of camera work in India, China, and Burma for the U.S. Office of War Information, he was convinced that photography and film were the visual media of the twentieth century. He never returned to painting.

Although it took a dozen years for one medium to supplant the other in Gutmann's affections, the preconditions that made this possible were well in place before he reached California. When he left Germany, he lost his appetite for European culture – too much art, too much past, too much *schlagsahne.* When one painted, there were too many giants over the shoulder. By comparison, California seemed to have no past at all. In such a raw culture, one was free to begin again. What better way than by adopting a new medium, especially one with so little recognized artistic tradition? Moreover, the leap from Expressionist painting to photography was perhaps more akin to a step than one first would have supposed. The artists of Die Brücke (Ernst L. Kirchner, Erich Heckel, Karl Schmidt-Rottluff, and Max Pechstein, among others) were prodigious printmakers. Their medium, like photography, produced multiple originals. Most Die Brücke prints were as small and monochromatic as photographs. Both media involved a reduction to visual essentials. Early Die Brücke prints were unsigned and unattributed: they had the same collective anonymity as photographs. Like photographers, the members of Die Brücke used their annual publications to disseminate their work. Although once in California Gutmann continued to paint, his work became increasingly precisionist, and some of his later works were renderings of his photographs. When the two media eventually met, photography swallowed up painting.

From the moment he landed, Gutmann began to stake out a territory that the established California photographers totally ignored. Mortensen's book *Monsters and Madonnas* (1936) was basically a Pictorialist process "cookbook." In the Purist camp, Imogen Cunningham was doing formal portraits and flowers, Weston was cutting up vegetables and combing farm country, while Adams was hiking in the mountains. Unaware of them all, Gutmann tramped the city streets.

San Francisco streets were full of cars that he just couldn't get over. As a child in Breslau, he had often taken long trips in his father's sky-blue automobile. Like any successful German who could actually afford a car, his father never drove it himself. When luxury cars like his weren't actually on the road, chauffeurs were kept busy polishing the fenders. Yet in America, everybody had one, even the impoverished Okies that Dorothea Lange was recording in the California migrant worker camps. The ubiquitous cars were manifestations of American democratic culture – everyone's right to be mobile. People ate in them, slept and made love in them, and with the most casual disregard for the stylists in Detroit, remade them into whatever they needed. They became moving vans, living rooms, billboards, and pulpits. In their turn, these buggies remade the landscape. Vacant lots became auto-parks, and when restaurants and movie theatres moved onto them, the drive-in was born.

Gutmann, the outsider, photographed all these as exotica. His alien vision was reinforced by the knowledge that he must seek out that which was most American for his audience in Europe. In the process, he became a kind of New World Atget. A quarter of a century earlier, the aging French photographer had hurried to fill out his catalogue of Old Paris before the Baron Haussmans of the world demolished it all. In America, Gutmann had his own catalogue to fill out: Automobile Culture in the USA; Documents of the Street; Graffiti: Marks and Messages; The People; and The Depression. However, the urgency of Gutmann's project was an inversion of Atget's. The latter was racing the wrecker's ball, while in America Gutmann was breathlessly attempting to keep up with people's amazing inventiveness.

West of the Rockies there was no parallel to what Gutmann was doing. While Dorothea Lange's extensive record of the Depression in California did include a few urban soup kitchens and employment lines, they tended to depict what we might call the Depression generic: scenes of emblematic hope and despair. Gutmann's work, by contrast, was about culture and his amazement. It was not that he didn't share Lange's compassionate humanity; his purpose in artmaking was to interpret life. However, he was used to different standards. The economic collapse that had produced the four-wheeled diaspora to California did not seem that drastic to a child of Europe. He could dismiss the San Francisco intellectuals' dark talk of imminent revolution as humbug; the California life of the thirties was essentially extravagant. The only real misery he ever witnessed was among the blacks. Gutmann came to see his own Depression photographs as being not records of hopelessness, but rather images of people waiting for change.

The photographer Ruth Bernhard, also a German emigré in thirties California, has remarked that, "In the West, the creative photographer was influenced by the sea and the mountains, and the landscape in general. And on the East Coast, particularly [for] New York photographers, the influence is the mass of humanity and the tall buildings."[1] Although Gutmann rejected New York as a possible home – it was too Europeanized – Gutmann's work was, in fact, much closer in spirit to currents there than in the West. He came from a highly urbanized culture and the artistic milieu in which he'd reached maturity was thematically focussed on the cities. Although his teacher Otto Mueller was largely devoted to gypsy subjects and nudes, Kirchner and the other Die Brücke Expressionists had painted urban scapes almost exclusively after their drift to Berlin. Their work, a response to the profound social and cultural dislocations of twentieth century life, used the European city as a symbol of their emotional reaction and rebellion. They protested the extreme refinements of contemporary life by attempting to become uncivilized. The late Gothic woodcut and the Primitive sculpture, particularly masks, became their points of departure. Like these models, their art depicted figures that were symbolic and generic, rather than individual. Gutmann's photography was, in part, an extension of these attitudes. His work was urban and few of the figures and faces in his photographs emerge from symbolic anonymity to become distinct individuals. It is mostly in his images of women that we begin to see traces of individuality. Even so, many of the women wear veils, turn away, and become not a woman, but "Woman." Their faces tend to be as stylized and impenetrable as those on the dozens of primitive carvings that fill Gutmann's San Francisco home.

By contrast, the contemporaneous photographs of Roy Stryker's Farm Security Administration (F.S.A.) photographers, though intended to portray the representative, give emphasis to the individual. Working on projects that were part of Roosevelt's New Deal, Dorothea Lange, Russell Lee, Ben Shahn, Jack Delano, and Walker Evans, along with half a dozen others, fanned out across America between 1935 and 1943. Their legacy has provided everyone's image of Depression America. However, as befits an agency connected with the Department of Agriculture, the archive produced by director Roy Stryker's photographers was overwhelmingly rural in its coverage. Although the style of the work ranges from the crude, intimate Leica photography of Ben Shahn to the sophisticated and distanced 8 x 10 view camera work of Walker Evans, there is nothing in the F.S.A. files even remotely resembling John Gutmann's images. His Expressionistic angles, truncated torsos, and densely packed surfaces are totally alien to the level, descriptive views of the F.S.A. photographers. Moreover, when their content overlaps, it becomes clear that their attitudes were totally different. If Walker Evans, whose choice of subjects influenced all others on the project, saw a commercial sign as the subject for a picture, it was because he appreciated its homespun character and its patina. Bernarda Shahn once described one of her husband's F.S.A. photographs as being "...as characteristic a photograph as possible. It contains all possible elements: a person, a sign, and folk art."[2] However, the signs that crowd into Gutmann's pictures are usually of the corporate present: billboards, product wall murals, and declarations of opinion. Collectively, they assured his European viewers that this was indeed a picture from America. When Russell Lee photographed an ornamental radiator cap in Laurel, Mississippi, it was because of its implied politics. It depicted a man gleefully thumbing his nose. Gutmann made pictures of hood ornaments in appreciation of their dynamic industrial forms and because they were American icons.

All F.S.A. photographs were fundamentally political. They were made to create public awareness of social and economic problems in America that would provide a groundswell of support for Roosevelt's reforms. The photographers went out into the field after an extensive briefing on the geography, economy, and social structure of the region they were to visit. For Gutmann, politics were totally secondary. When political content appeared in his photographs, it was usually in the form of an ironic aside on America's naïveté in international affairs. He was much more interested in documenting and decoding an exotic culture.

While Stryker's team was driving out of Washington to discover rural America, individual photographers were independently taking on that most daunting of American subjects, the city of New York. In 1929, Berenice Abbott returned from a seven-year exile in France determined to put aside her career as photographer of the literati of Paris to become a portraitist not of people, but of the city itself. To some extent, her exile, like Gutmann's arrival, gave her the distance that enabled her to see the extraordinary transformations that were taking place in New York. Like Gutmann, she had turned away from a traditional art to take up photography. Although she had learned the basics of photography while working as Man Ray's assistant in Paris, she soon rebelled against his kind of Surrealism and gradually found her own way as a Classical Realist.

There was much in Abbott's attitude that Gutmann, had he known her, would have found sympathetic. In 1928, she told an American reporter: "I have willingly abandoned sculpture, finding in photography a new, if not finished art, and one that at least has equally great possibilities – and a form better suited to the times."[3] She dismissed discussions about whether photography was an art as being totally unprofitable – she cared little whether she was labelled an artist. Photography was a medium that recorded content; the important thing was to choose a subject of significance that could be probed and explored.

Her portrait of New York as it evolved between 1930 and 1939, when her book *Changing New York* was published, was based on the documentation of architecture. As she wandered the streets of New York recording both the old and the new she frequently photographed subjects – store fronts, commercial signs, and automobiles – that were also intrinsic to Gutmann's work. However, in a Gutmann photograph the subject is everything that is in the photograph: the street, the people, the cars, the signs, and buildings. In Abbott's photographs, these become details that are secondary to the grand theme of architecture. Her work was not about the people of New York, nor was it a catalogue of uniquely American iconographic situations: it was architectural documentation pure and simple. Her views are clear, level descriptions of appearances. There is none of the restless formal experimentation that is so marked in Gutmann's first decade of photography.

In 1936, Gutmann set out on a journey across America that can be compared to that of the Swiss emigré photographer Robert Frank almost two decades later. His immediate task was to find a new agency to handle his pictures, as Presse-Foto was reselling his material without acknowledgement or payment of residuals. Gutmann turned this business trip into an odyssey. The Depression kept the buses on which he travelled almost empty, so the drivers were happy to stop whenever he wished to photograph. The negatives that he still prints from that trip are largely of the great cities of the Midwest: Chicago and Cleveland and especially Detroit, the ground zero of car culture, which struck him as the quintessentially American city. In New York, Gutmann walked the streets with his camera, photographing the cars and cops of Harlem. It was a good time to have come. Henry Luce had just launched *Life*, the greatest of the American picture magazines, and he had engaged another German exile, Alfred Eisenstaedt, as staff photographer. Eisenstaedt set up the Pix

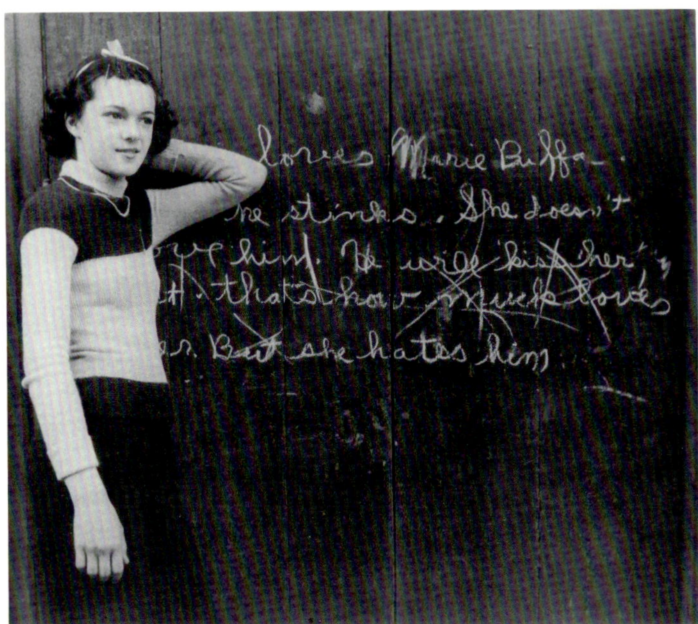

fig. 1
Love-Hate Graffiti. New Orleans, 1937.

agency to feed the burgeoning magazine business and took on Gutmann as one of his agency photographers.

After six months in New York, Gutmann began his long bus journey back to San Francisco. Although he made various stopovers along the way, none was more productive than his encounter with Mardi Gras in New Orleans. It would be the richest creative period of his life: every third or fourth negative he made there was worth printing. The dark narrow streets, the masked figures, and the fierce partying in the penumbra of the approaching war, all suggested the conditions that had sustained Die Brücke thirty years before. It was archetypal material for his sensibility. At the same time, he made one of his earliest graffito photographs there, showing a girl on the edge of womanhood shyly vamping beside a scrawl about love and hate (fig. 1).

Back in San Francisco, life took a new turn for Gutmann. He began teaching painting part time, and by 1938 he had a permanent position at San Francisco State College. This first official recognition of his status as a painter and teacher did not put an end to his photography, however. Working between classes and on weekends, he did as much, if not more, photographic work than before. A curious tension began to emerge in his photographs: as his style became plainer, less sensuous and expressionistic, the content became more mysterious, what he was to call the surrealism of life itself. Walls were covered with anxious messages, but people hurried by them. Individuals became performers and vanished into roles: geisha, majorette, soldier, and circus grotesque. The streets filled up with empty cars: the world was still waiting.

Working through Pix for the next couple of decades, Gutmann would supply photographs to *Newsweek*, *Look*, *Life*, *National Geographic*, *McCalls*, *Redbook*, *Holiday*, *Saturday Evening Post*, and *Parents Magazine* and to numerous rotogravure newspaper supplements including the Toronto *Star Weekly* (fig. 2). Although these publications generally made rather uninspired edits of his work and mutilated photographs on the page, a few of the thirties magazines were quite sophisticated. *Ken*, a publication of the Esquire organization in Chicago, commissioned writers like Ernest Hemingway to write strongly opinionated pieces on American foreign and domestic policy and culture. It featured many photographs on its large and well printed pages. During the forties the small-format magazine *Coronet* was frequently a vehicle for Gutmann's American images.

By signing with Pix, Gutmann entered the highly competitive world of American magazine journalism. It was a world of exiles. Eisenstaedt, Andreas Feininger, and Martin Munkacsi had all worked on the German illustrated weeklies. One of the few homegrown stars of the period was Margaret Bourke-White. From the thirties through to the fifties, her photographs appeared regularly in Luce's *Life* and *Fortune*, as well as other publications. Her style became a paradigm of the magazine photography of the day.

She began her career in the late twenties doing industrial photography in Cleveland. Her pictures celebrated the "wonders of the mechanic age" in images that were romantic, theatrical, and not without a lingering residue of Pictorialism. Her autographic style, the relentless search for the strong graphic and the heroic, stands in marked contrast to Gutmann's attempts at transparency – to be a window for the marvellously ordinary. Her people became isolated timeless monuments: Gutmann's were always firmly anchored in time and the real world. Years later, when Dorothea Lange looked back at her own early work she concluded that, "Now I feel I was mistaken, and think that, to have any real significance, most photographs have got to be dated."[4] When we look at Gutmann's photographs of the thirties and forties we can see that he understood this from the beginning.

Life magazine, which was largely modelled on the German illustrated weeklies of the twenties, quickly became a powerful voice in American photojournalistic circles. To be published in *Life* was to have arrived. However, there were other important loci in which New York documentary photographers worked. The Photo League was an offshoot of the Workers' International Relief, which was founded by the 1921 Communist International. It promoted a photographic vision that was many removes from the corporate one characteristic of Henry Luce's *Life*. The mix of amateur and professional photographers who worked with the League undertook New York documentary projects that produced many pictures similar in content to Gutmann's. While he was League president in the late thirties, Max Yavno made some wonderful photographs of commercial signage. So did his roommate of the time, Aaron Siskind. Siskind joined the League in 1933 and, later in the decade, organized its Features Group. His photographic contributions to the Group's documentary projects, particularly the *Harlem Document* and *Dead End: The Bowery*, often concentrated on popular culture – automobiles, advertising, graffiti, and the mix of language and picture – all subjects common to Gutmann's work of the period. However, if one looks at the images within the larger body of each man's work, as one always must with photography, it is clear that very different sensibilities lie behind them. Siskind was working within the context of the League, where pictures were vehicles for messages of social reform. If signs were in the photographs, they were supposedly there to give information about prices and the availability of goods and shelter.

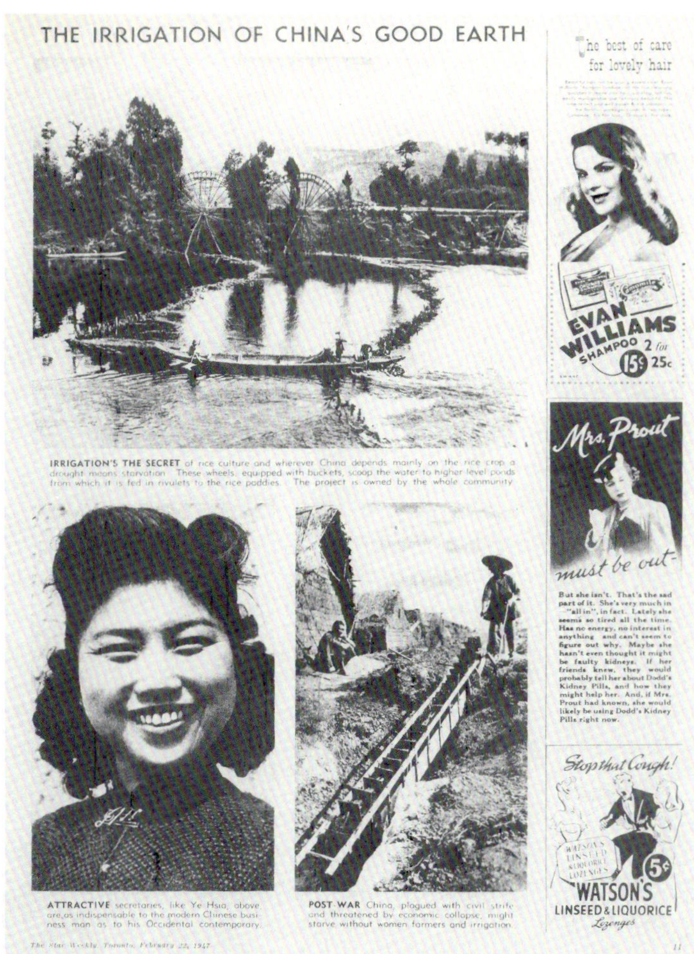

THE IRRIGATION OF CHINA'S GOOD EARTH

IRRIGATION'S THE SECRET of rice culture and wherever China depends mainly on the rice crop a drought means starvation. These wheels, equipped with buckets, scoop the water to higher level ponds from which it is fed in rivulets to the rice paddies. The project is owned by the whole community.

ATTRACTIVE secretaries, like Ye Hsia, above, are as indispensable to the modern Chinese business man as to his Occidental contemporary.

POST-WAR China, plagued with civil strife and threatened by economic collapse, might starve without women farmers and irrigation.

The Star Weekly, Toronto, February 22, 1947

he best of care for lovely hair

EVAN WILLIAMS SHAMPOO 2 for 15¢ 25¢

Mrs. Prout must be out-

But she isn't. That's the sad part of it. She's very much in—"all in", in fact. Lately she seems so tired all the time. Has no energy, no interest in anything and can't seem to figure out why. Maybe she hasn't even thought it might be faulty kidneys. If her friends knew, they would probably tell her about Dodd's Kidney Pills, and how they might help her. And, if Mrs. Prout had known, she would likely be using Dodd's Kidney Pills right now.

Stop that Cough!

5¢ WATSON'S LINSEED & LIQUORICE Lozenges

fig. 2
Page from *The Star Weekly*, February 22, 1947.
Courtesy of Toronto Star Newspapers Ltd.

In the later thirties, as Siskind began to reject the Social Realist line of his colleagues, his photographs of these same subjects increasingly became somewhat veiled metaphors for his turbulent emotional life at the time. Seen in the context of his other work, a Siskind photograph of a word-cluttered storefront before which a man turns his back to the camera, is clearly about his alienation and distress. A Gutmann photograph of a parallel situation simply asserts presence: it tells us what once existed. As the thirties wore on, Siskind's photographs seemed to become progressively darker while Gutmann's remained clear descriptions of a popular culture that he continued to find amazing. By the forties, the two men were on entirely different paths. Siskind was pursuing a singularly personal movement into a formal but very sensuous "abstraction." He worked exclusively outside New York while Gutmann remained loyal to the street.

In 1943, he volunteered for overseas duty so that he could enroll at the motion picture school of the Signal Corps in Astoria, New York. When his training was complete, he was assigned to Stilwell's Y-Force in China. Soon the U.S. Office of War Information requested him for their Kunming Operation. For two years, he photographed leaflet- and rice-dropping flight missions over Japanese-occupied China, the opening of the Burma Road, and many other assignments in Southwest China, Burma, and India. While much of this was motion picture work, he was also given still-photography assignments. All but a small fraction of it promptly disappeared into government files. After the war, he assembled some of the film that he had taken for himself, and created two movies on China. In 1949, the productions were completed, shown on American television, and sold to various libraries. As American curiosity about China crested in the wake of the revolution, Gutmann culled the stills that remained in his possession for a large exhibition at the M.H. de Young Museum in 1947. Pix placed many of these images internationally and in an essay on the Kunming Pilgrimage published in a *National Geographic* issue of 1950.

Although the immediate post-war years were a time of recovery and consolidation for Gutmann – he was busy setting up a department of photography at San Francisco State College – he continued to complete editorial assignments. He was a regular West Coast contributor to the *Saturday Evening Post* until 1954, and through Pix, new Gutmann photographs continued to appear in many American magazines of the decade. However, his sensibility is seldom evident in these published stories. His captions were usually cast aside and the images radically cropped to fit the column widths of the magazines. Nor were the topics assigned to him (for example, an essay on camping for *Parents Magazine*) the most congenial vehicles for his sensibility.

Yet he continued to work throughout the decade. In 1957, while on a sabbatical from teaching, he spent eight months in Europe making a film about modern architecture. Architecture had long been a significant subtheme in his photographs and he wanted to document the growing rebellion against the cool, corporate formalism of the International Style. Not surprisingly, his sympathies lay with the structurally radical organicism of Pier Luigi Nervi and Le Corbusier. Gutmann's failure to secure a completion grant from the American Institute of Architects meant that the film was never released, however. Soon after this, Gutmann began to slow down. During the greater part of the sixties, his production was severely reduced as he struggled with health problems resulting from the time he had spent in China twenty years earlier. When his health returned in the early seventies, he began to put his archives in order.

After retiring from teaching in 1973, Gutmann was able to devote himself entirely to the task of organizing and editing four decades of photographic work. His archives revealed that most assignments had generated more than a hundred negatives. They were a mix of exposures that he had made purely for himself, various exploratory approaches to his subject, and a number of straightforward descriptive views that anticipated the predispositions of magazine picture editors. Deadline pressures and simple economics had generally dictated that he would send only fifty of the total, Pix usually edited down to approximately twenty, while the magazines often published fewer than ten. Three-quarters of this massive archive had never been printed because it failed to meet the immediate needs of agencies and editors.

Photography is an editing medium. Beginning with the complex of decisions made through the viewfinder – in a sense, an editing of the world – and through to the final selection of negatives to be printed, the photographer makes himself. Now, for the first time, Gutmann was free to make his own choices. As he worked his way through more than ten thousand negatives and forty years

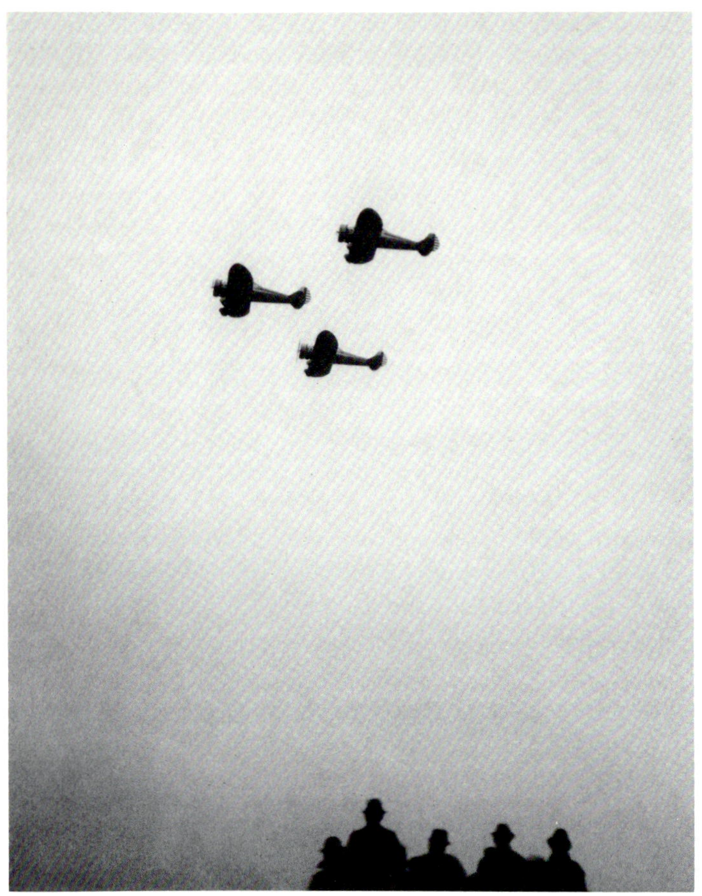

fig. 3
Omen. 1934.

of his life, he began the long process of discovering and rediscovering himself. He could now invent an artist.

There is a deprecatory joke that photographers occasionally exchange with their colleagues. It is framed by the question, "What is the difference between painters and photographers?" The answer is that painters don't sit around all day talking about paint brushes. Photographers do talk frequently about cameras, but they are seldom forthcoming about the extent to which the type and format of their chosen camera determines what they can do and how they will see. The twin-lens Rollei on which Gutmann apprenticed and matured makes its own unique assertions. Its ground glass is on the top of the body, an arrangement that forces the user to look at the world from below the level of the eye. It also greatly facilitates photography from ground level, as the photographer need not prostrate himself. This low level of view is a persistent element in Gutmann's visual syntax. So, too, is the influence of the square frame. The square, a very stable visual form, is also an unnatural one. It bears little relationship to the horizontal scanning activity of the eye and encourages a kind of compression of elements within its borders. It is totally self-contained. Although Gutmann was no purist – he cropped his negatives whenever good structure demanded it – the legacy of the square persisted. His photographs used every part of the frame; every element had its own business. If there was a blank space – sky or wall – there was only enough to emphasize the form of the object before it. The Rollei is a kind of hybrid, part-view camera – the master tool of the nineteenth century – that also incorporates features of the 35mm miniature camera so ubiquitous in the twentieth. From the former, it takes the large ground glass, a viewer that permits the arrangement of a substantial amount of information within the frame. Without it, photographs so dense with text, so precise in their descriptions of surfaces, photographs that can describe buildings, messages, cars, and people in a single view would have been impossible. One only has to compare the 35mm photographs that Henri Cartier-Bresson or André Kertész made in the thirties with Gutmann's of the same period to see the radically different constraints and freedoms the different formats imposed. The photographs of Kertész and Cartier-Bresson rely upon timing and clear obvious design, rather than information density, to achieve their photographic effects. Gutmann's rely upon description, while still exploiting the rapid-roll film camera's grasp of the moment. The view camera, on the other hand, while capable of great descriptive powers, is slower to work with, and less capable of comprehending the instant. It is the camera of calculated contemplation; it gives no second chances. The choice of a camera that partook of the qualities of both extremes informed Gutmann's notion of what a photograph could be and do, while at the same time setting his work apart from that of his American colleagues who were still wrestling big-view cameras about the country. Although Gutmann worked with both larger and smaller cameras than the Rollei during the forties and fifties, he soon returned to his original camera and has used it ever since.

While John Gutmann's photography was shaped by many factors – his schooling as a painter, his journey from Europe to America, even the equipment that introduced him to the medium – it was also shaped by the requisites of professional photojournalism. Initially, his job was to describe for European eyes that which was uniquely American, a mandate that only served to reinforce his outsider's vision. He learned that photographs, unlike paintings, always require a text. Without captions, photographic images float free of specific meaning; the inherent ambiguity of photographs becomes uncontrollable. As a professional, he always supplied carefully written captions as part of his assignment material. Later, when he was free to recontextualize his pictures for his own expressive purposes, he remained true to this practice. However, the captions changed – they became titles. Their function was no longer to render the images specific, but rather to make them suggestive and resonant. They drew the viewer to details that might otherwise have been overlooked, details that could function as signs. His titles often subverted the literal and fostered ambiguity. The strategy of *Omen* (fig. 3) or *Death Stalks Fillmore* (fig. 4), two of his most famous pictures, is an inversion of the documentary principle. The title does not anchor; it frees.

Walking the streets with a camera, Gutmann was a man witnessing things and events so extraordinary that he considered the act of making a record statement enough. His photographs of an emerging popular culture signalled his determination to avoid the reflexiveness of painting. He did not want to impose the self upon the image. With a few exceptions, his photographs declared a culture, a time, and place. Yet as the body of work grew, as picture butted against picture, even the most transparent photographs began to combine into a portrait of a singular man walking through his part of history. This man was curious, sensual, and emotional. He was passionate about life and, yet, like all artists, preoccupied with death. Contrast is the essence of his life. It is also the core of his art. Harlem blacks enter the rich man's Cord, the two races alternate in line, before and after, fat and thin, and, at the core of life itself, man and woman. Gutmann's men often disappear beneath hats and long coats. They become shapeless shadows that stand alone. His women – sensuous and palpable – are all physical presence. They have bodies that even clothing can't contain. They are the target of desire, the very life force itself, yet they remain always the other. Naked, they are so self-contained as to be unapproachable: dressed, they wear veils, turn away, or commune with each other. The photographer, barred from participation, can only observe. Black and white, man and woman, the self and the other – always a contrast, but never a dialectic. Time and life pass. The only possible transformation is the fixing of the observed into a permanent statement. Make a photograph and create a memory.

Michael Mitchell

Notes

1 Louis Katzman, *Photography in California 1945–1980* (New York: Hudson Hill Press/ San Francisco Museum of Modern Art, 1984), p. 19.

2 Hank O'Neal, ed., *A Vision Shared: A Classic Portrait of America and Its People, 1935–1943* (New York: St. Martin's Press, 1976), p. 36.

3 Hank O'Neal, *Berenice Abbott: American Photographer* (New York: McGraw-Hill Book Co., An Artpress Book, 1982), p. 13.

4 Beaumont Newhall, Commentary by, *Dorothea Lange Looks at the American Country Woman: A Photographic Essay by Dorothea Lange* (Amon Carter Museum, Fort Worth/The Ward Ritchie Press, Los Angeles, 1967), p. 5.

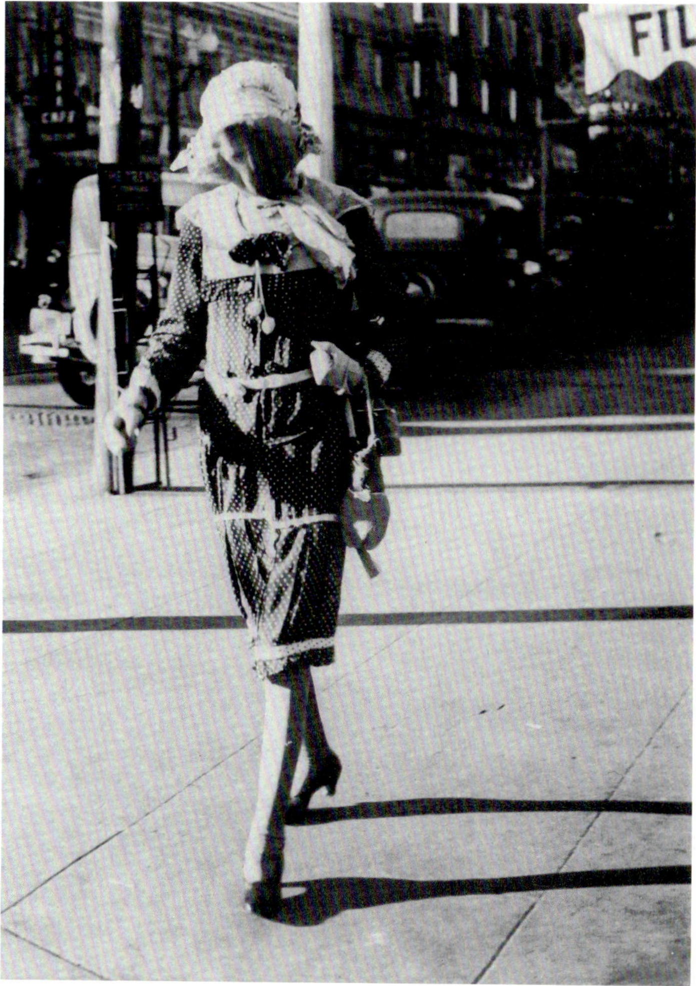

fig. 4
Death Stalks Fillmore. 1934.

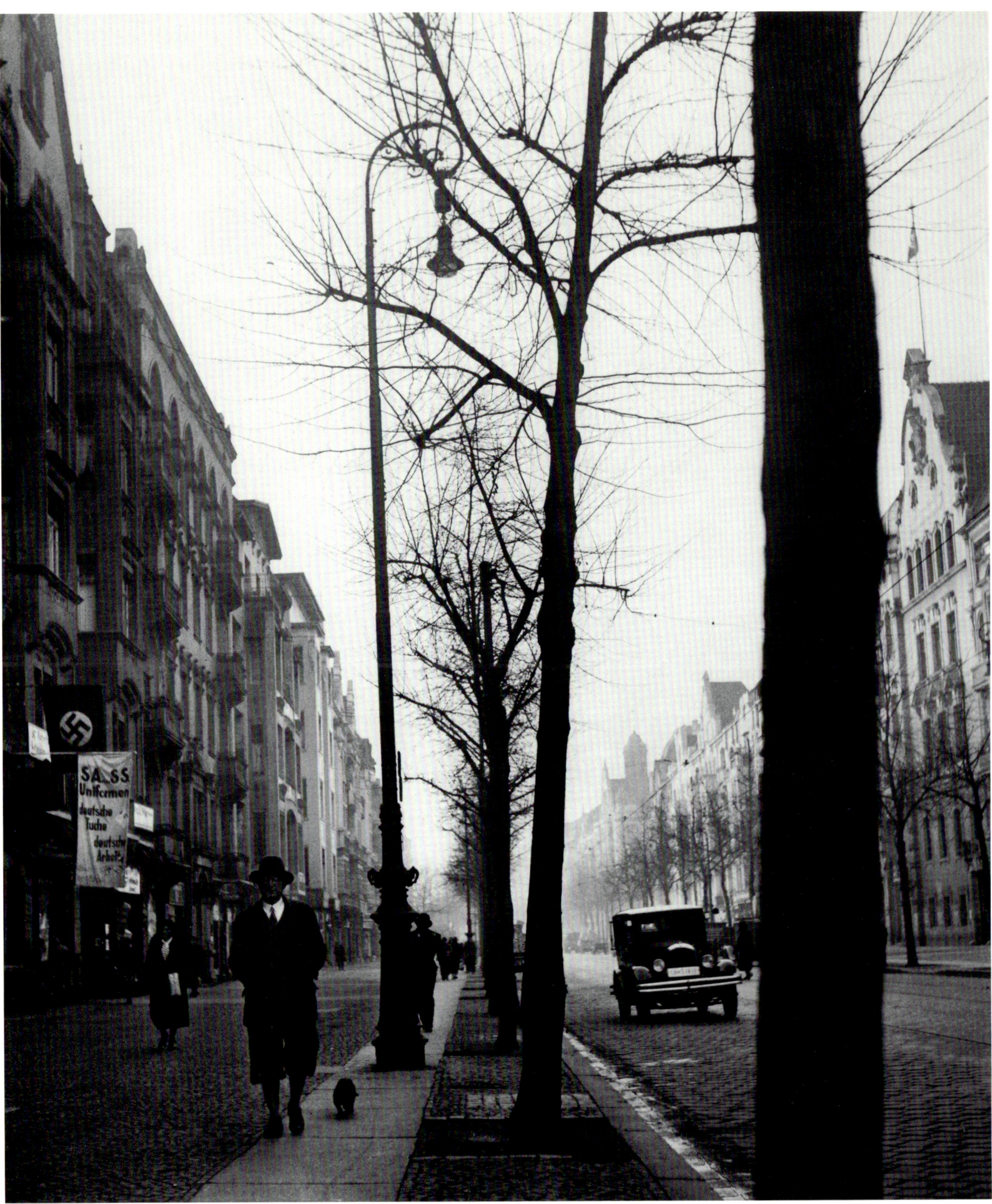

1 *Autumn in Charlottenburg*. Berlin, 1933.

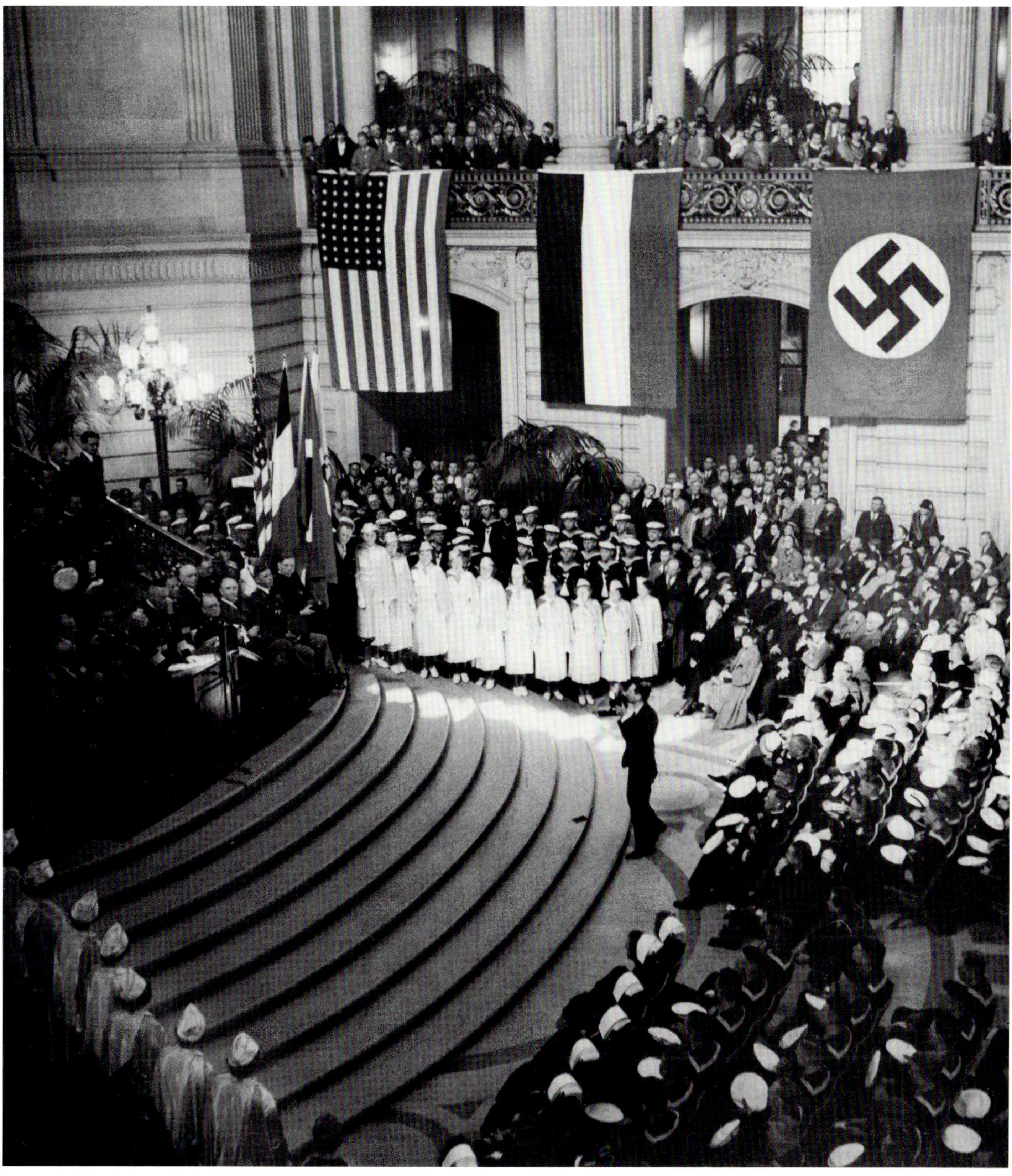

18 *The News Photographer*. San Francisco City Hall, 1935.

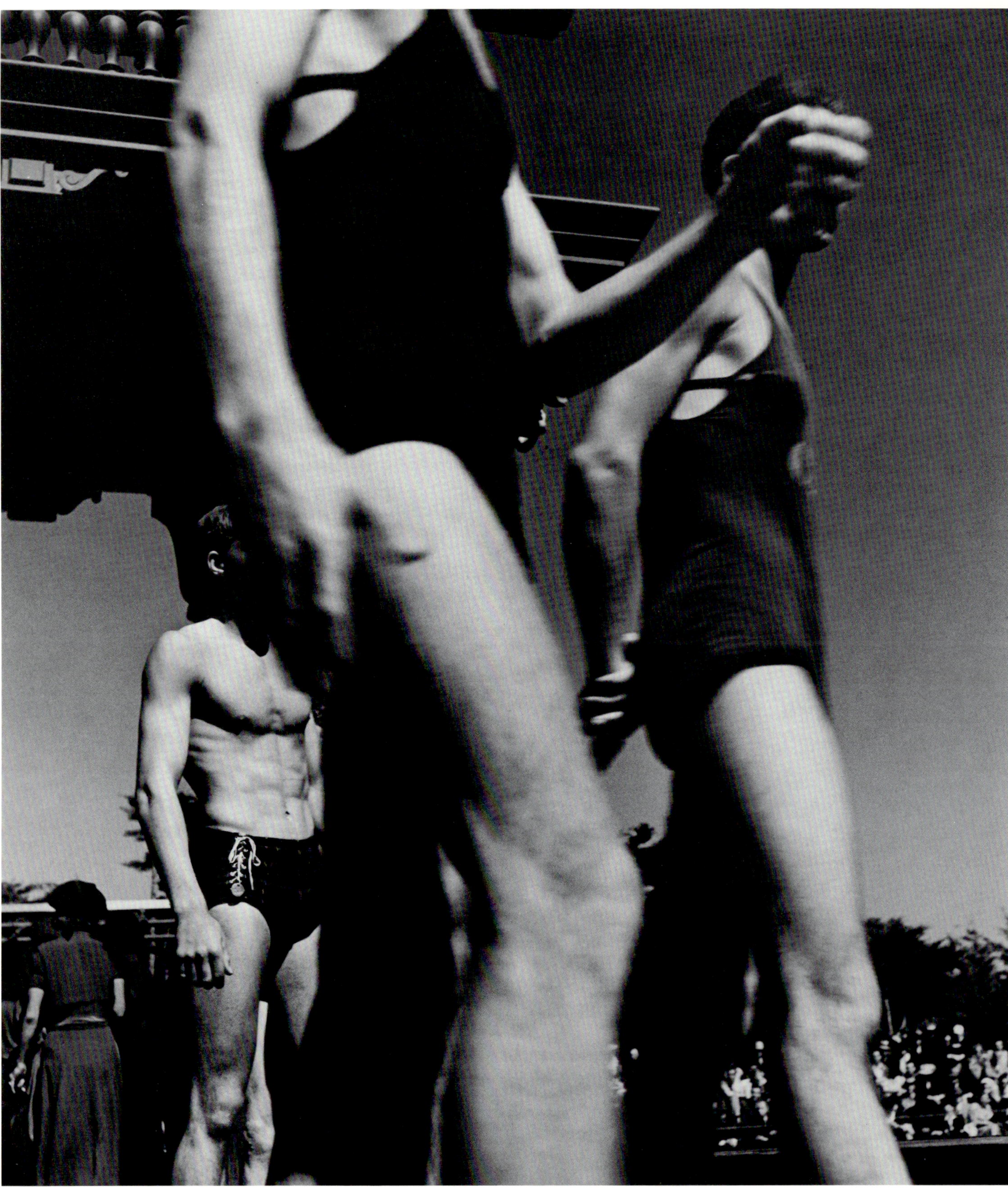

8 *Towards the Pool.* San Francisco, 1934.

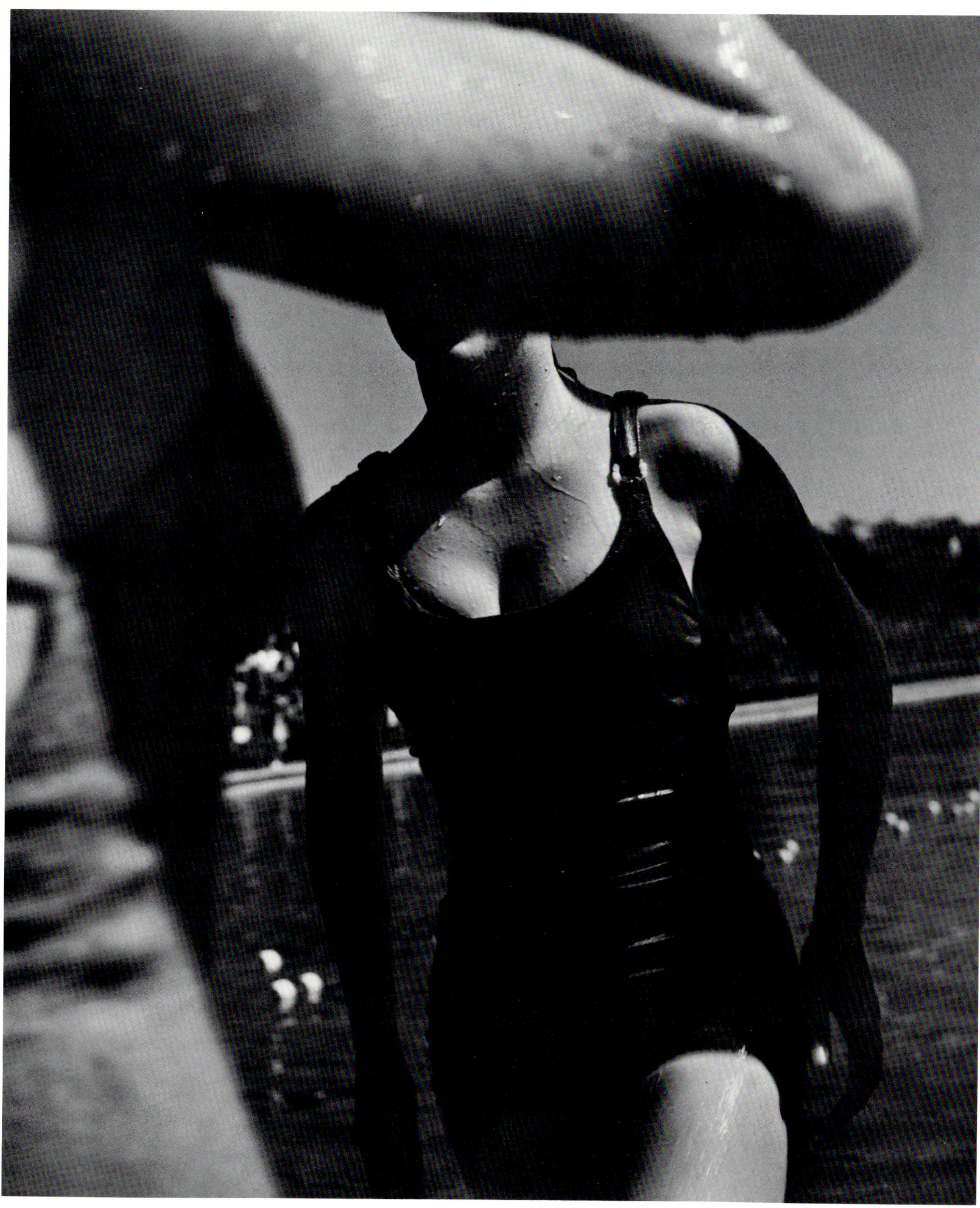

7 *Out of the Pool.* San Francisco, 1934.

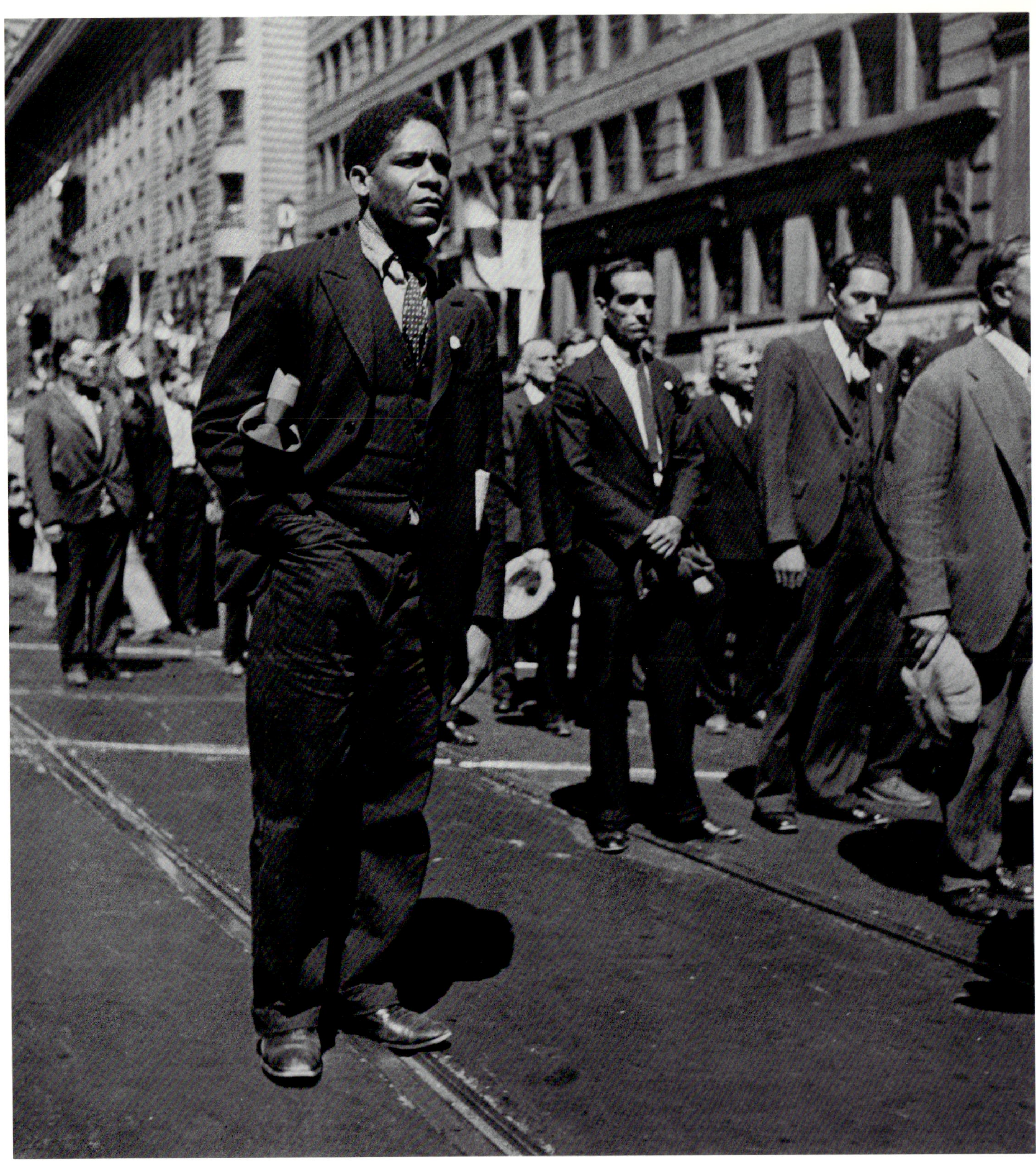

11 *Black Man Alone. Union Members in the Funeral Procession for Killed Worker.* General Strike, San Francisco, 1934.

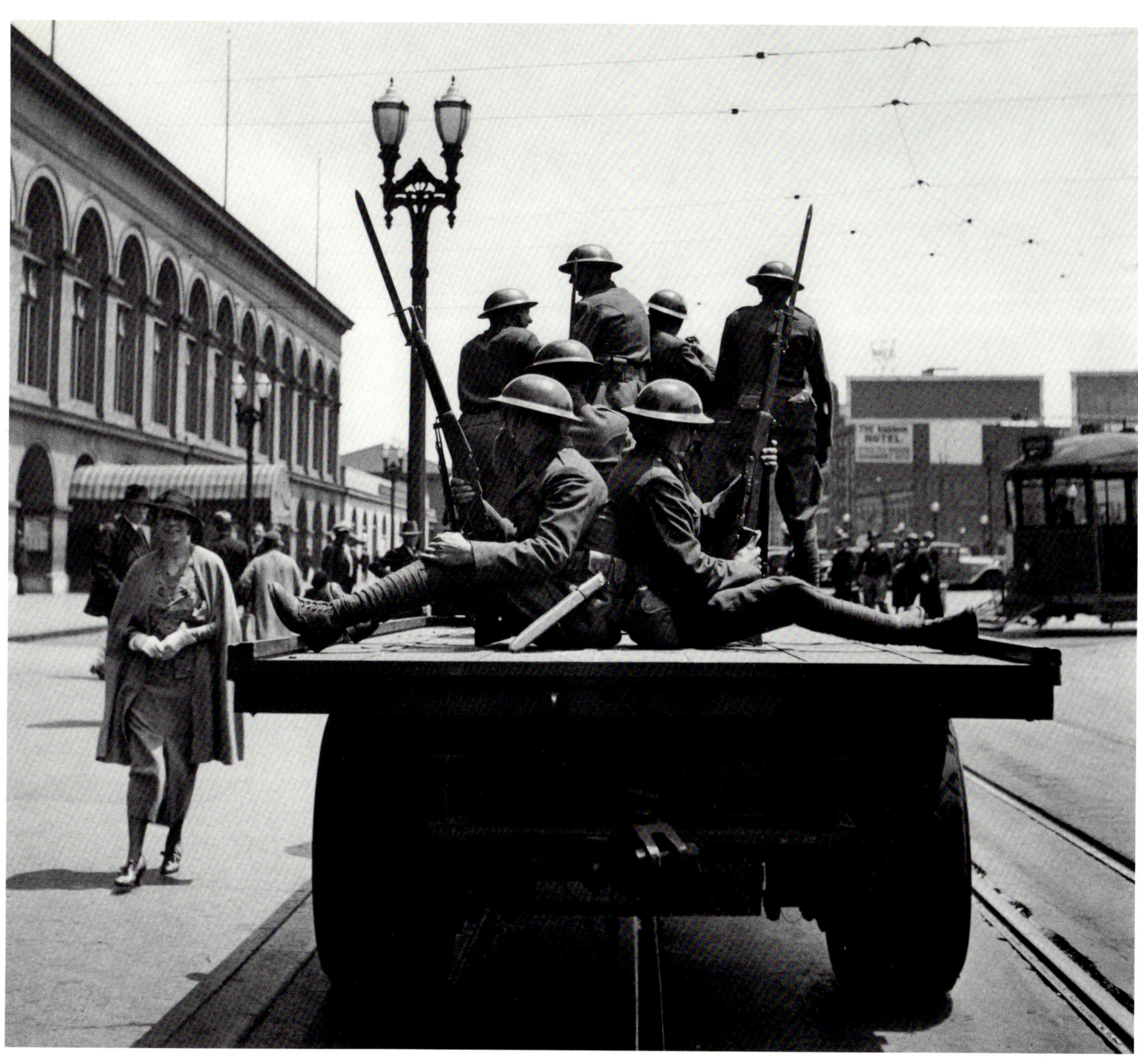

10 *National Guard on Truck Patrolling Waterfront.* General Strike, San Francisco, 1934.

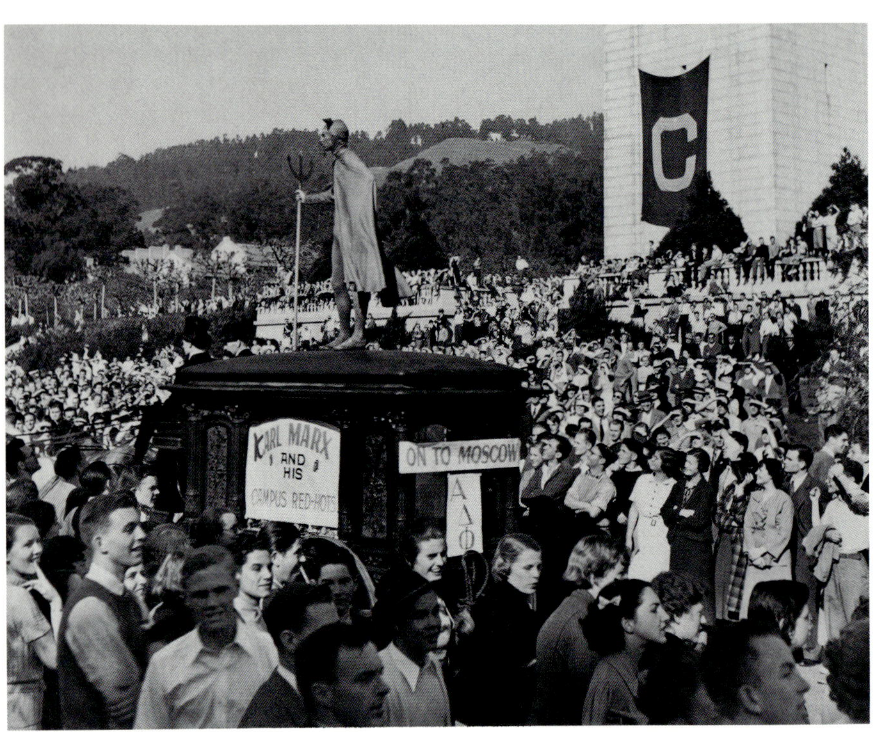

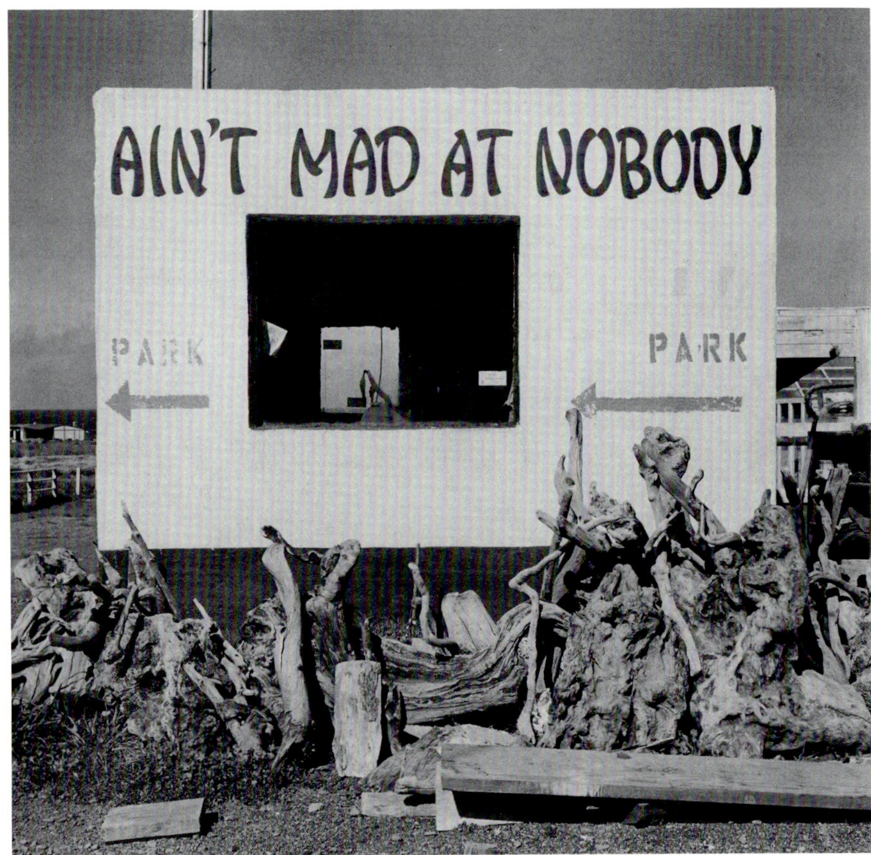

31 *Leap-Year Parade*. Berkeley, 1936.

117 *"Ain't Mad at Nobody"*. Oregon, 1960.

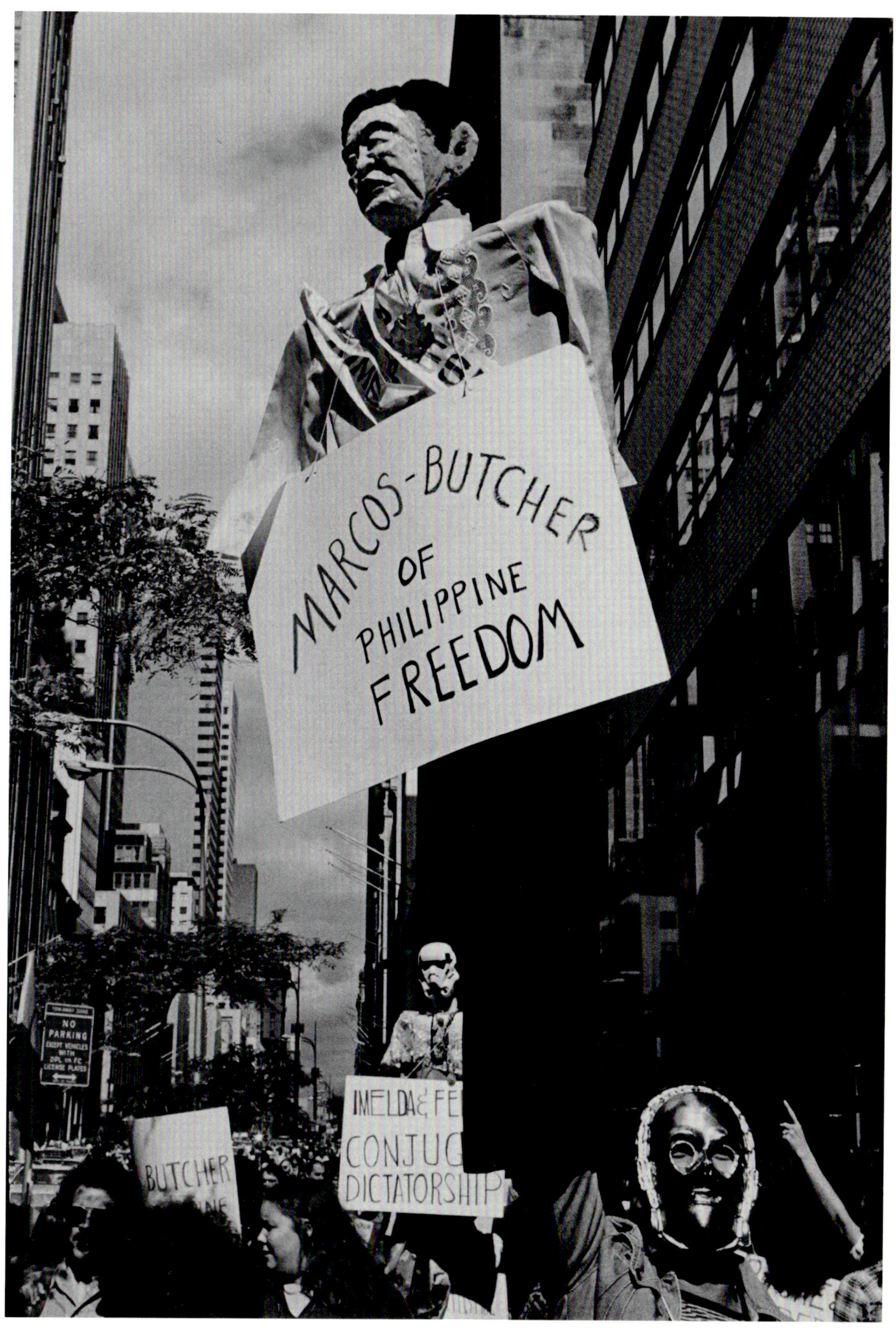

126 *Anti-Marcos Demonstration.* 5th Avenue, New York City, 1978.

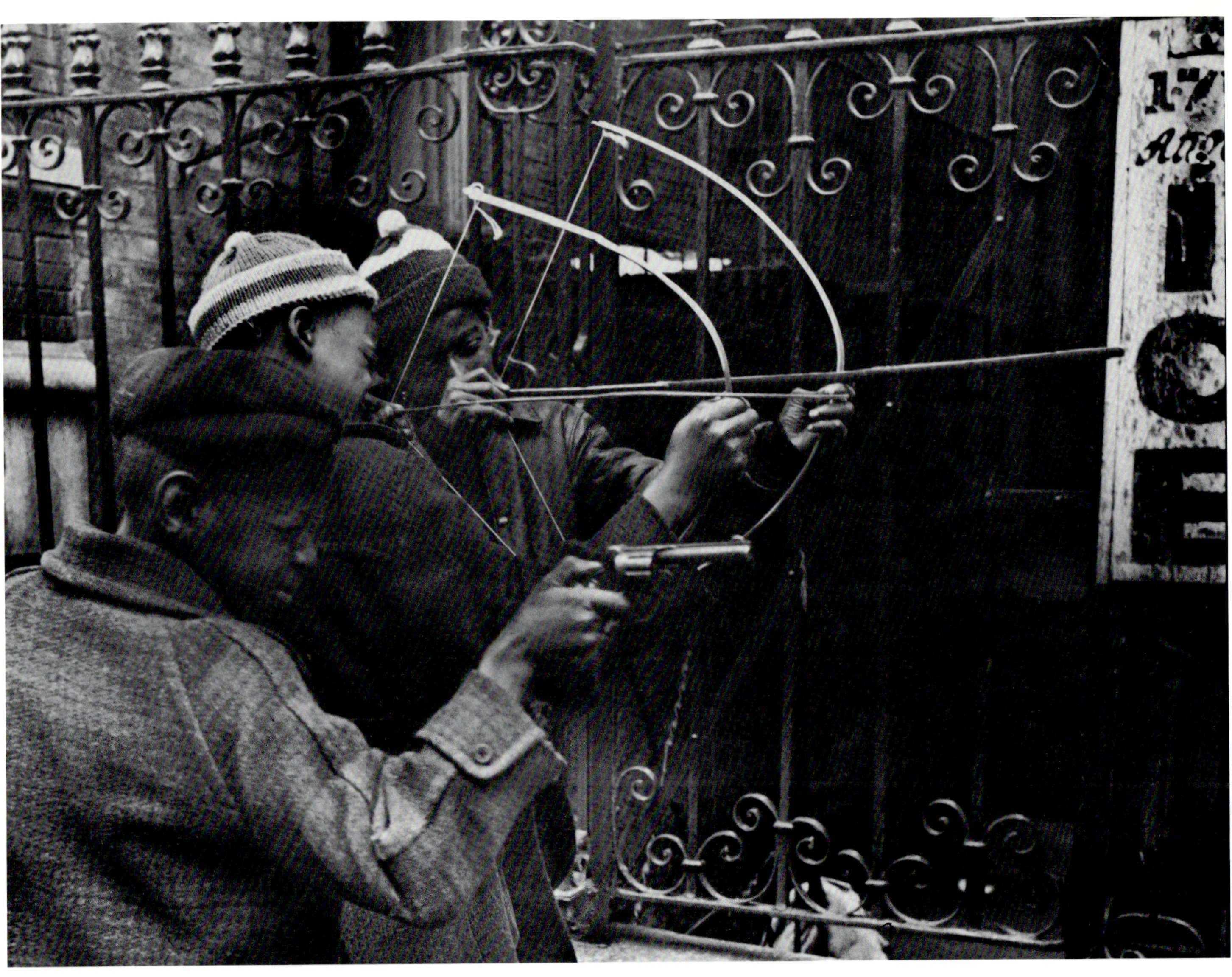

25 *The Sharpshooters.* Harlem, 1936.

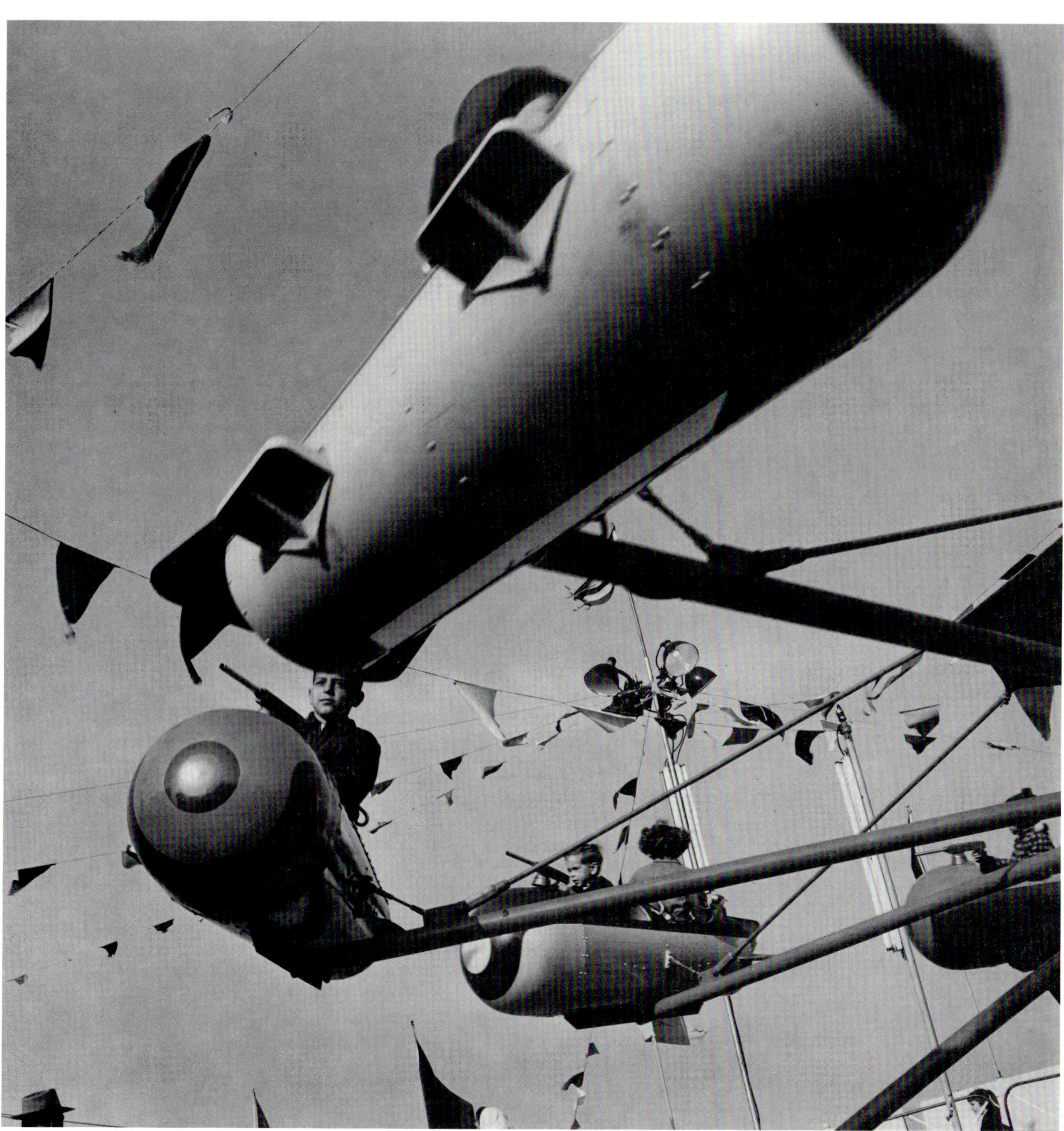

101 *Machine Gunners.* San Francisco, 1950.

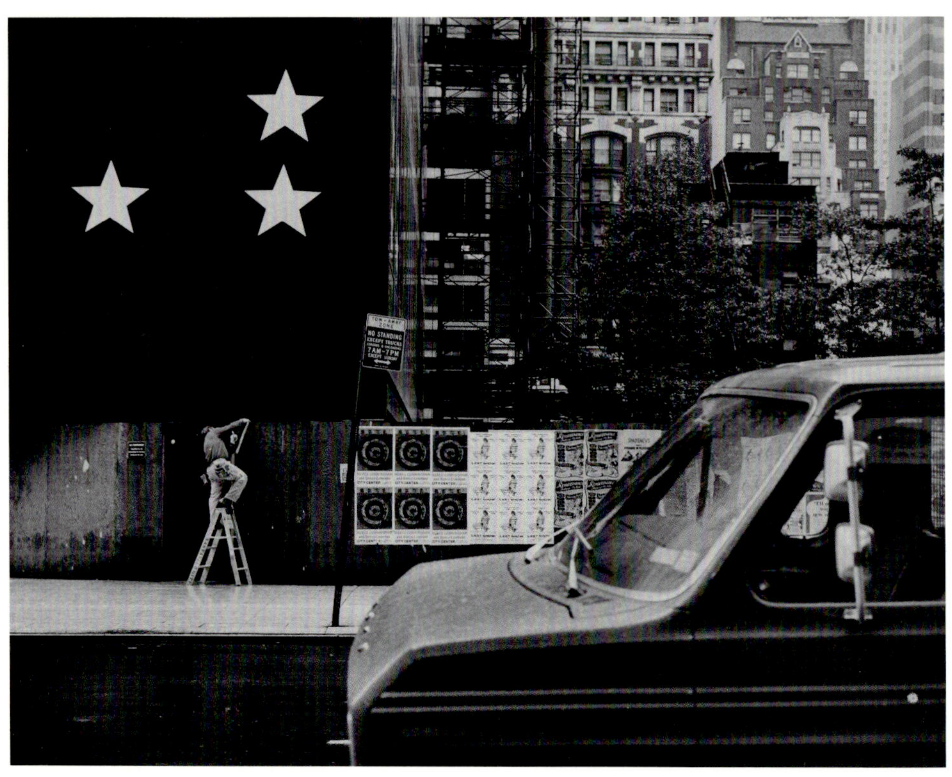

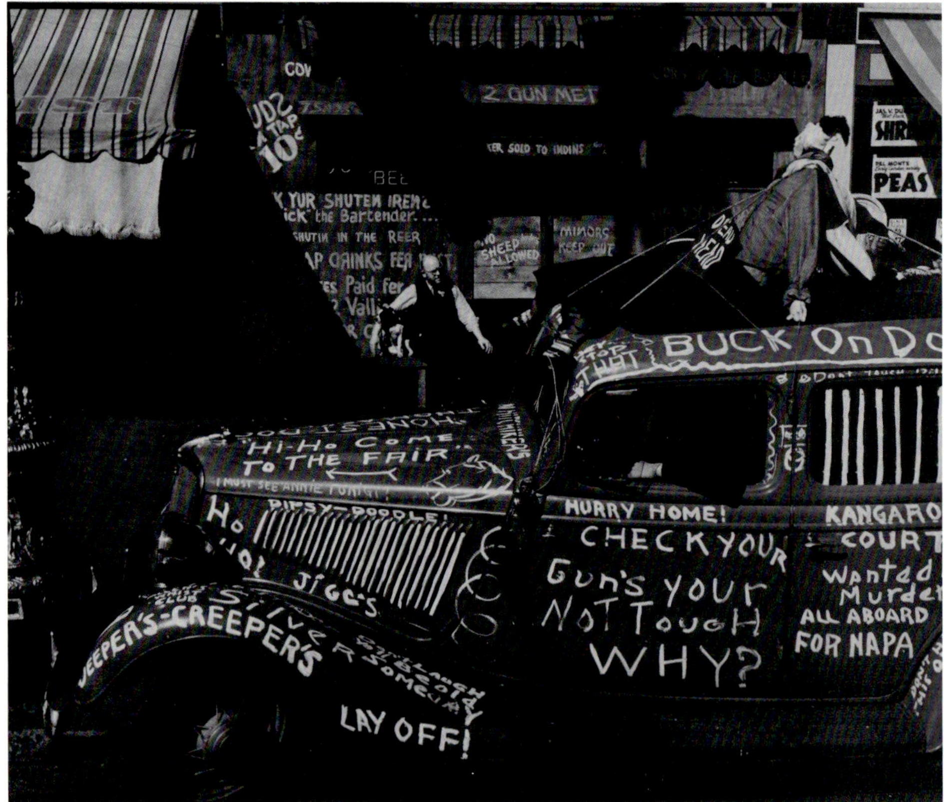

125 *Three Star Building and Fence with Jasper Johns Posters.* New York City, 1978.

56 *San Francisco Celebrates Opening of World's Fair.* 1939.

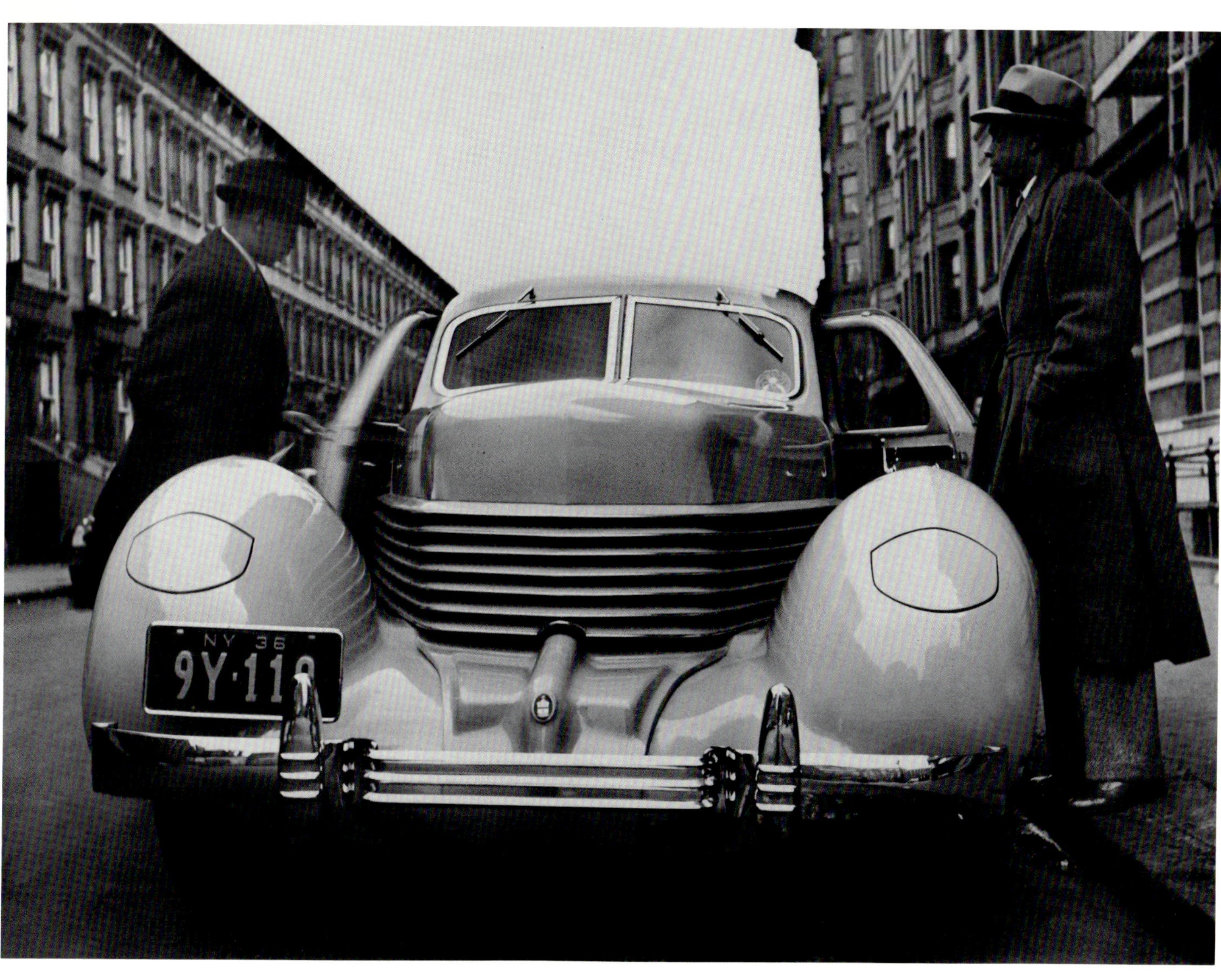

 Cord in Harlem. New York, 1936.

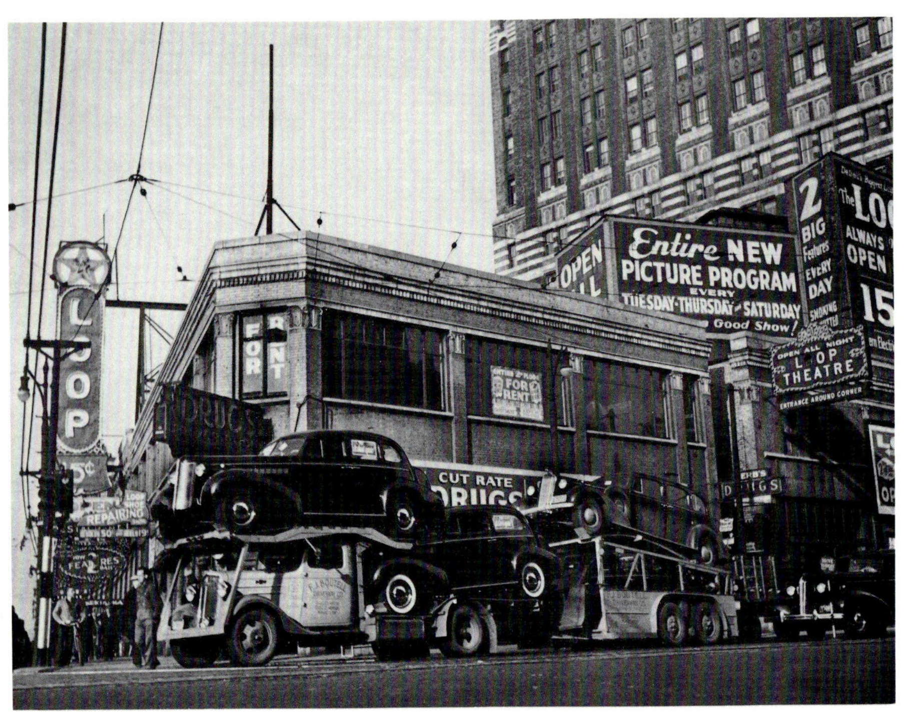

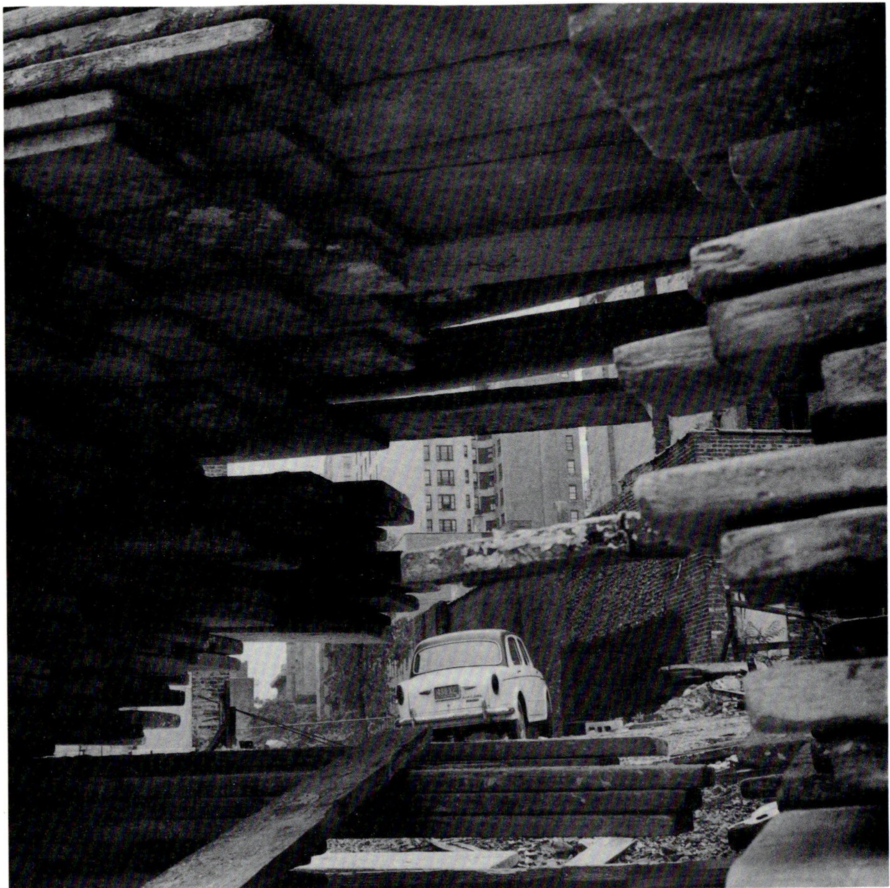

27 *Automobile Transport.* Chicago, 1936.

120 *White Car Away from Lumber Tunnel.* New York City, 1965.

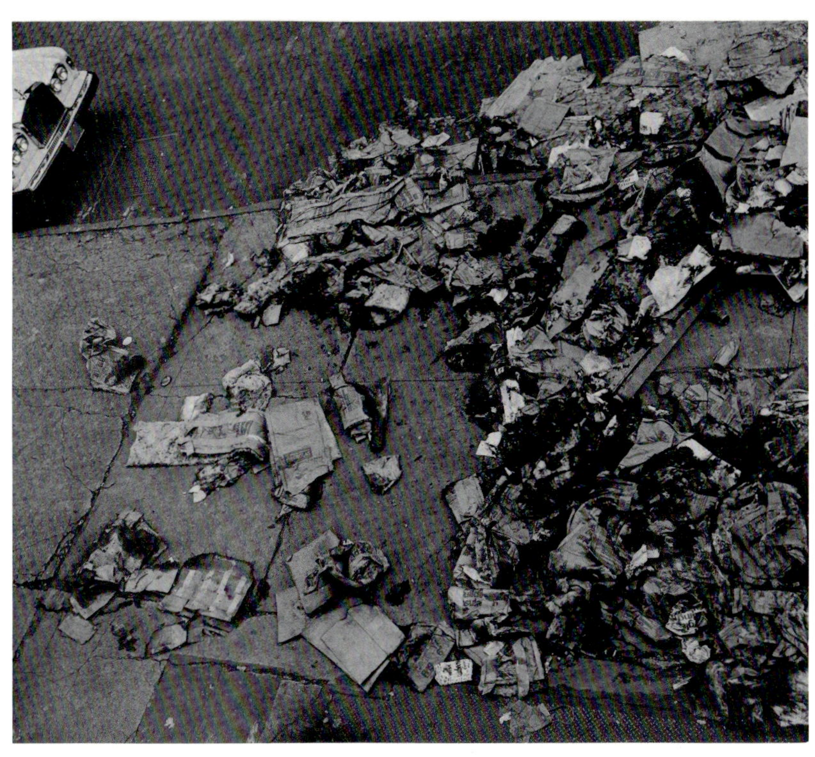

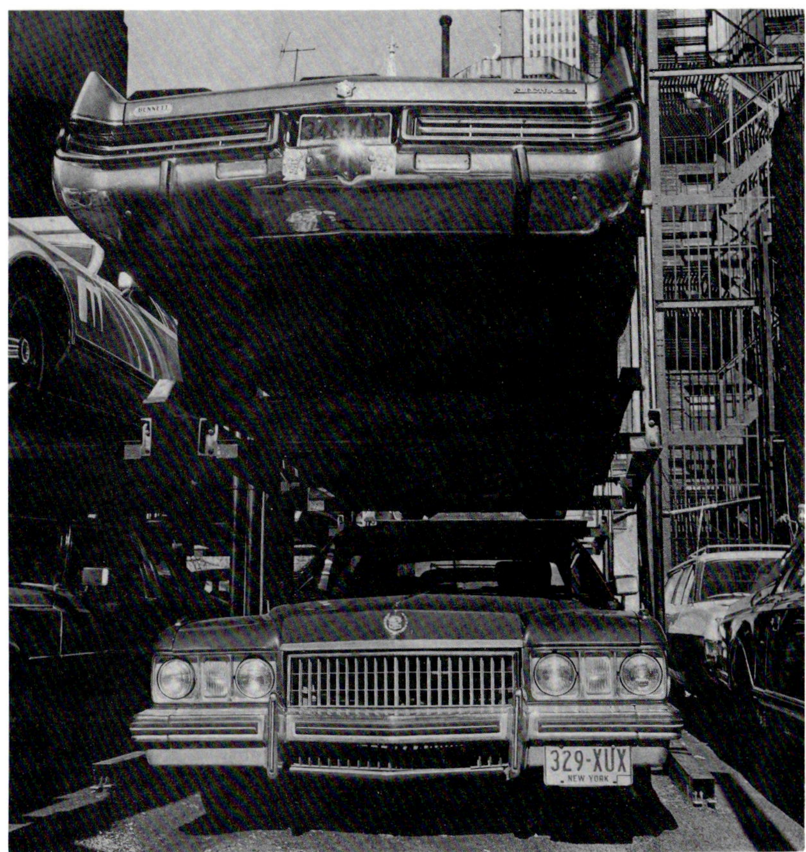

124 *Rolls Royce with Charred Garbage.* New York City, 1978.

123 *Elevated Parking.* New York City, 1978.

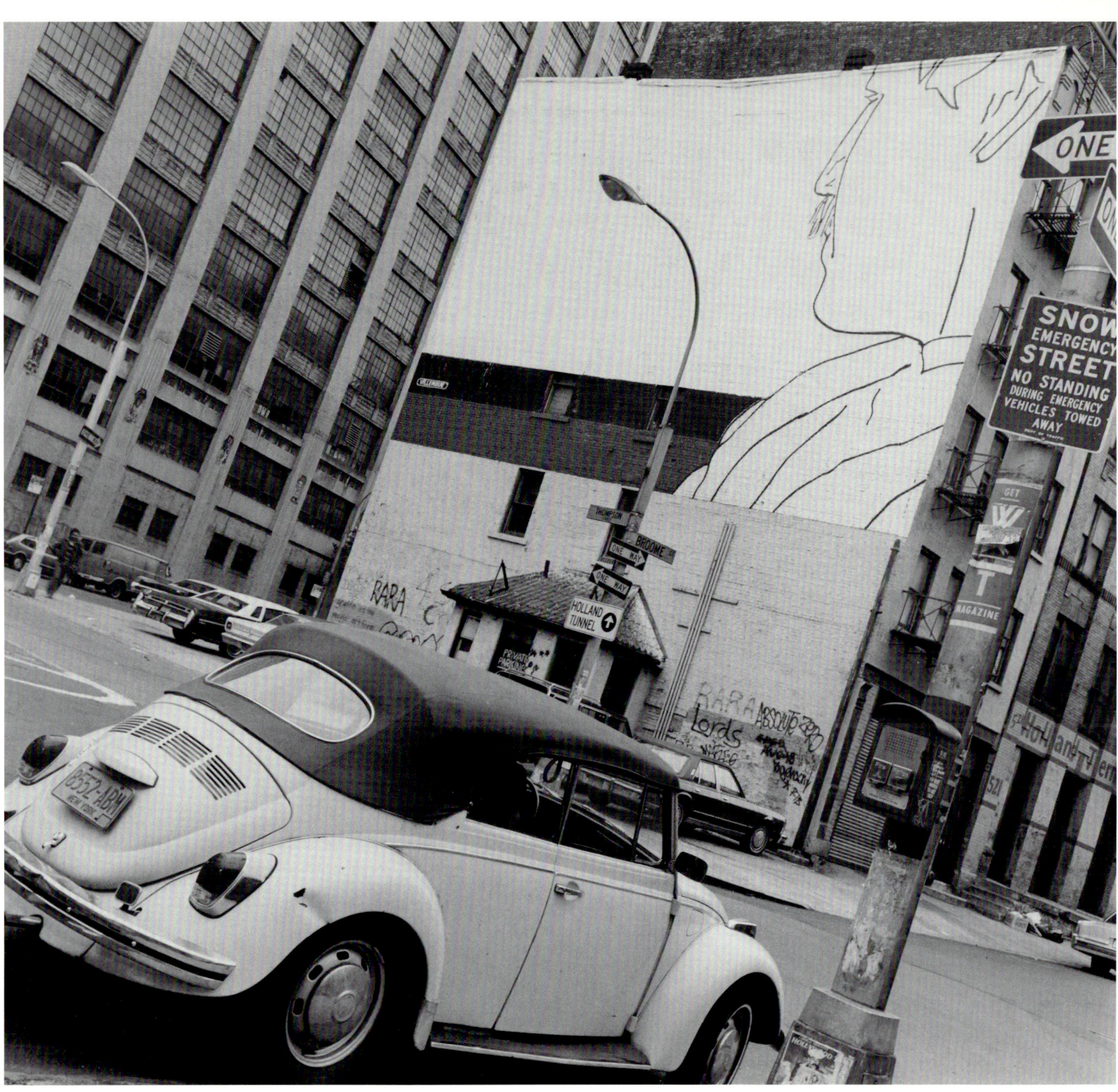

137 *Soho Mural.* New York City, 1981.

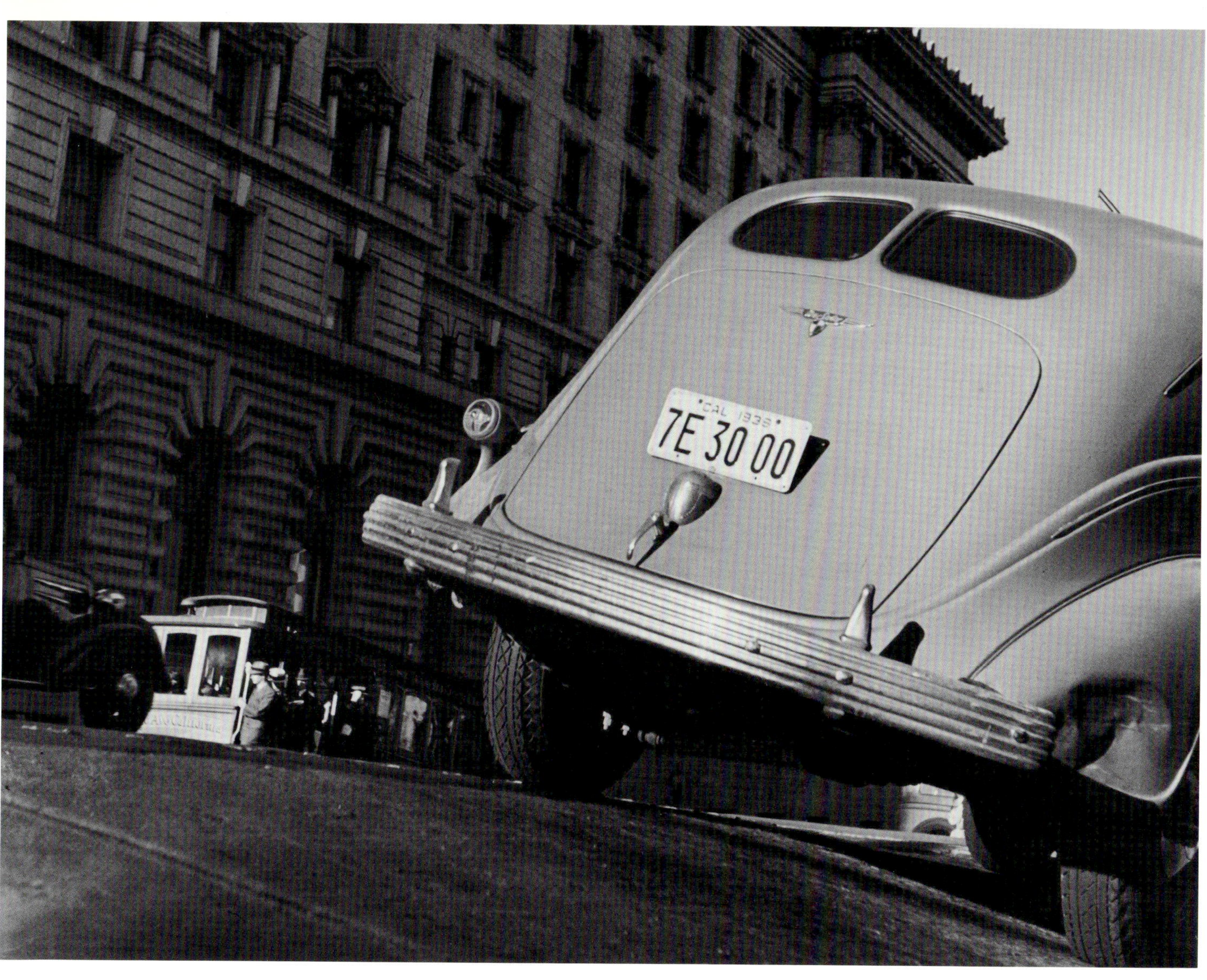

53 *Nob Hill.* San Francisco, 1938.

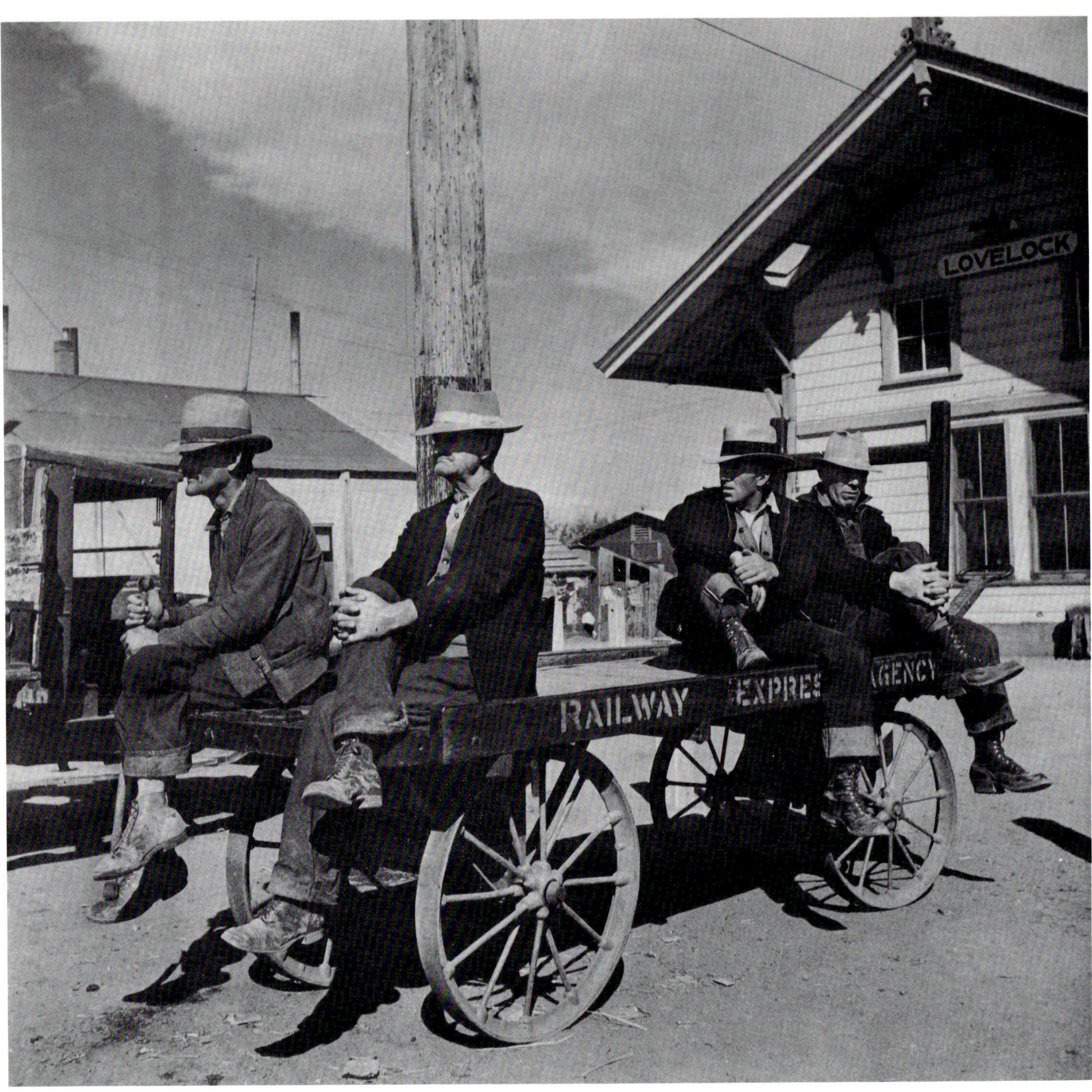

29 *"We're not Talking"*. Lovelock, Nevada, 1936.

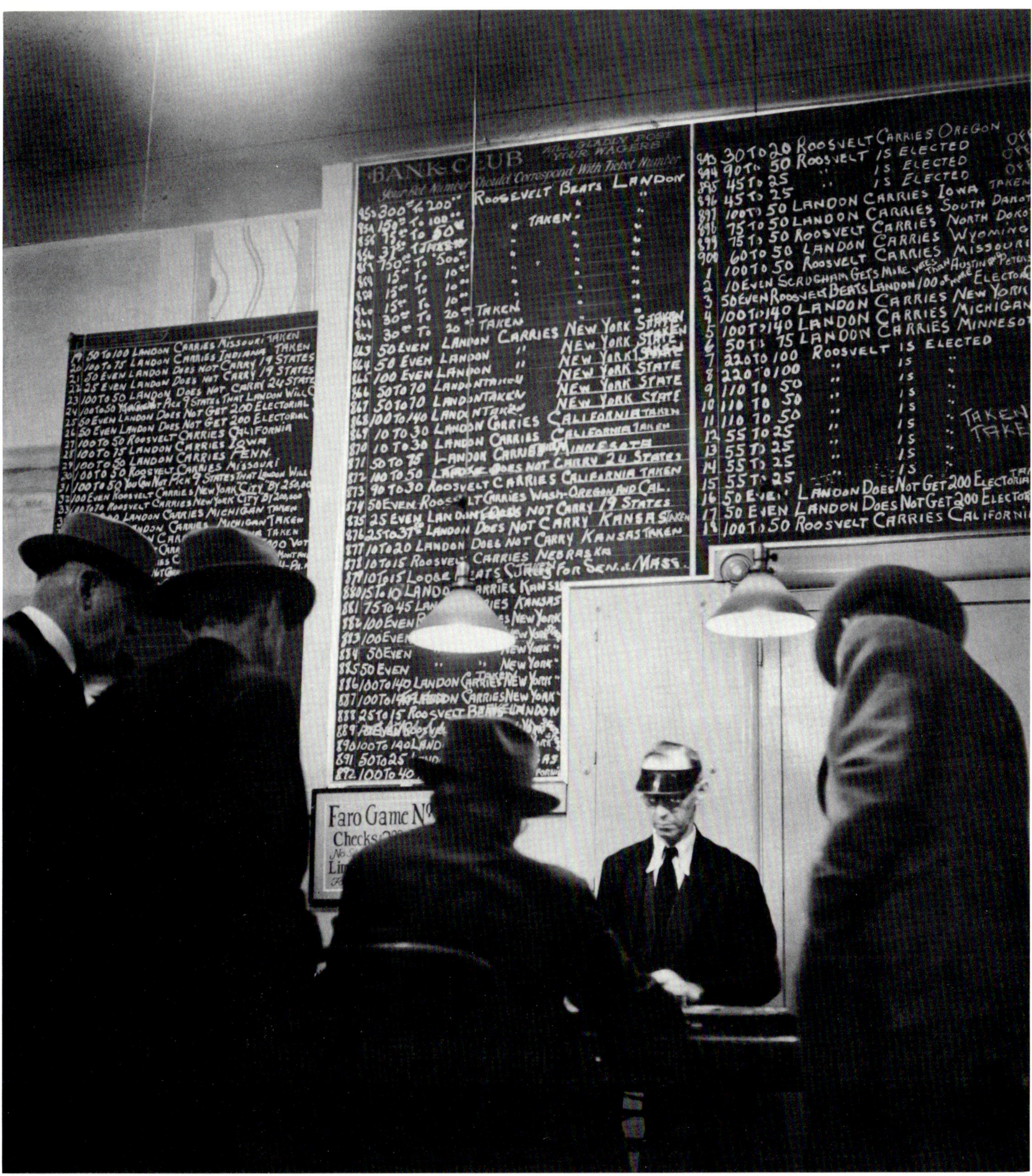

30 *Blackjack in Reno at Election Time.* Nevada, 1936.

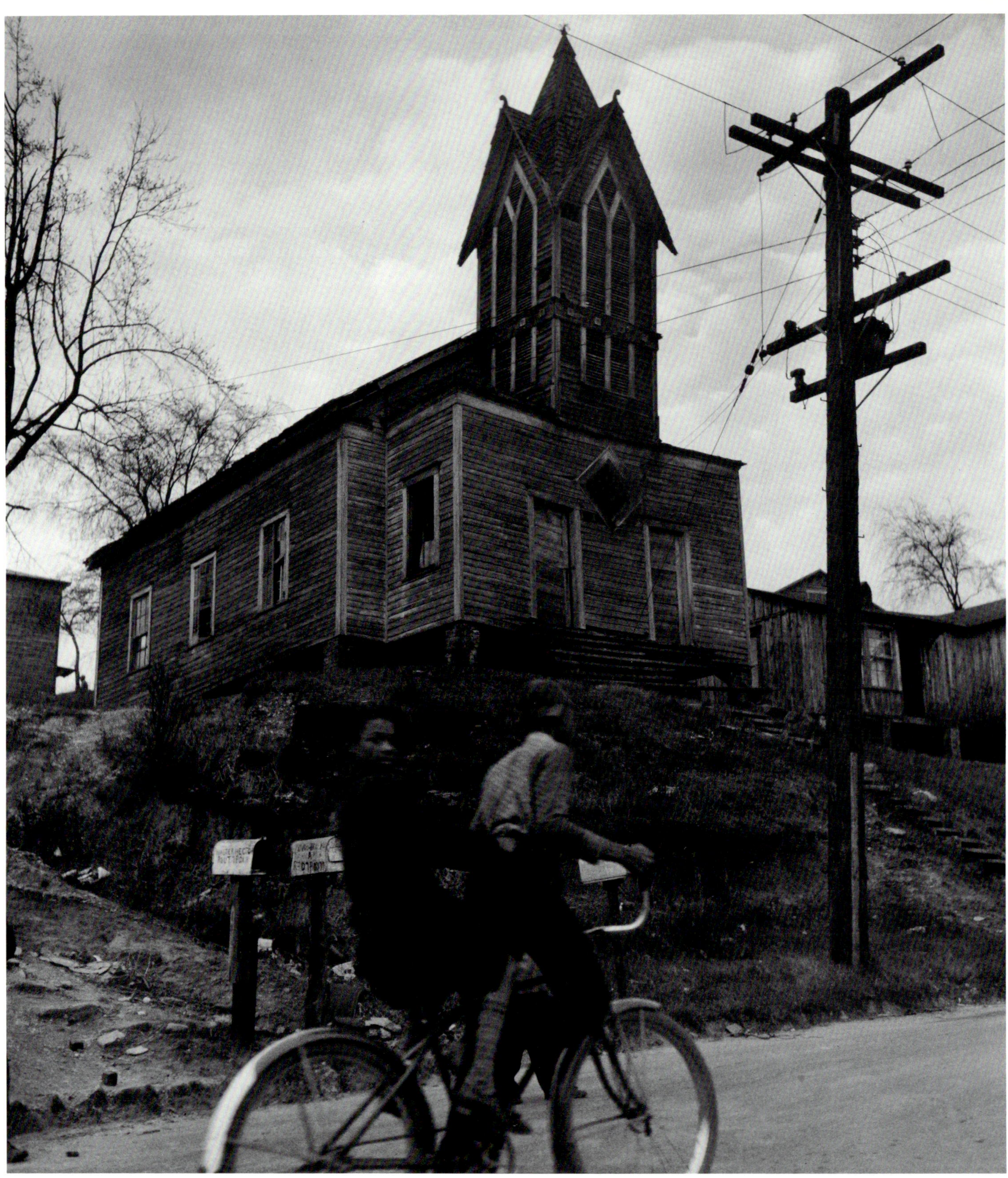

43 *Bicycling by the Old Village Church*. Georgia, 1937.

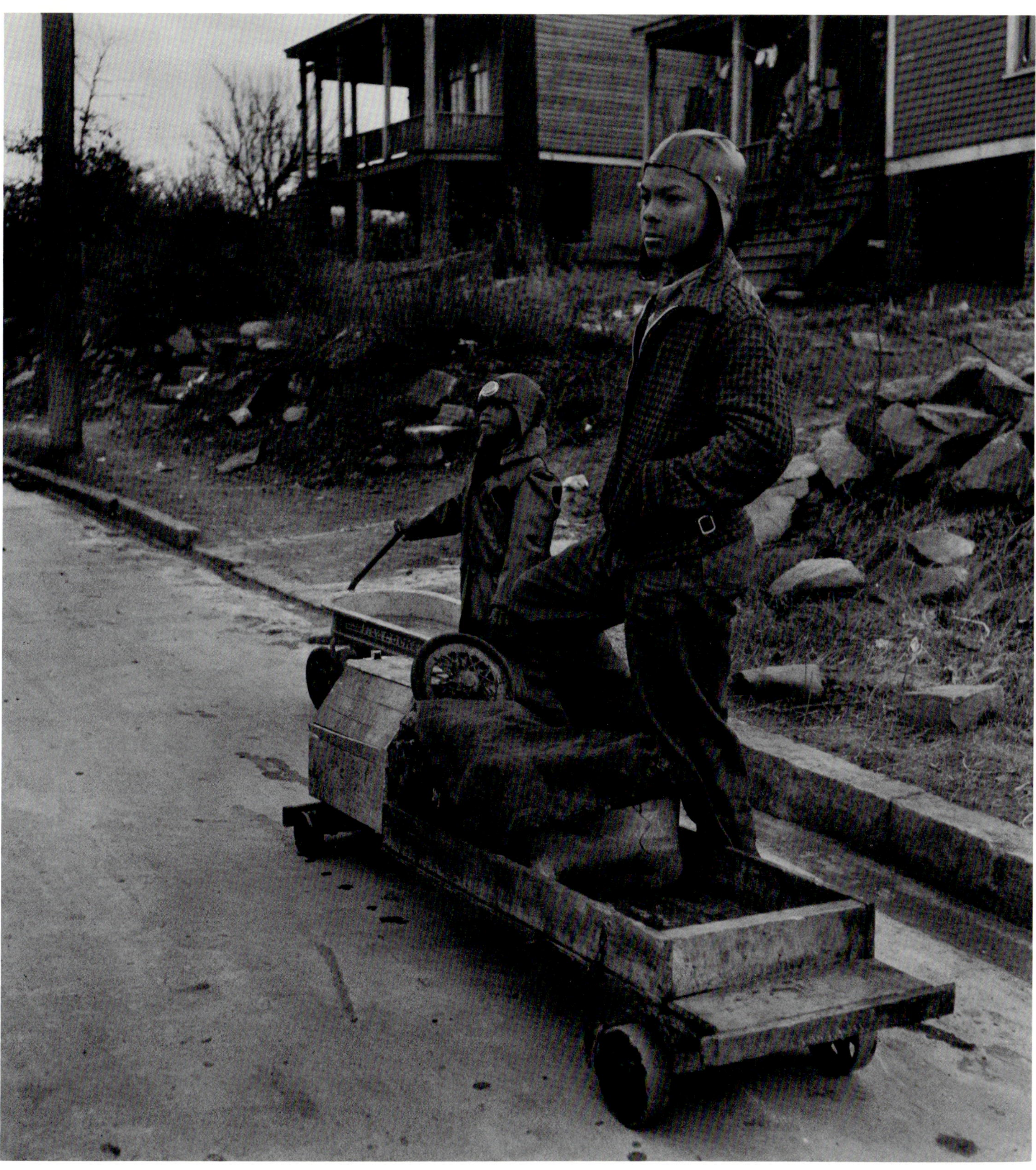

44 *The Soap Box Brothers.* Georgia, 1937.

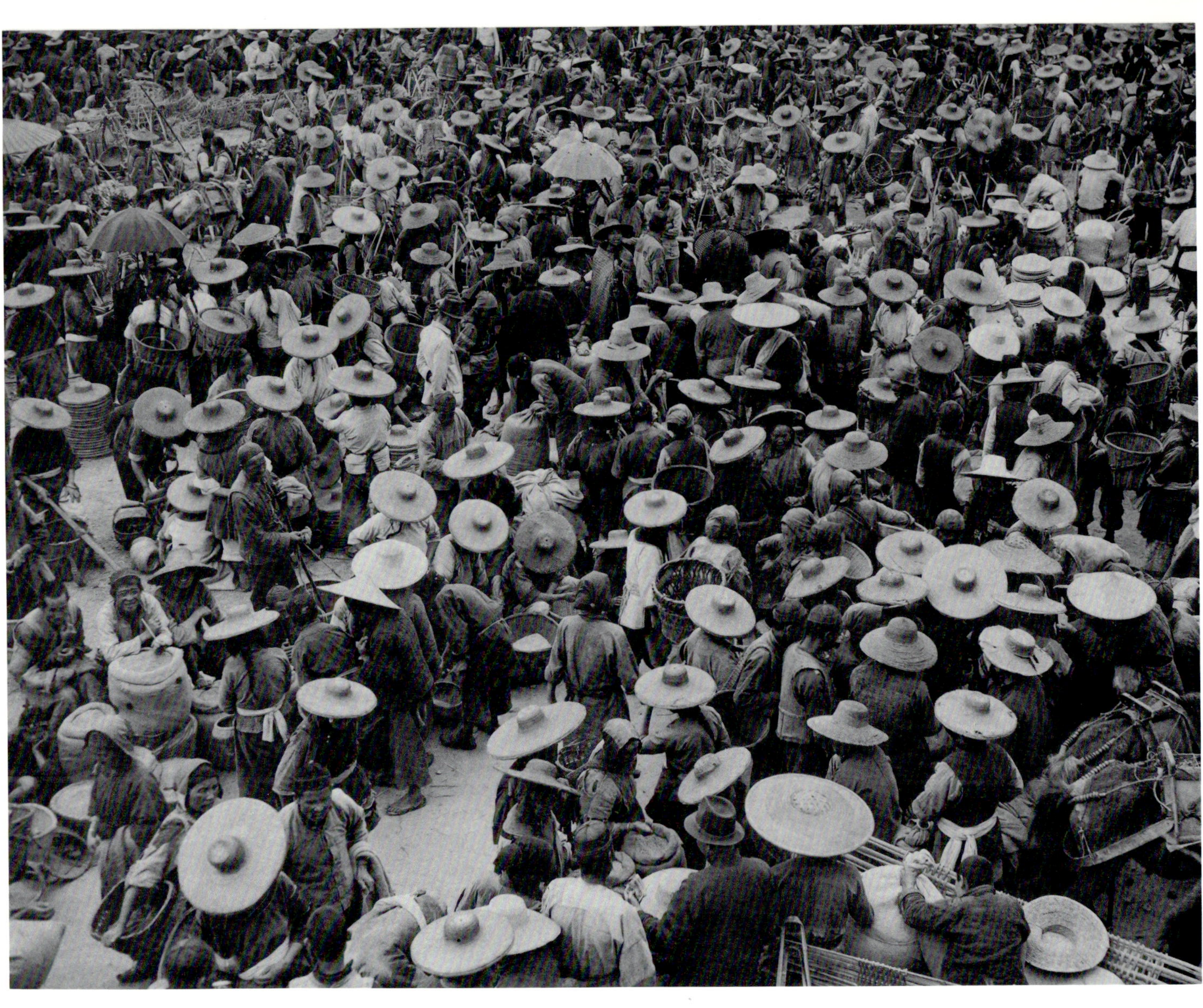

72 *Country Market at Cheng-Kiang.* Yunnan, China, 1944.

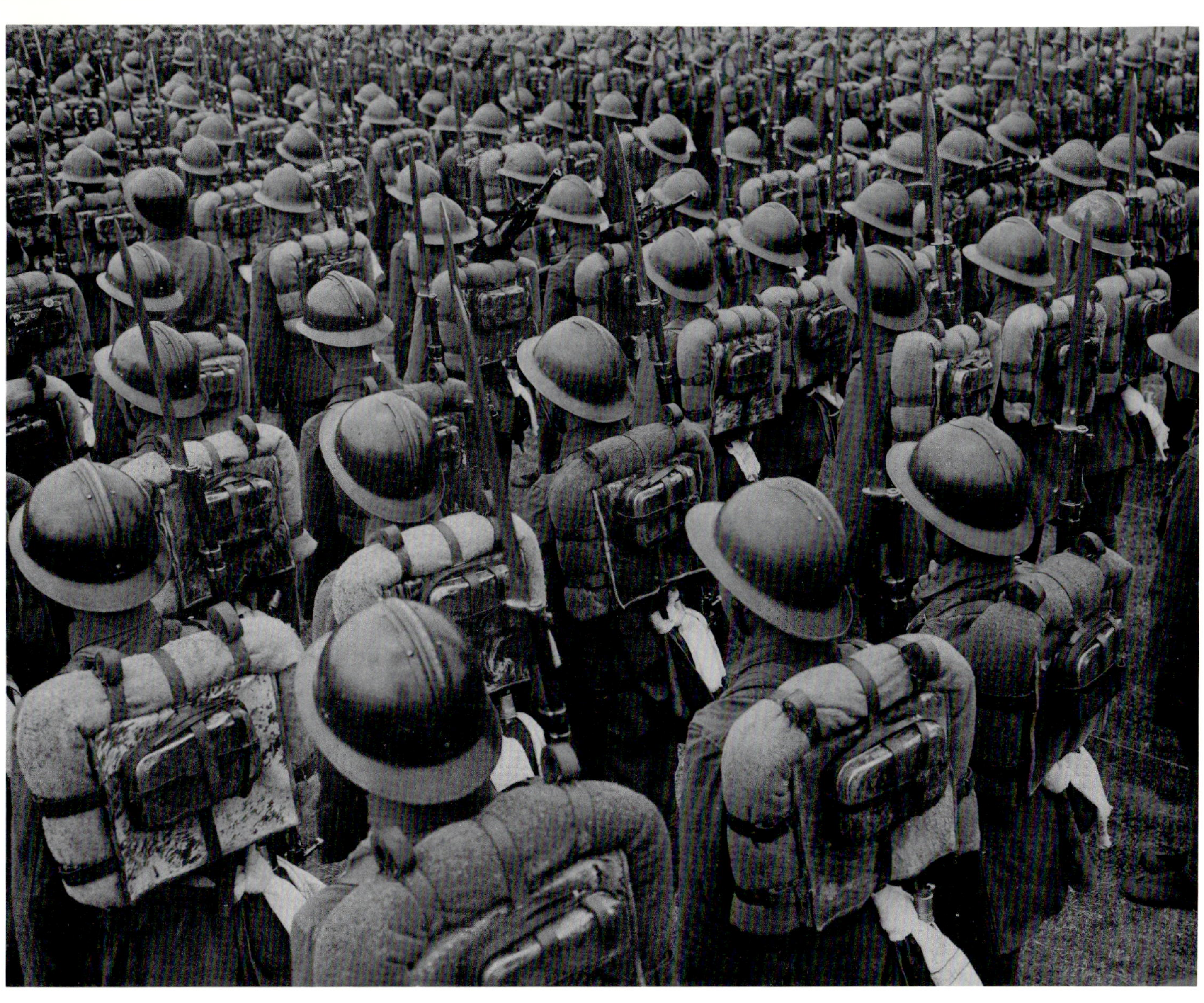

77 *European-Trained Troops of the Chinese Nationalist Army at Parade*. Kunming, China, 1944.

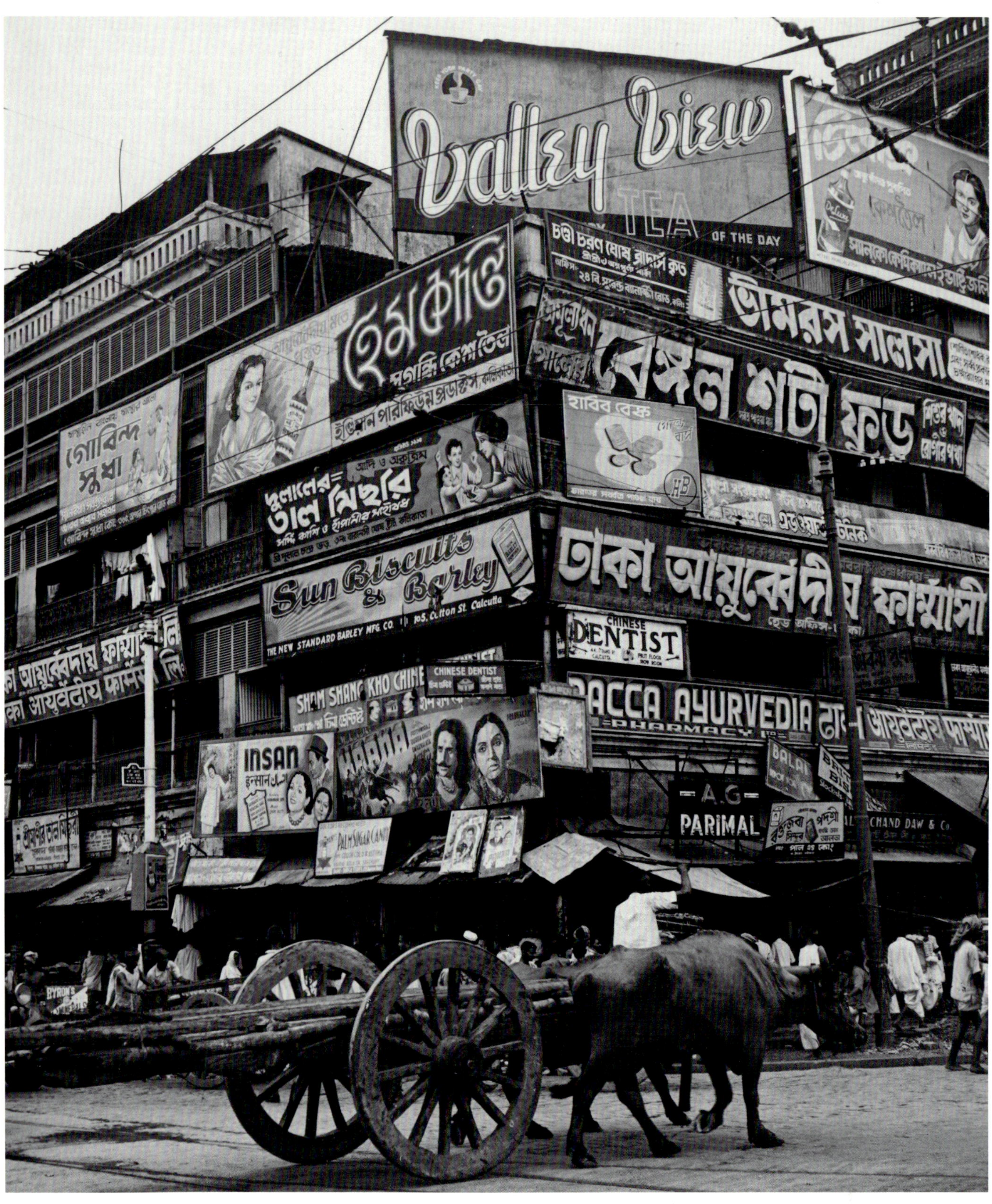

83 *Huge Posters Advertising Anything from a Hindu Movie Epic to a Chinese Dentist, Cover Buildings on Bowbazaar Street.* Calcutta, India, 1945.

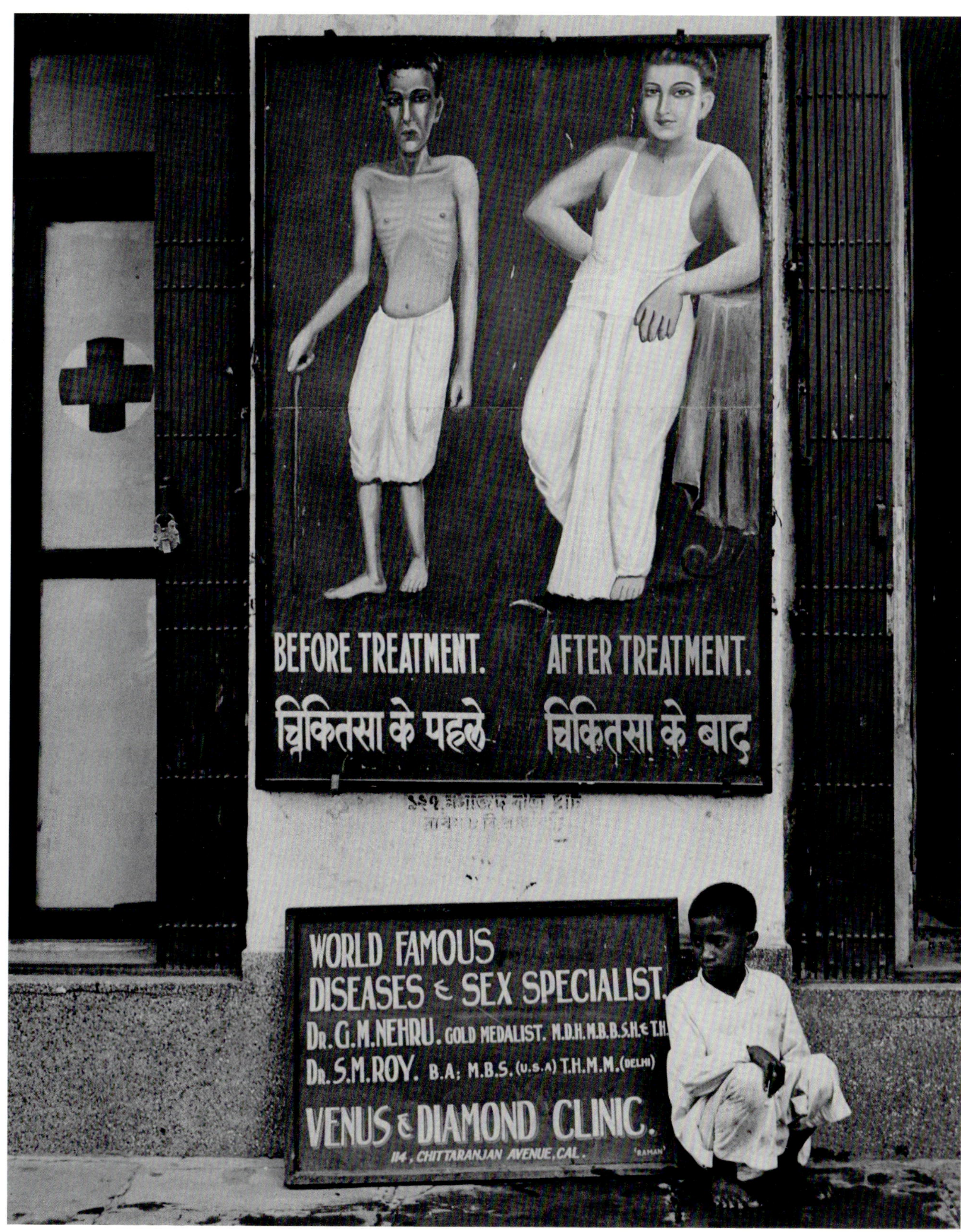

84 *Advertisement of a Sex Specialist for the Treatment of "World Famous Diseases"*. Calcutta, India, 1945.

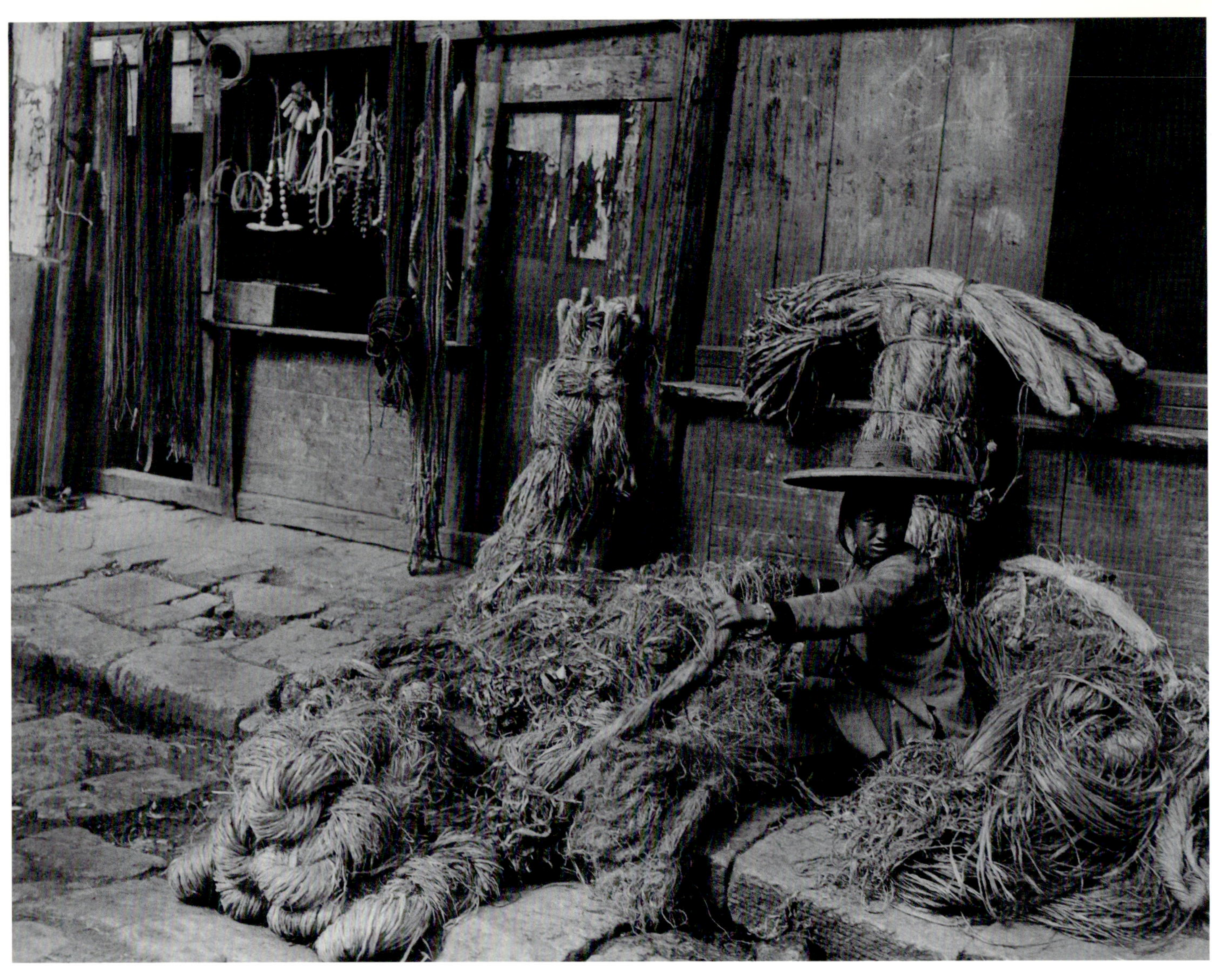

74 *Peasant Girl Selling Hemp in Kunming.* Yunnan, China, 1944.

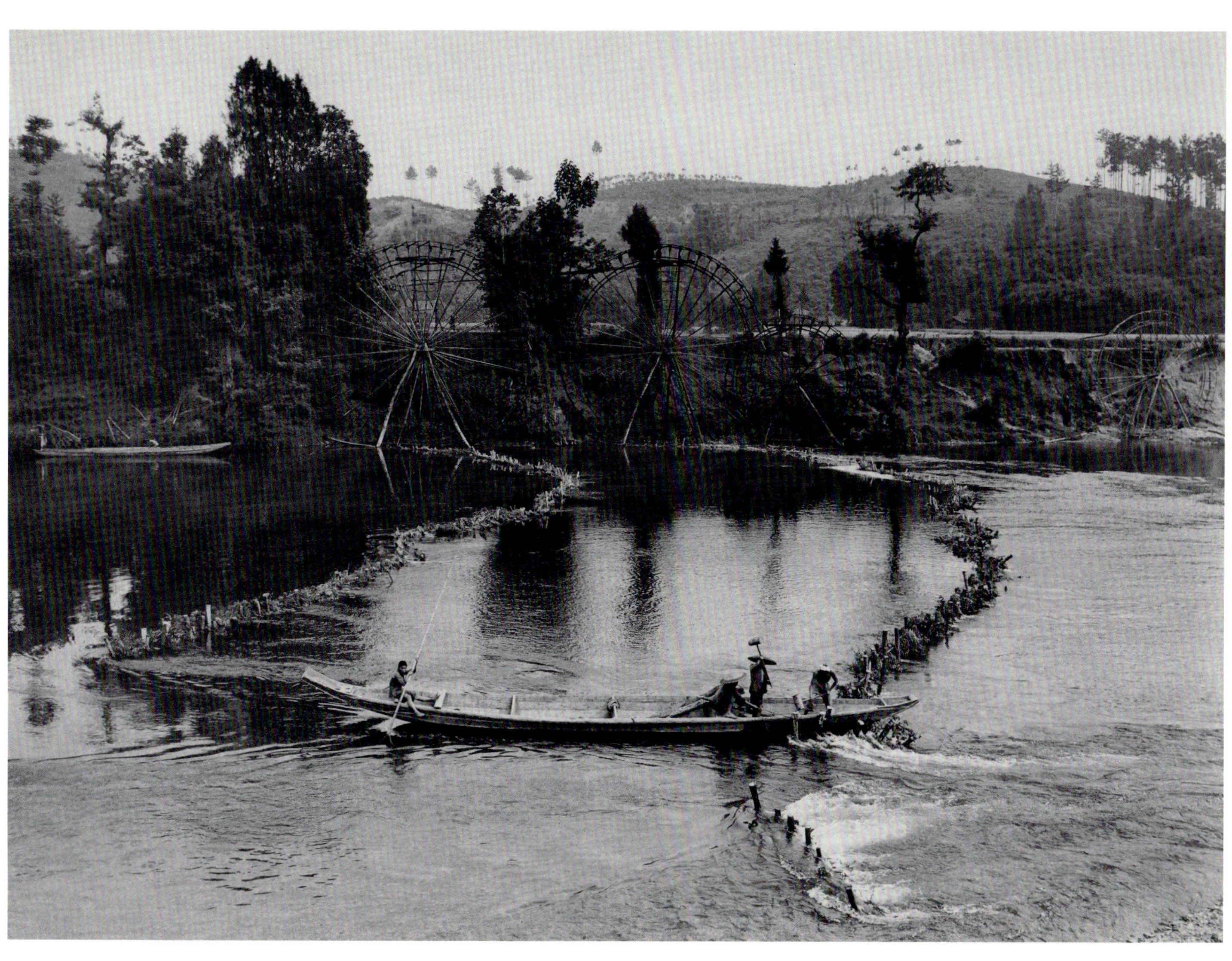

79 *Peasants Repair Dams across Yuan River for Irrigation of near-by Rice Fields.* Hunan, China, 1944.

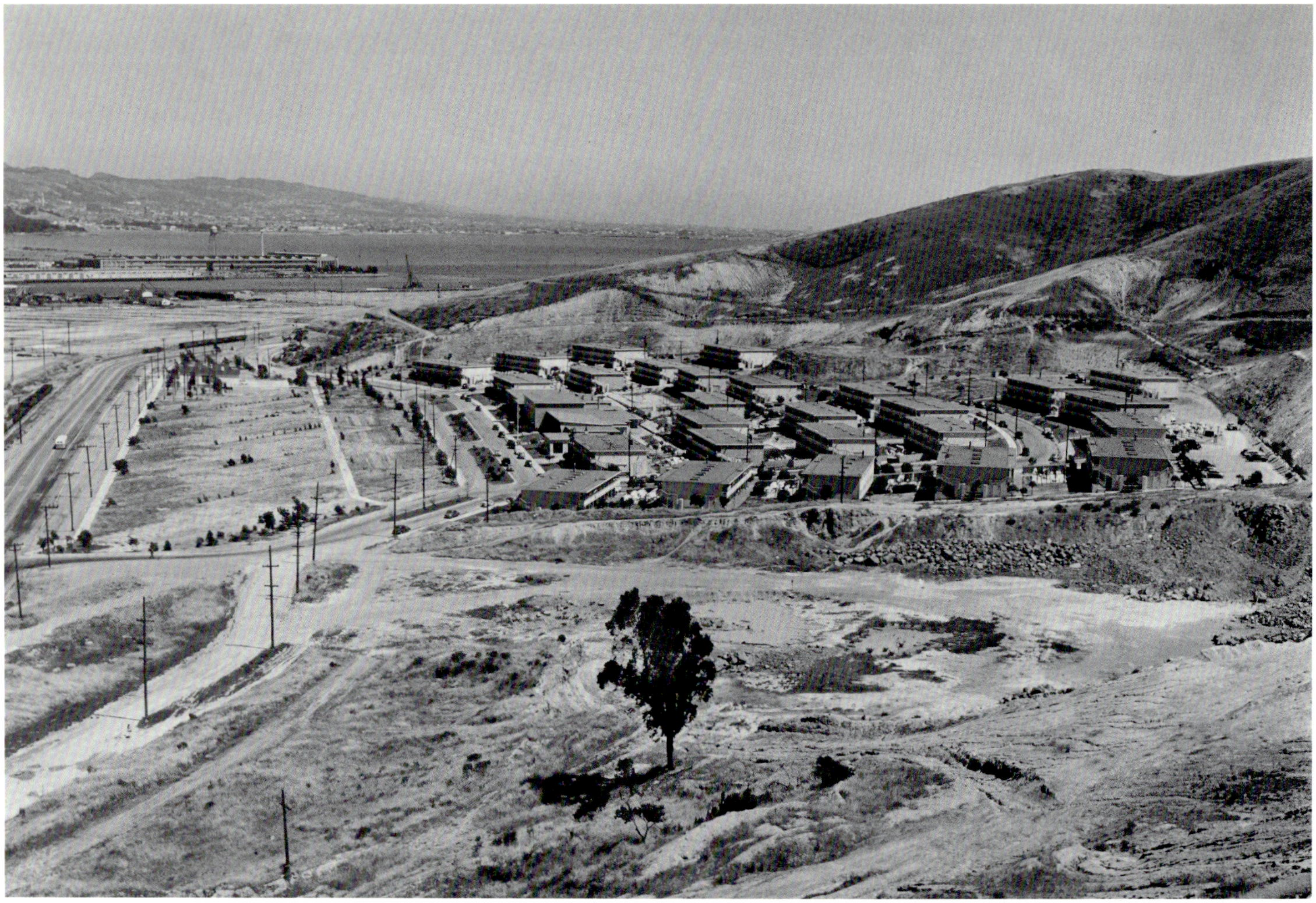

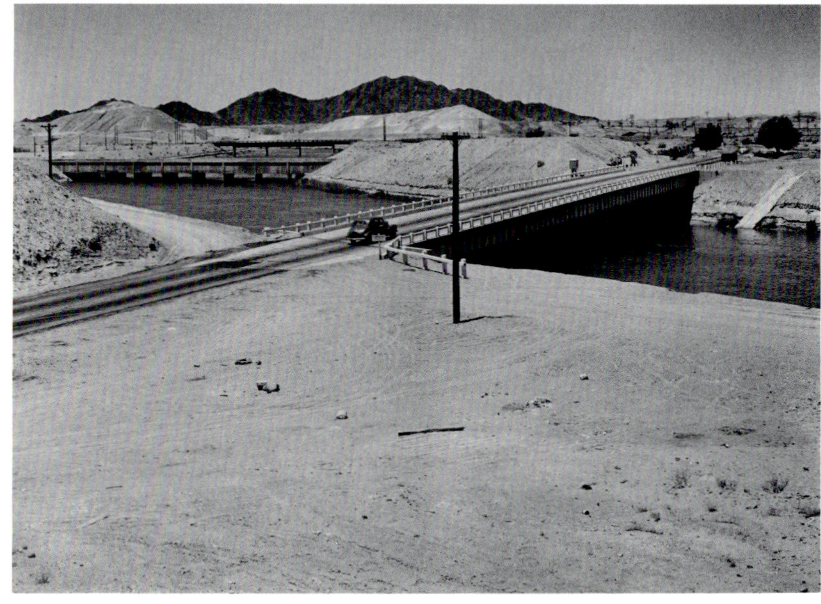

94 *A Tree at Hunter's Point.* San Francisco, 1948.

98 *Three Crossings.* The American Canal, California near the Arizona Border. 1948.

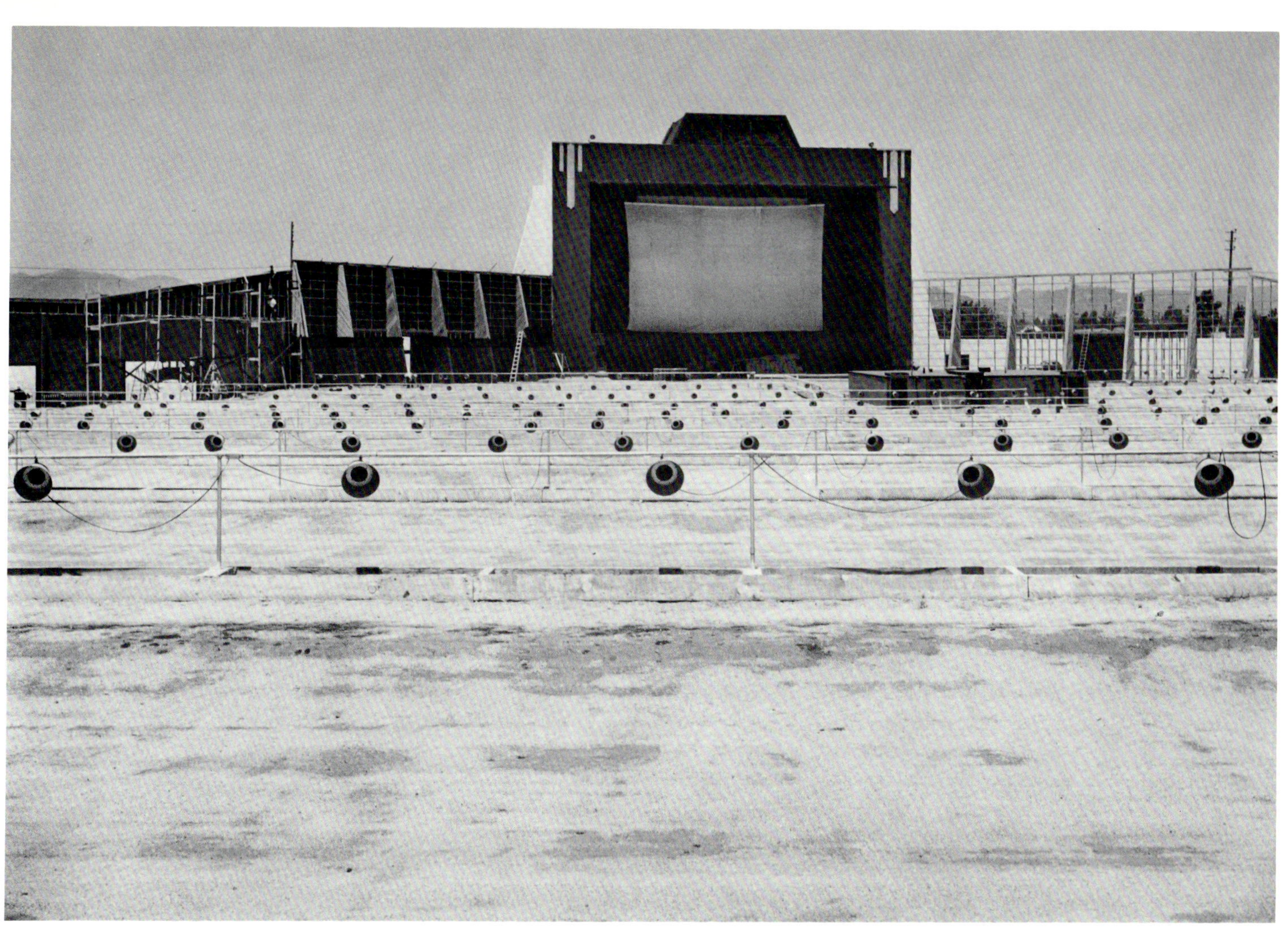

19 *Inside the First Drive-In Theatre.* Los Angeles, 1935.

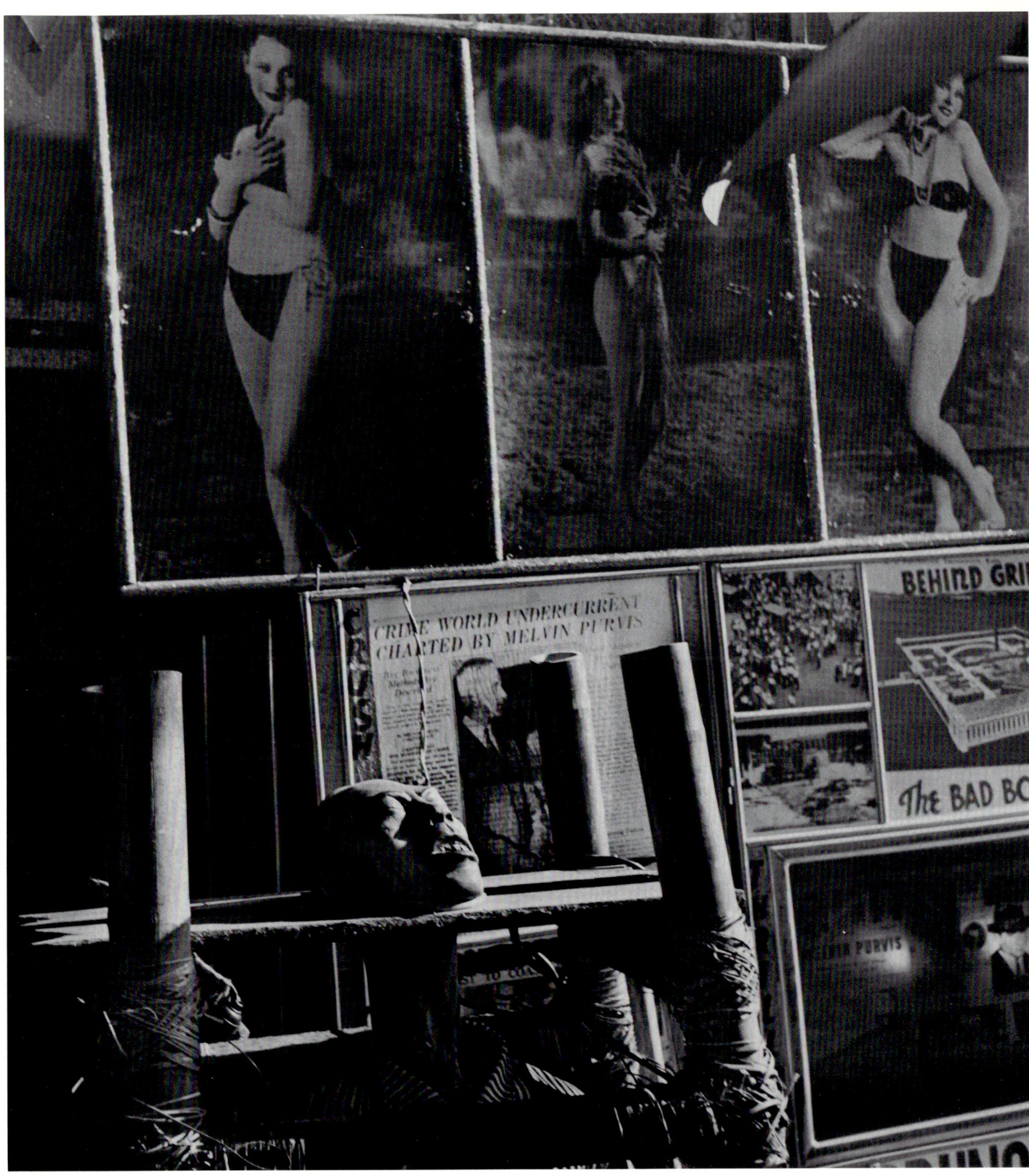

23 *Sex and Crime*. 1935.

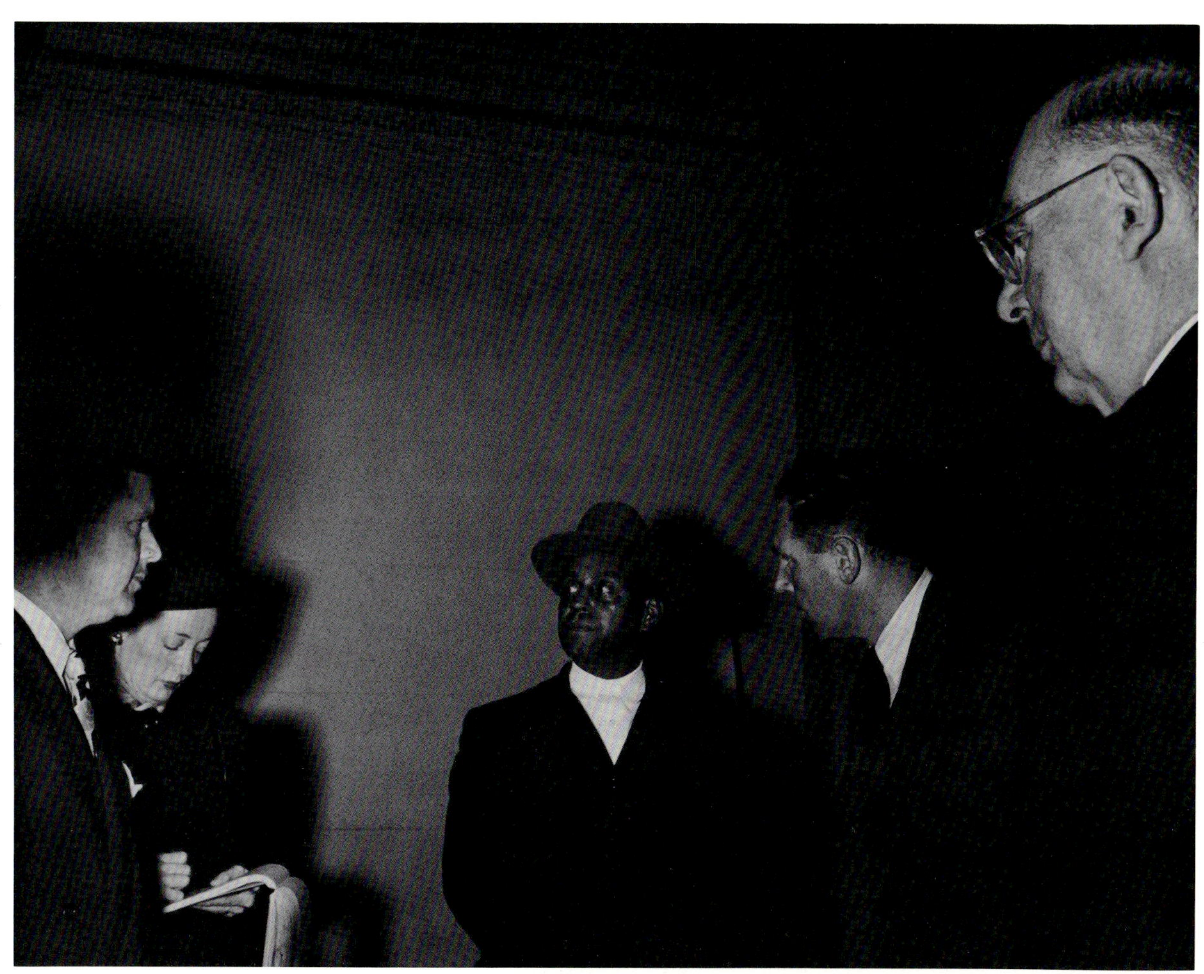

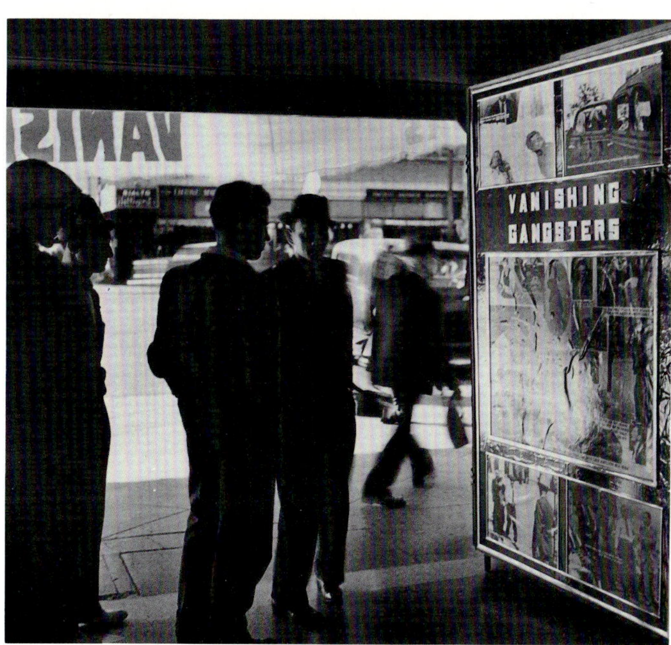

100 *The Killer.* 1948.

9 *"Vanishing Gangsters".* San Francisco, 1934.

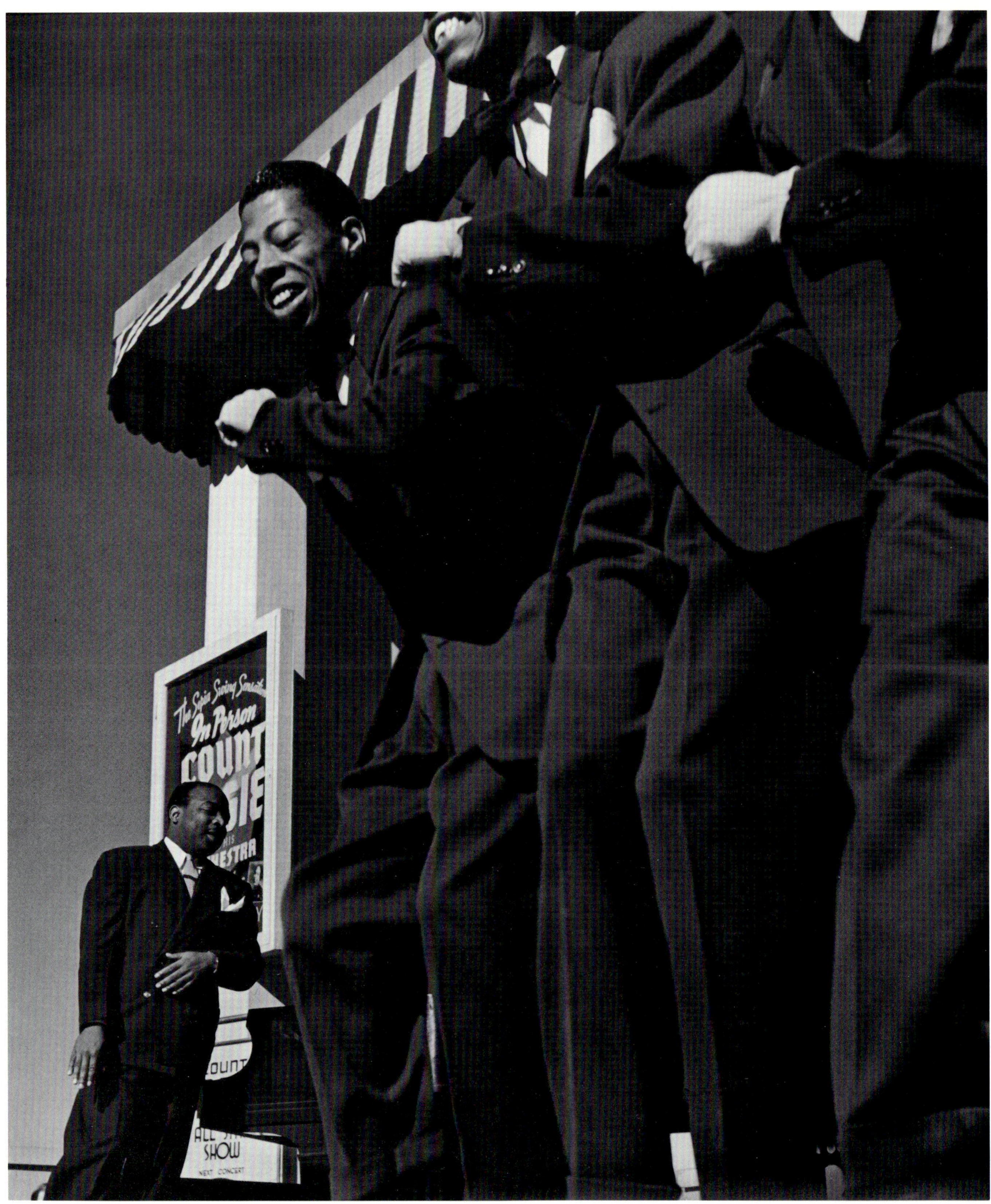

59 *Portrait of Count Basie.* San Francisco, 1939.

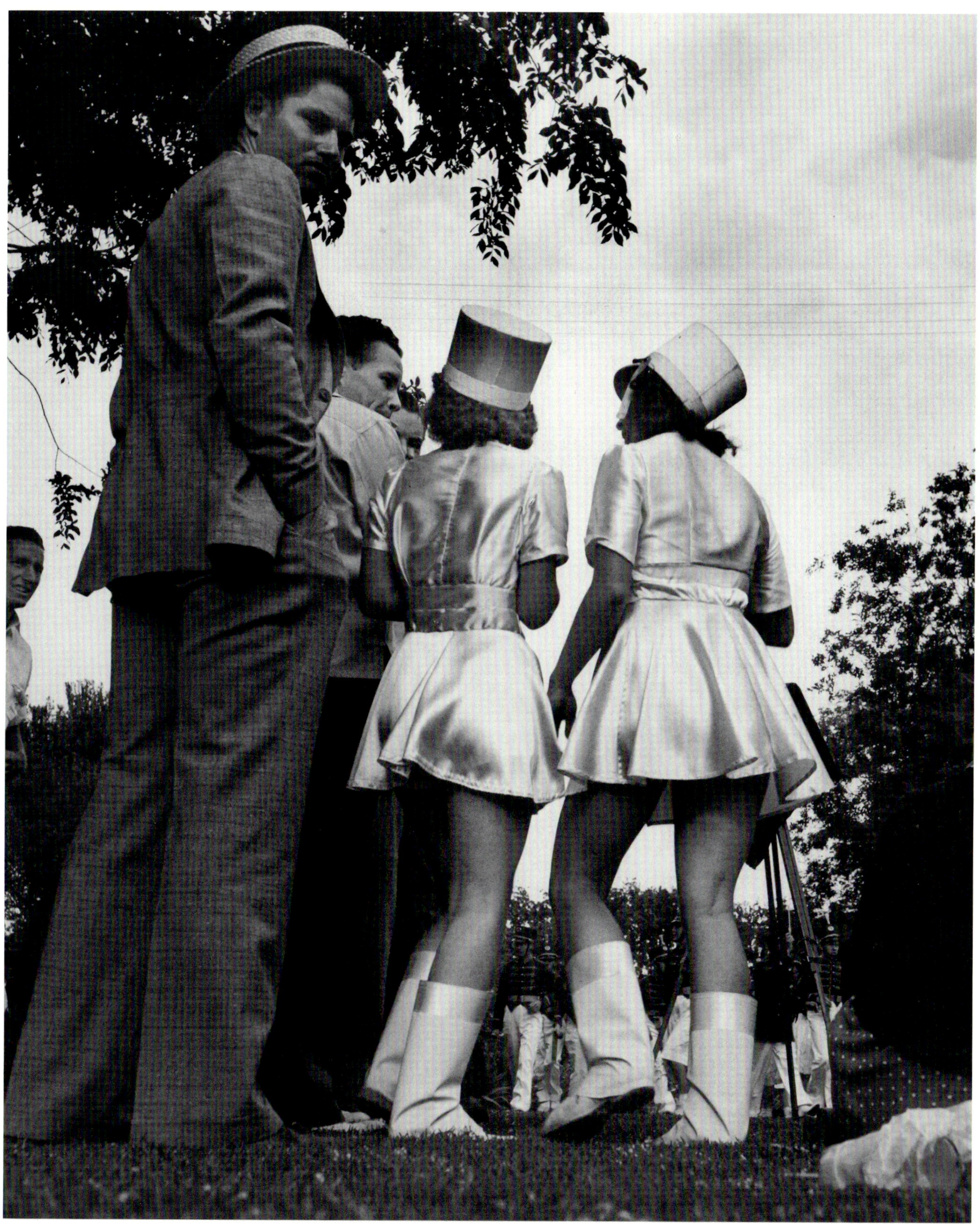

60 *Voyeur Alarmed*. California, 1939.

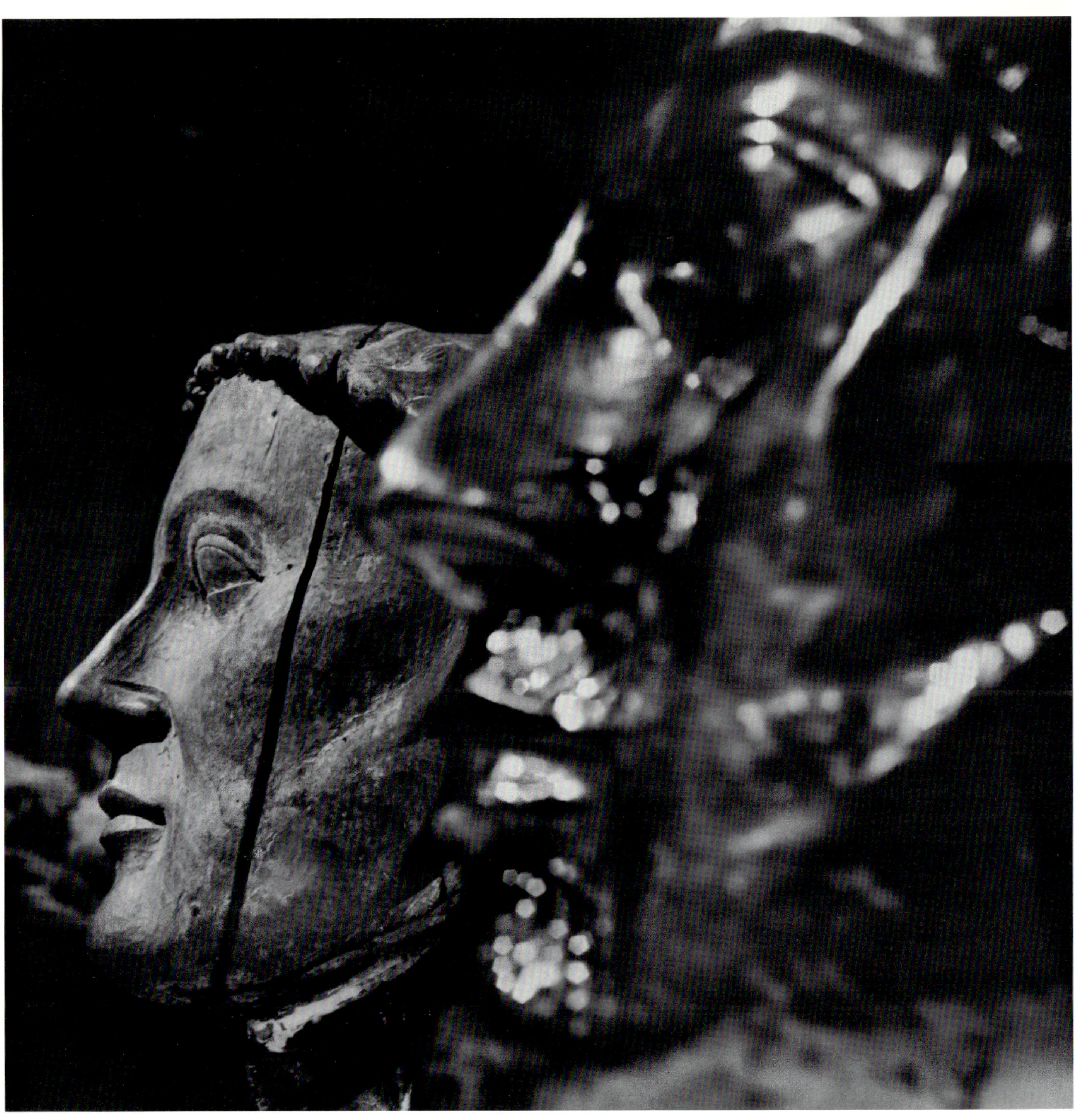

121 *Metal and Wood.* 1965.

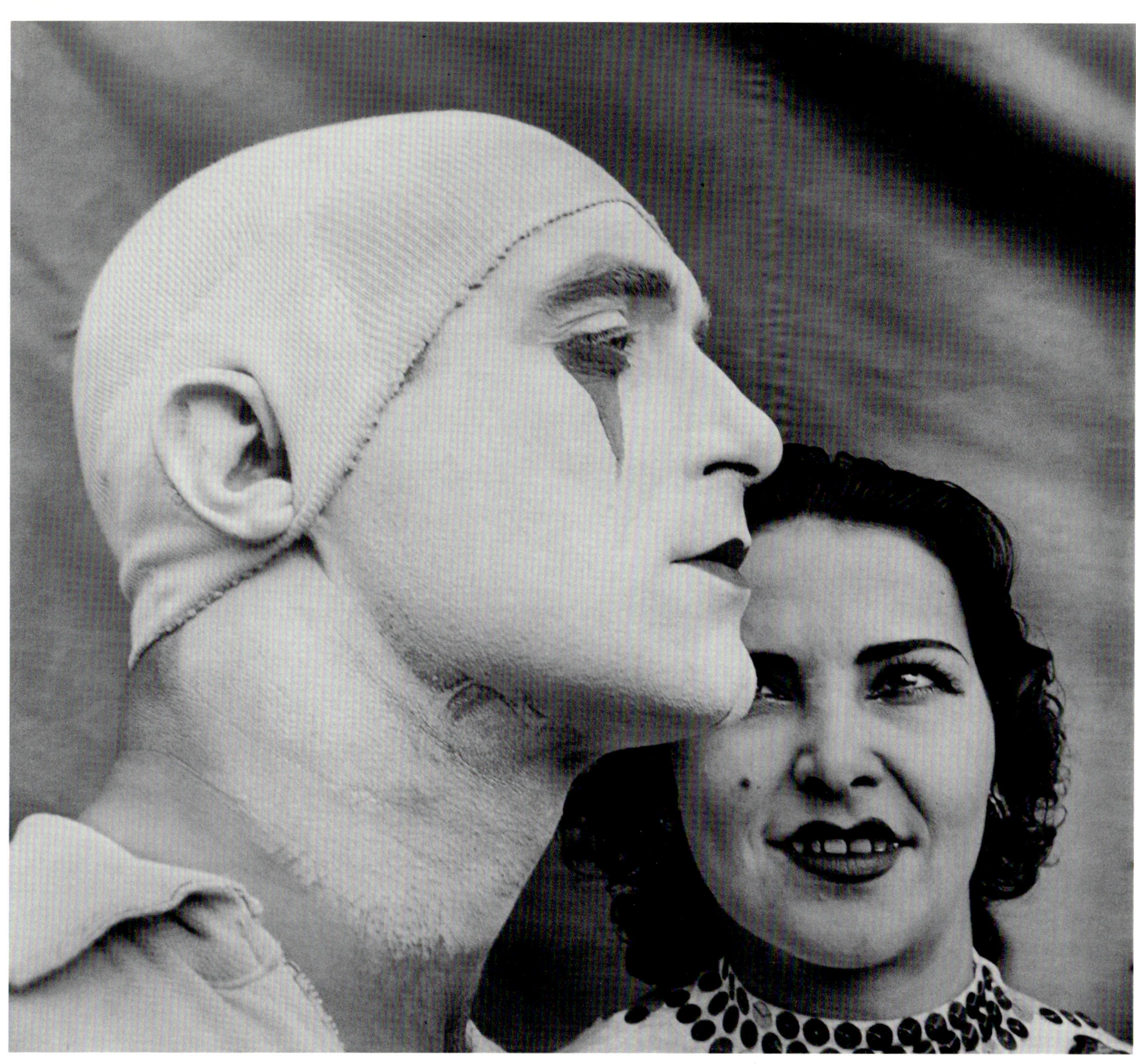

66 *The Beautiful Clown*. 1940.

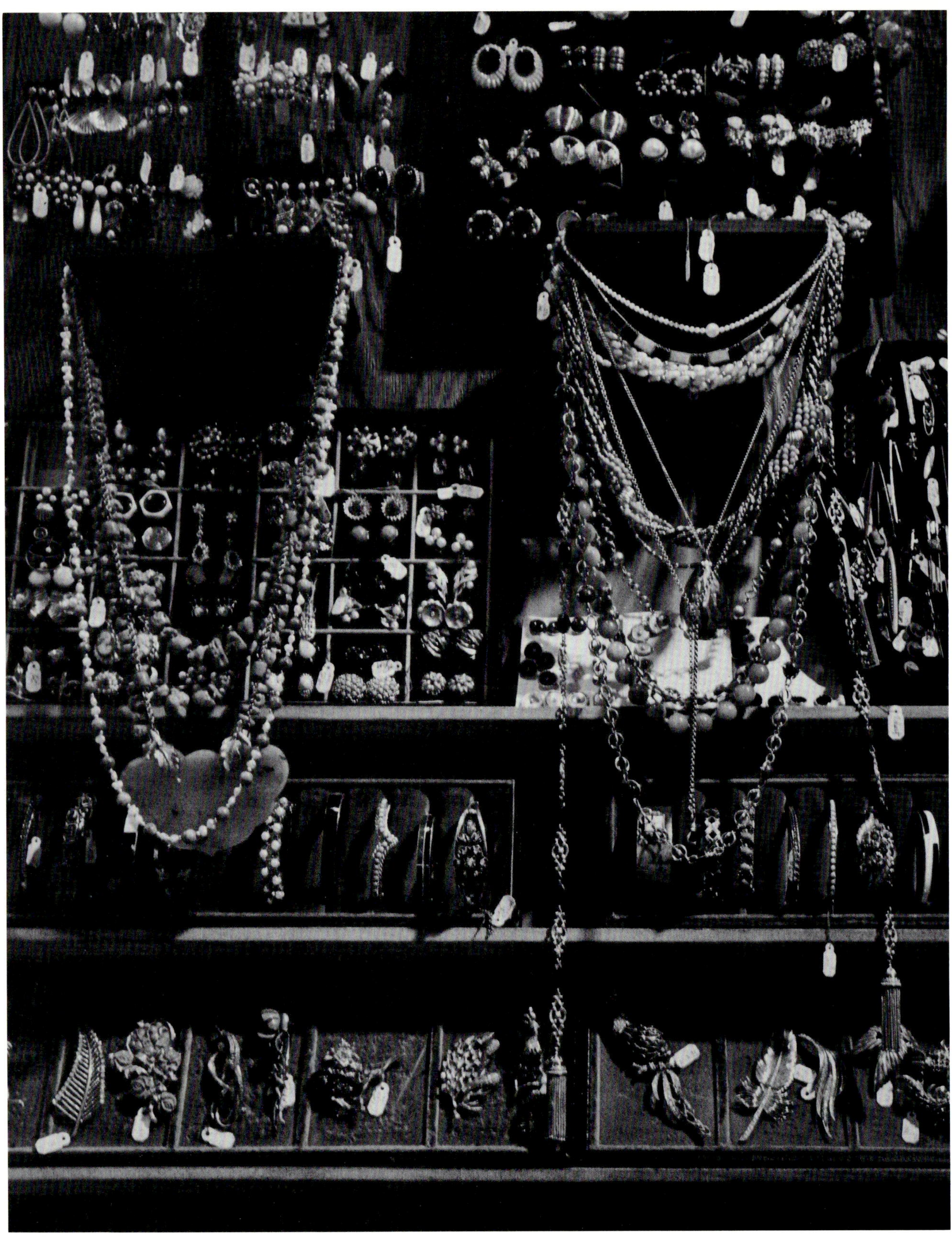

130 *The More the Better.* W. 47th Street, New York City, 1979.

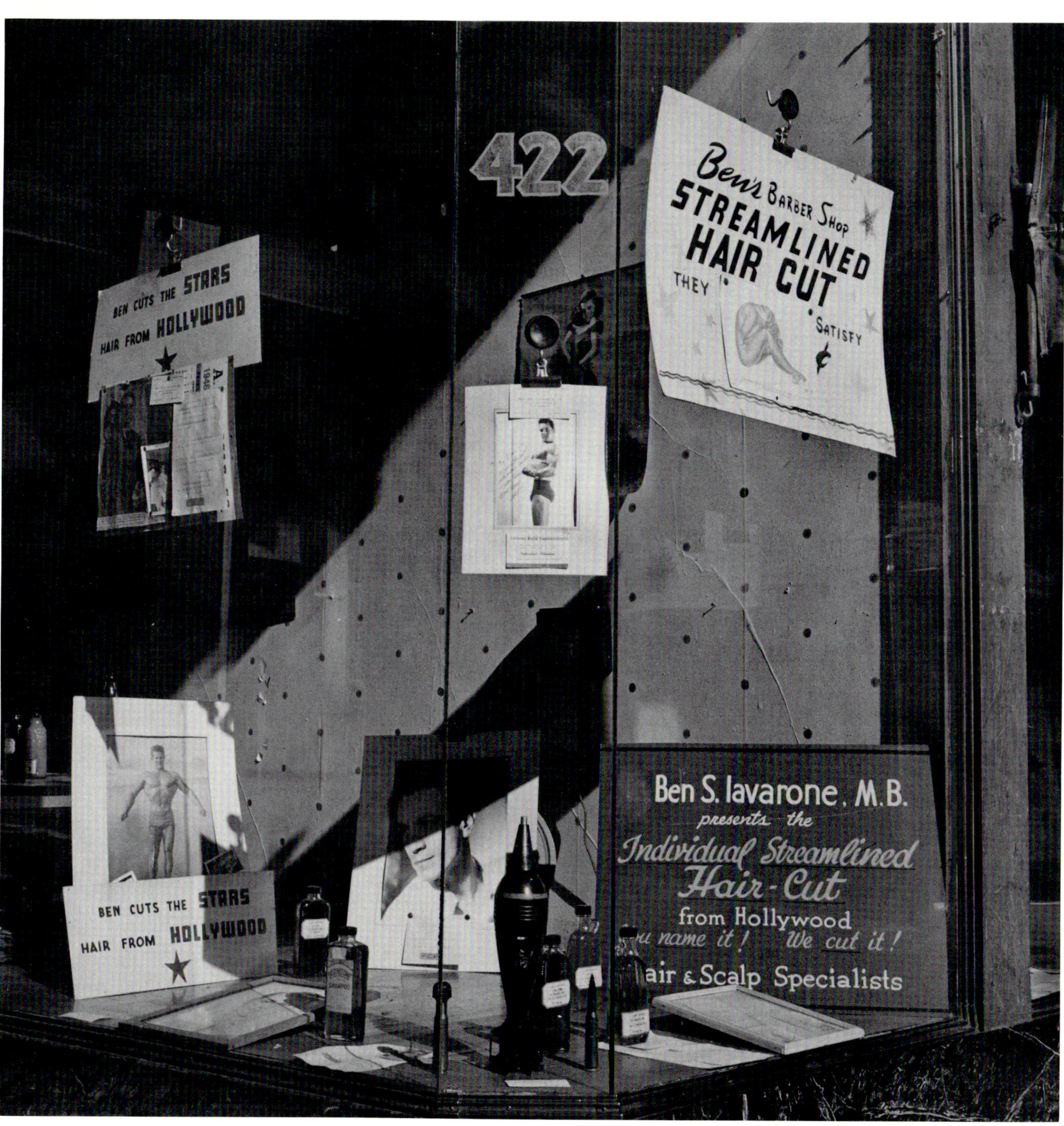

86 *Ben's Barber Shop Window*. San Francisco, 1946.

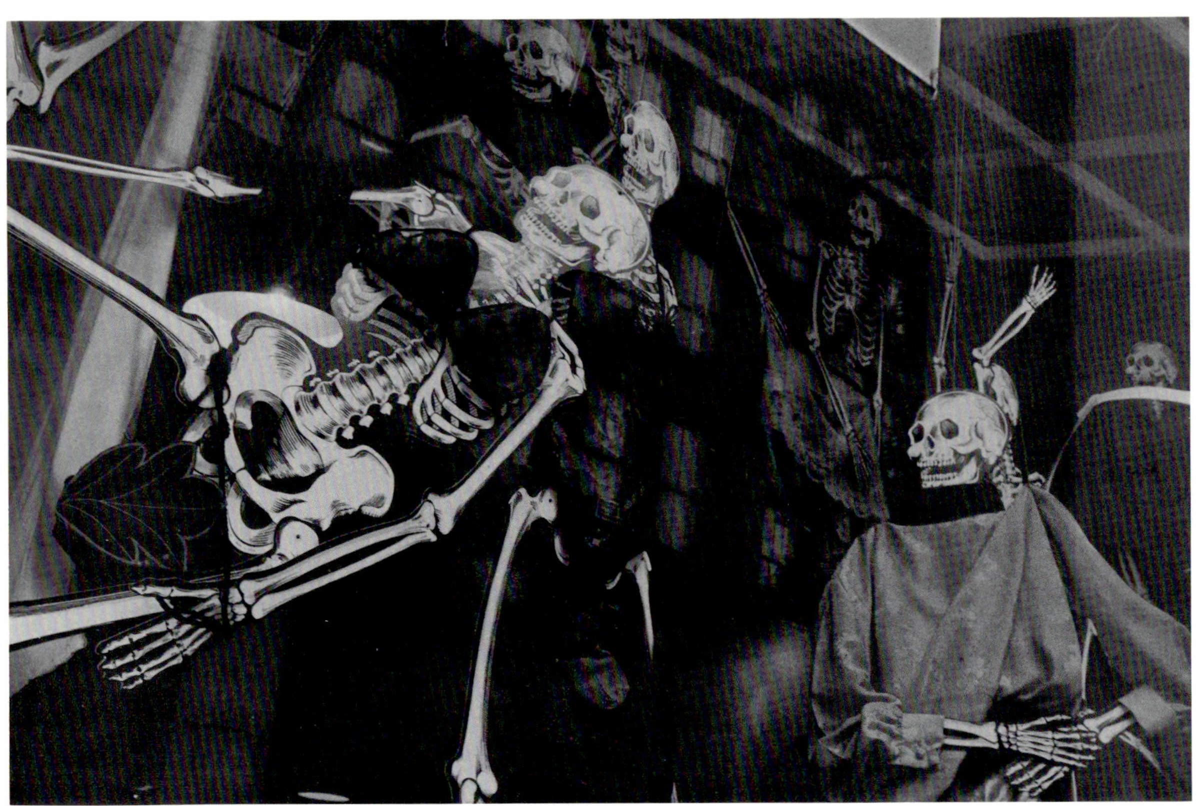

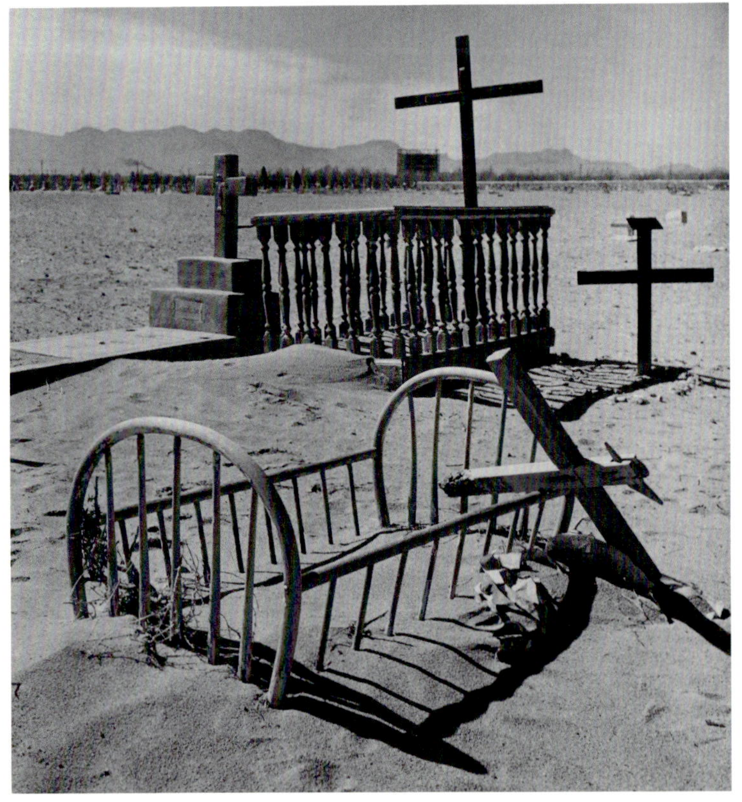

134 *Dance Macabre.* New York City, 1979.

46 *Child's Grave.* Mexican Cemetery, El Paso, Texas, 1937.

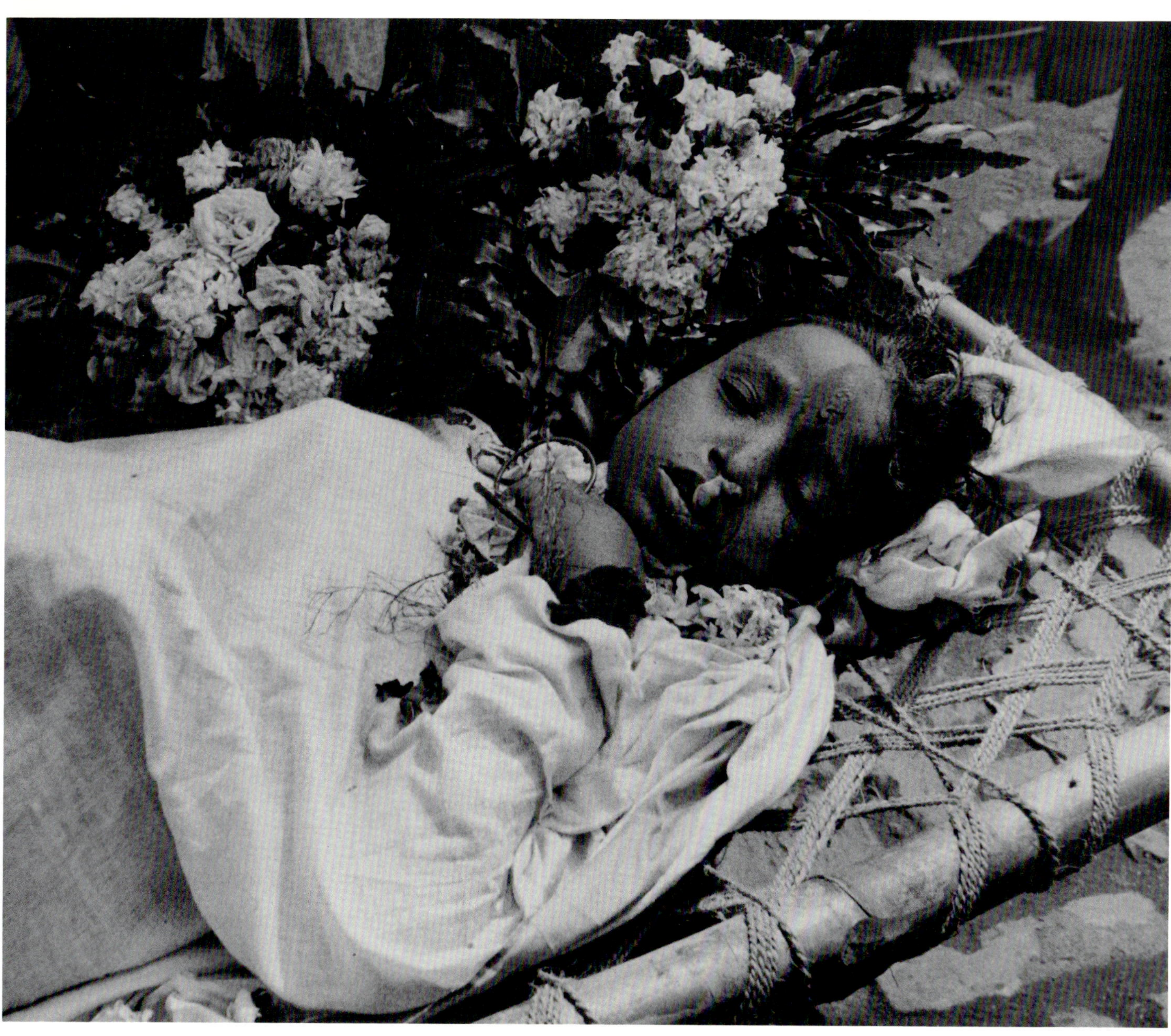

82 *Dead Hindu Girl Awaiting Burning at the Pyres of the Nimtolla Ghat.* Calcutta, India, 1945.

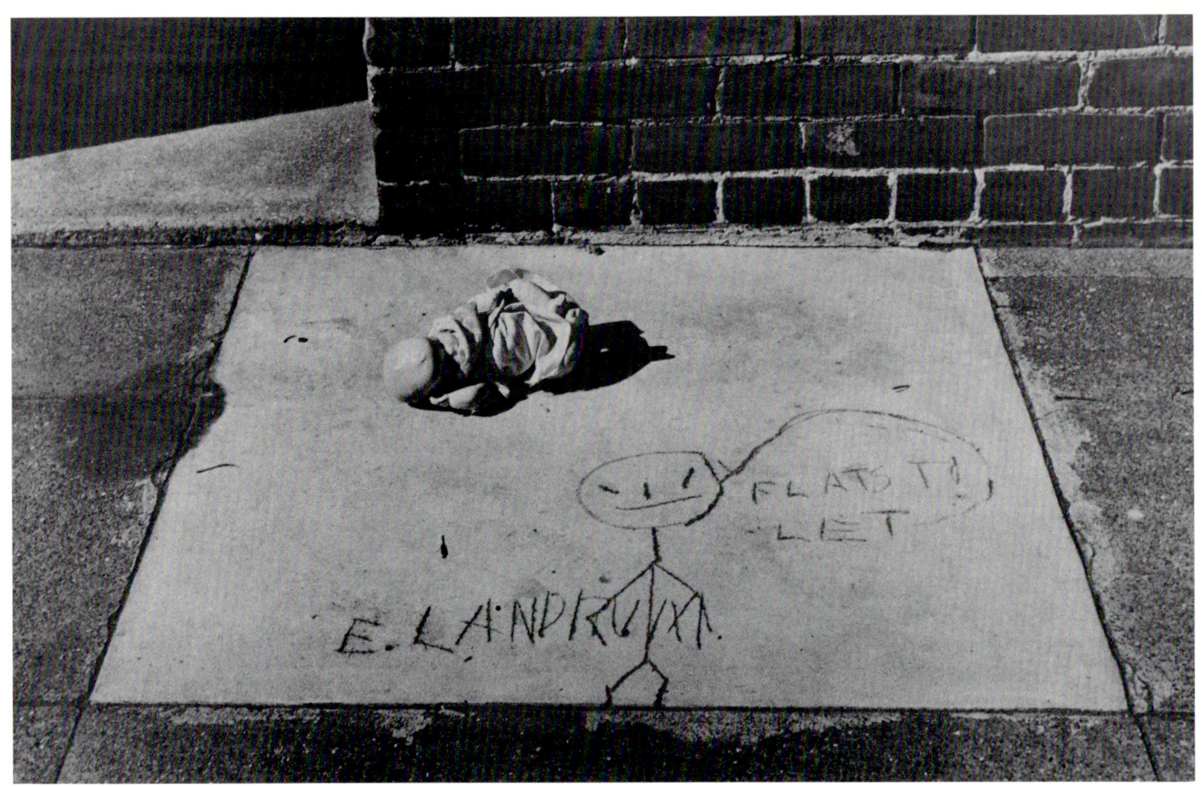

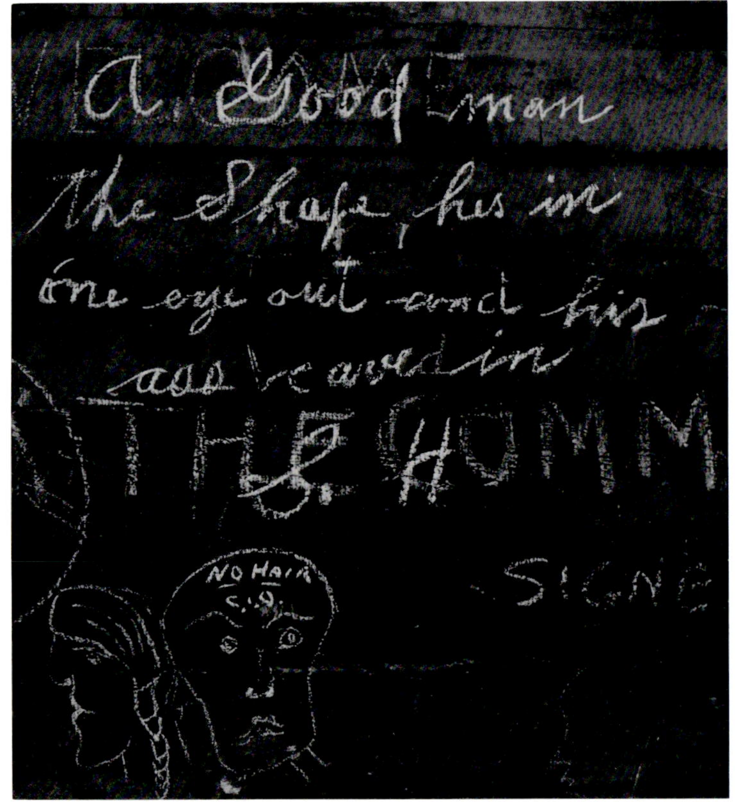

33 *The Landlady Graffiti*. San Francisco, 1937.

51 *Longshoreman's Poem*. Waterfront, San Francisco, 1938.

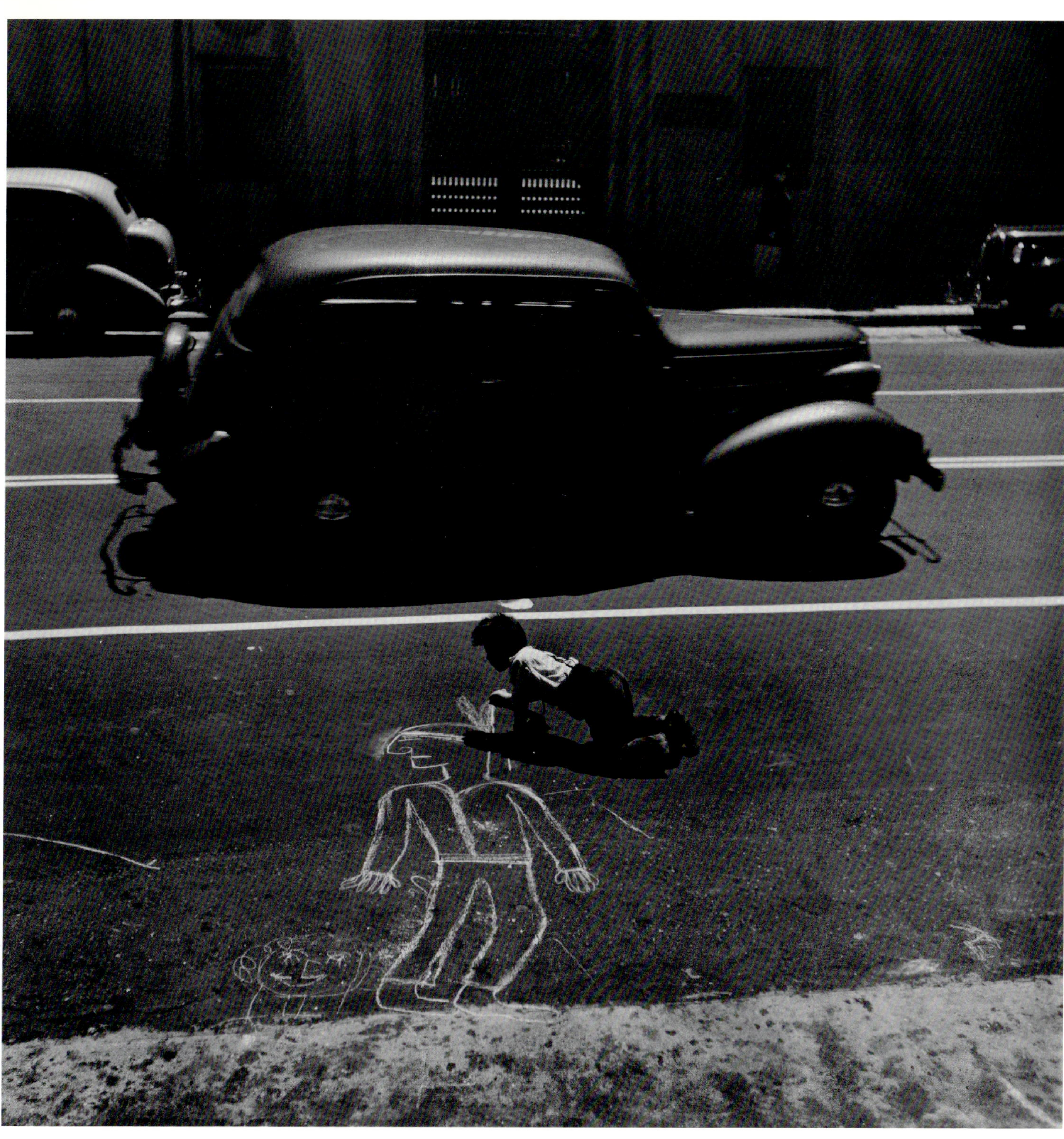

52 *The Artist Lives Dangerously*. San Francisco, 1938.

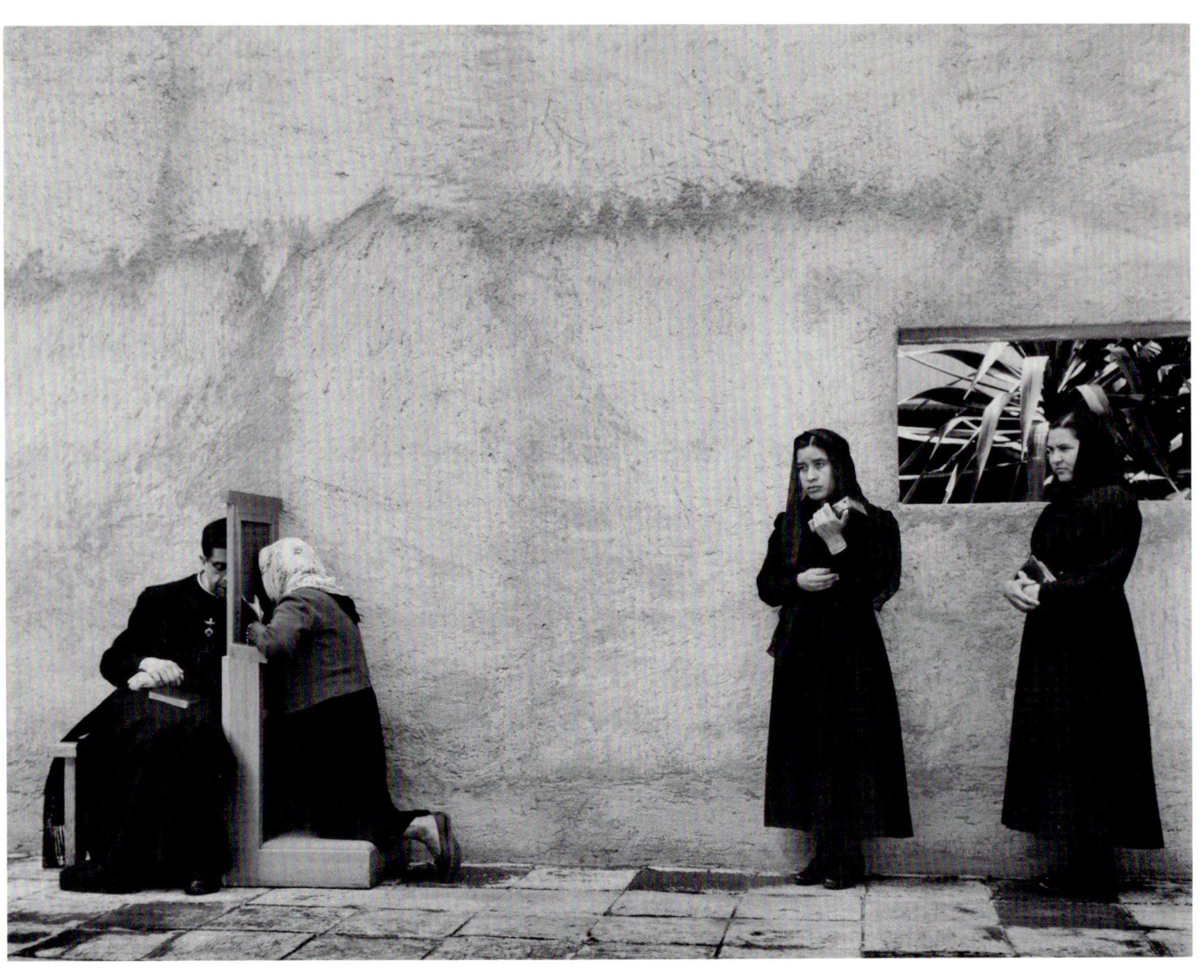

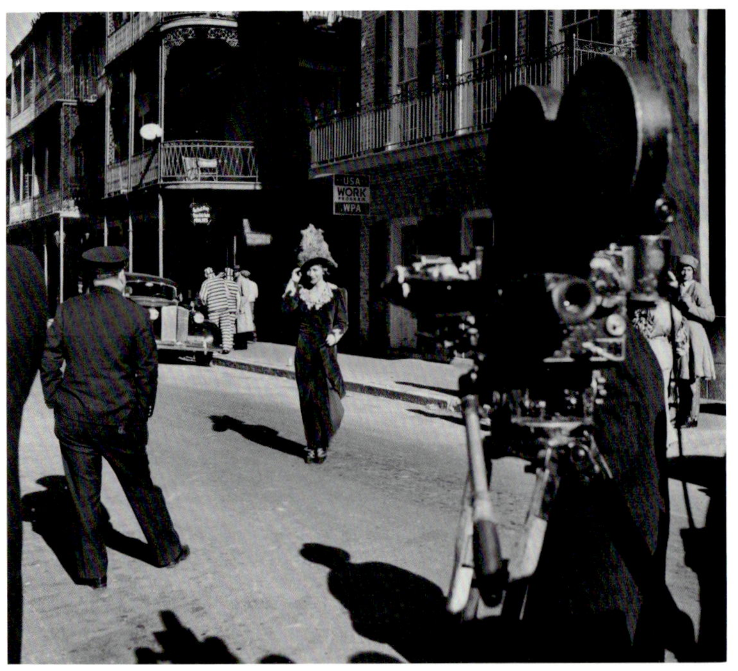

115 *The Confessional.* Mexico, 1960.

37 *Making a Movie in New Orleans.* 1937.

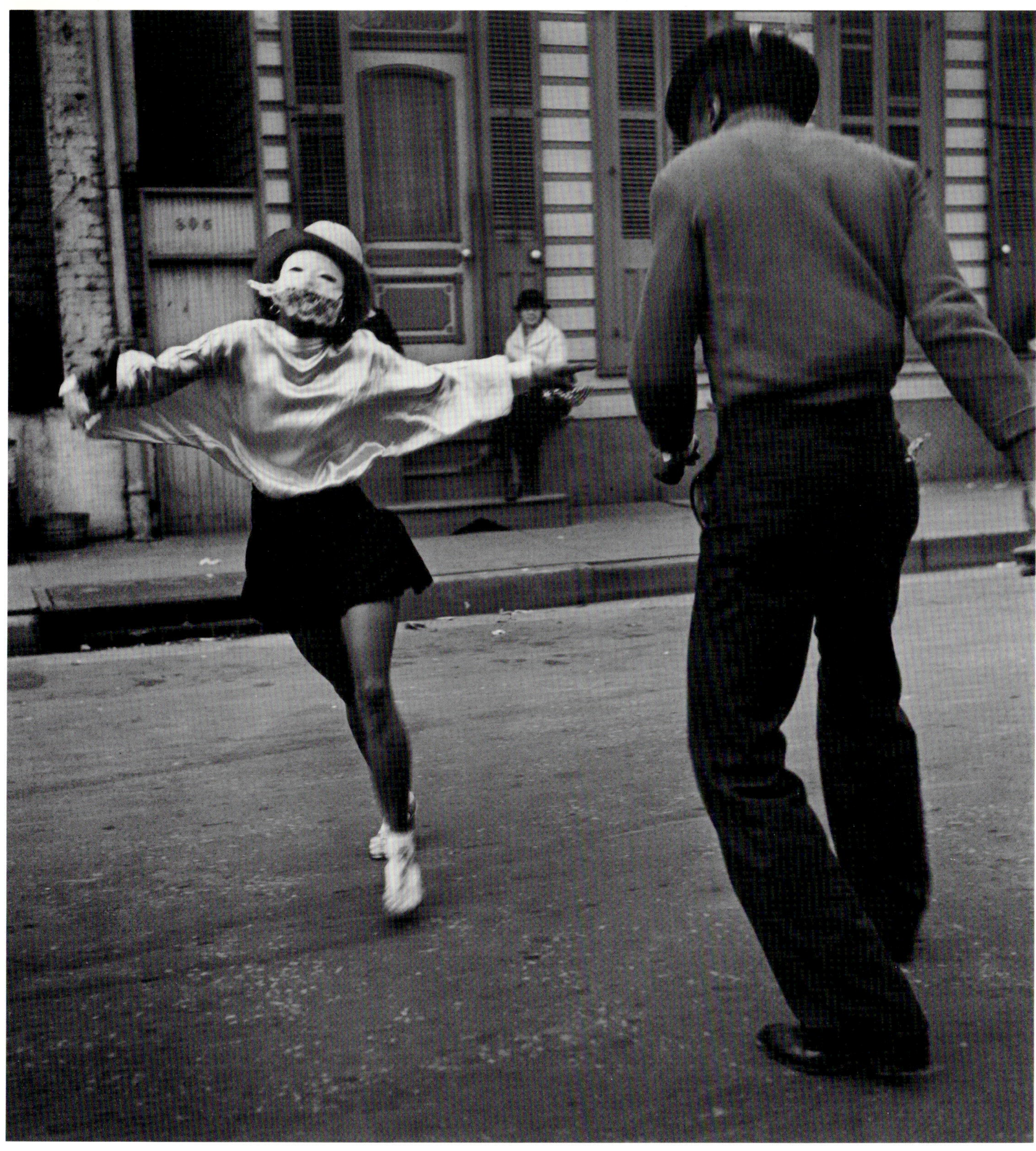

40 *Jitterbug.* New Orleans, 1937.

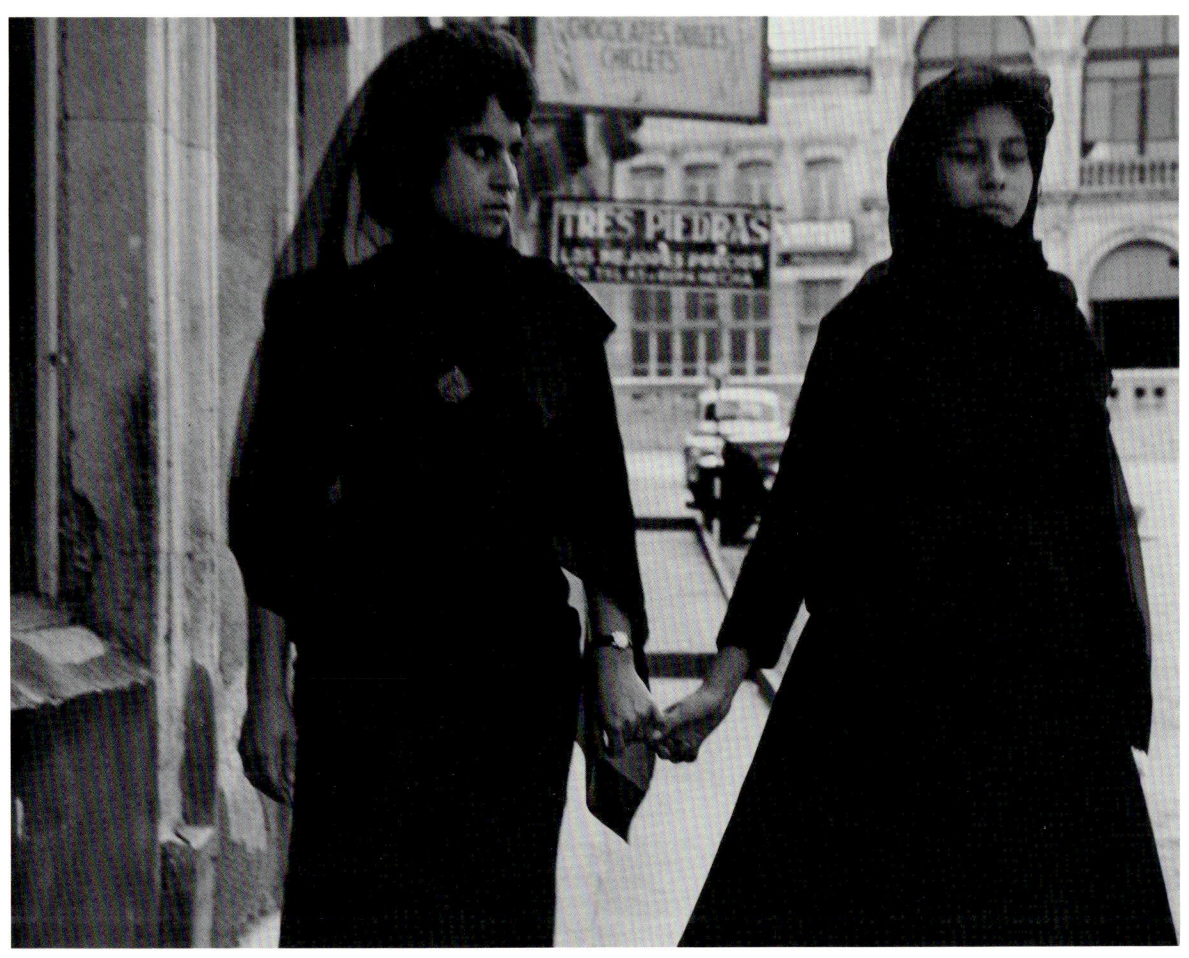

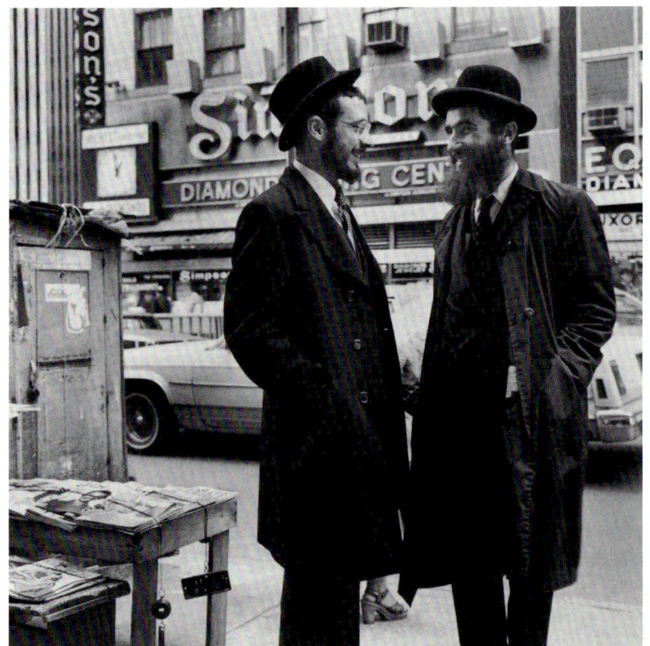

113 *The Sisters*. Mexico, 1960.

132 *A Funny Conversation*. W. 47th Street, New York City, 1979.

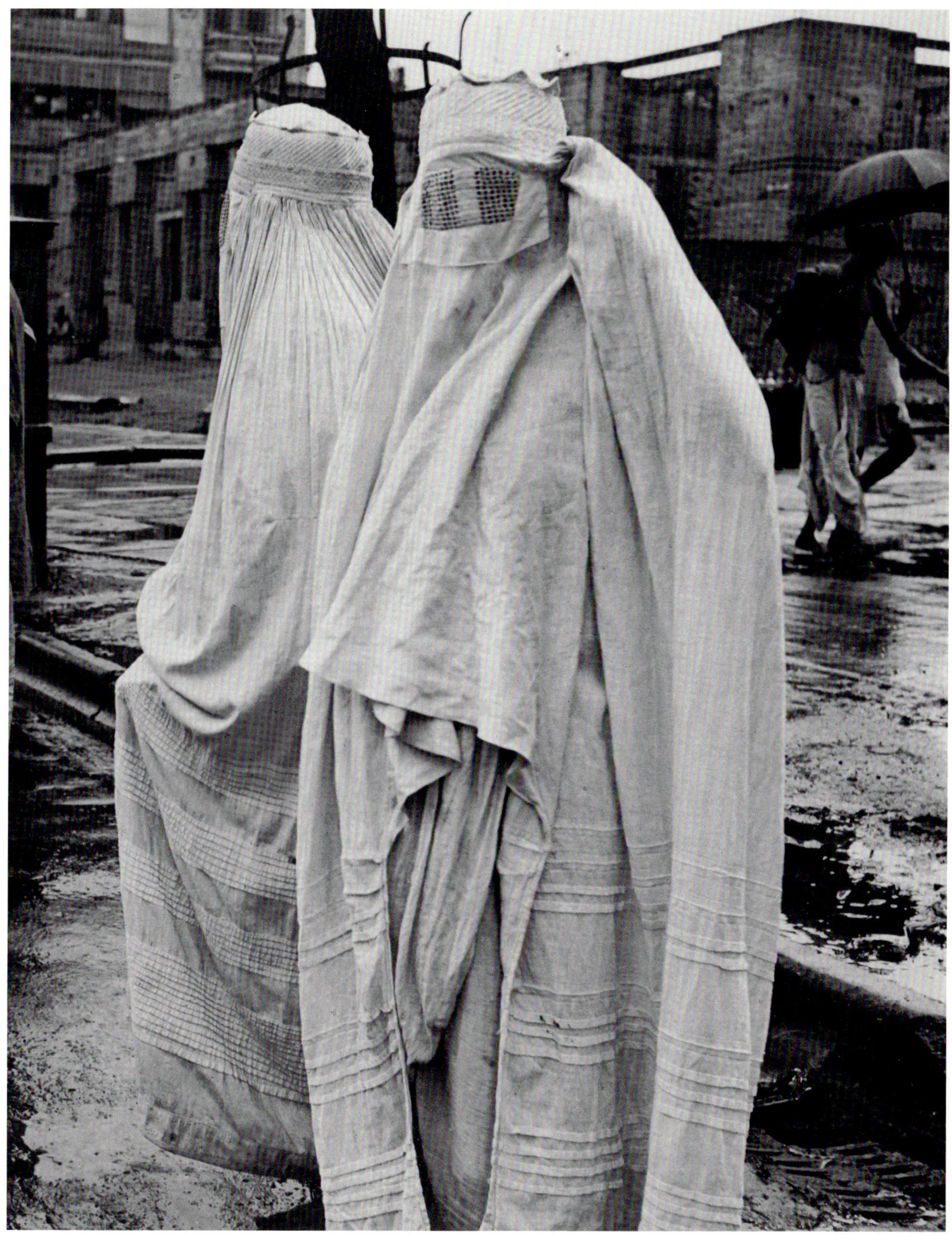

71 *Two Moslem Women on Monsoon Swept Calcutta Street.*
India, 1943.

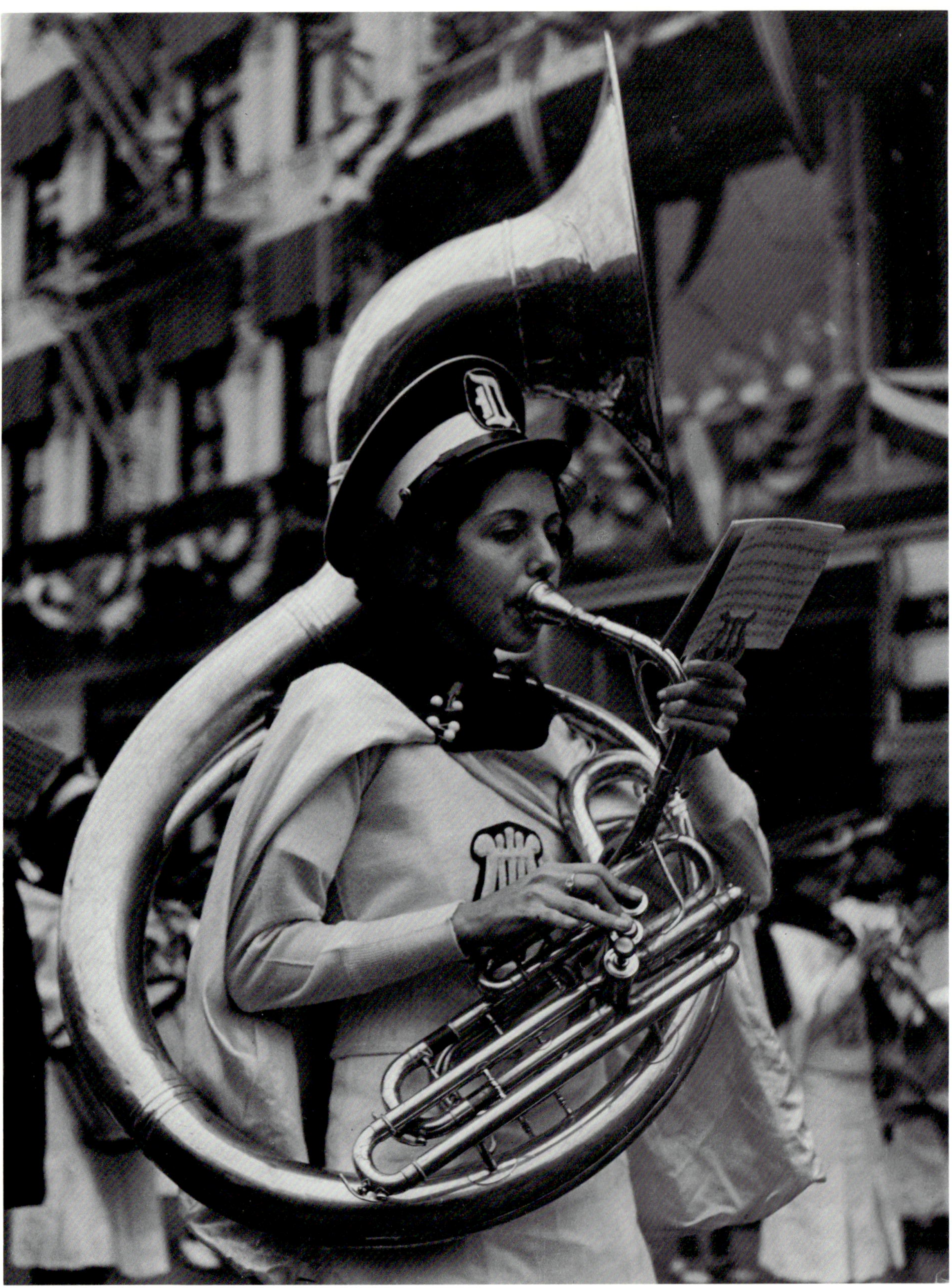

38 *Member of the Band.* New Orleans, 1937.

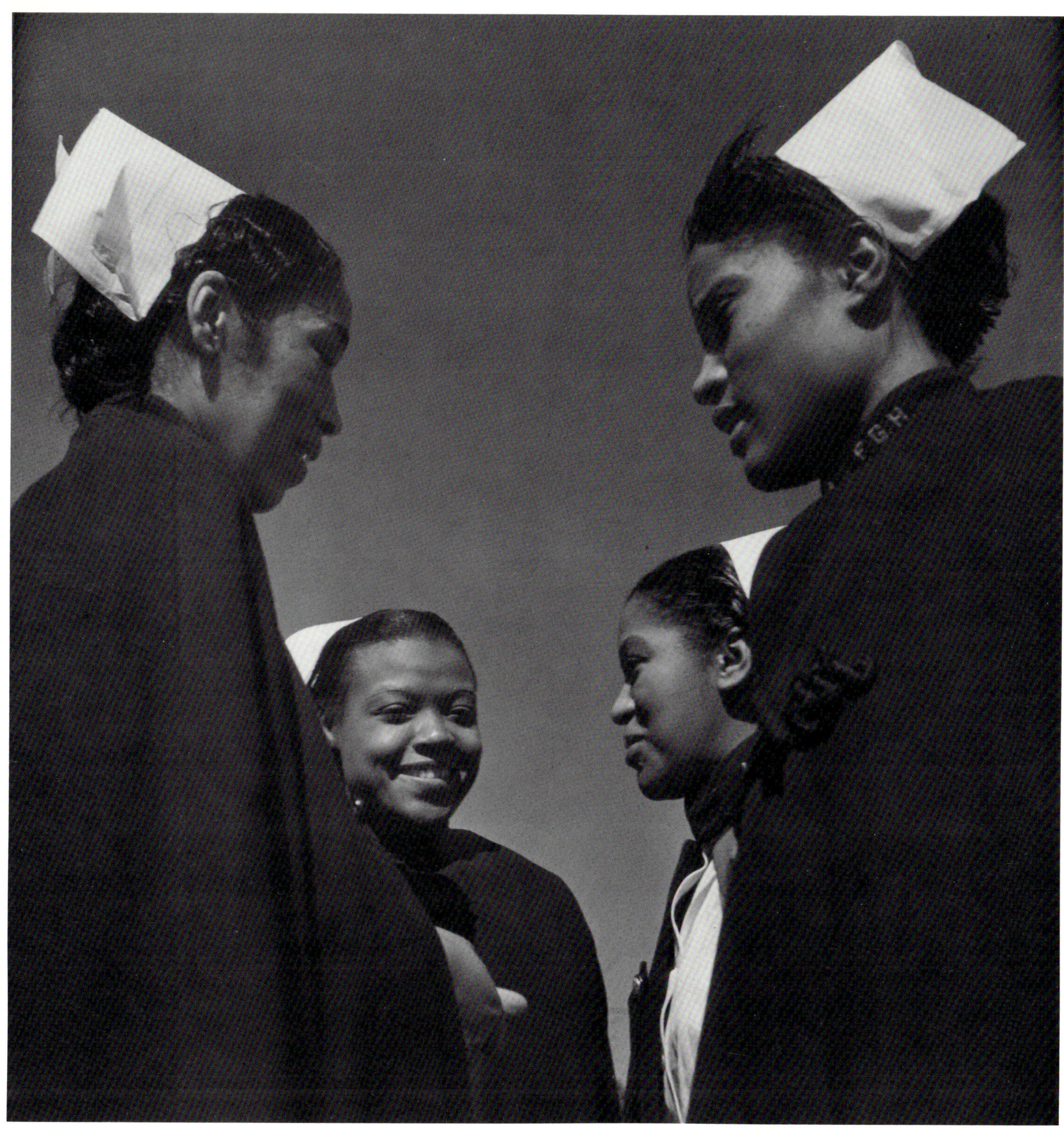

41 *Nurses of the All-Black Flint-Goodridge Hospital.*
New Orleans, 1937.

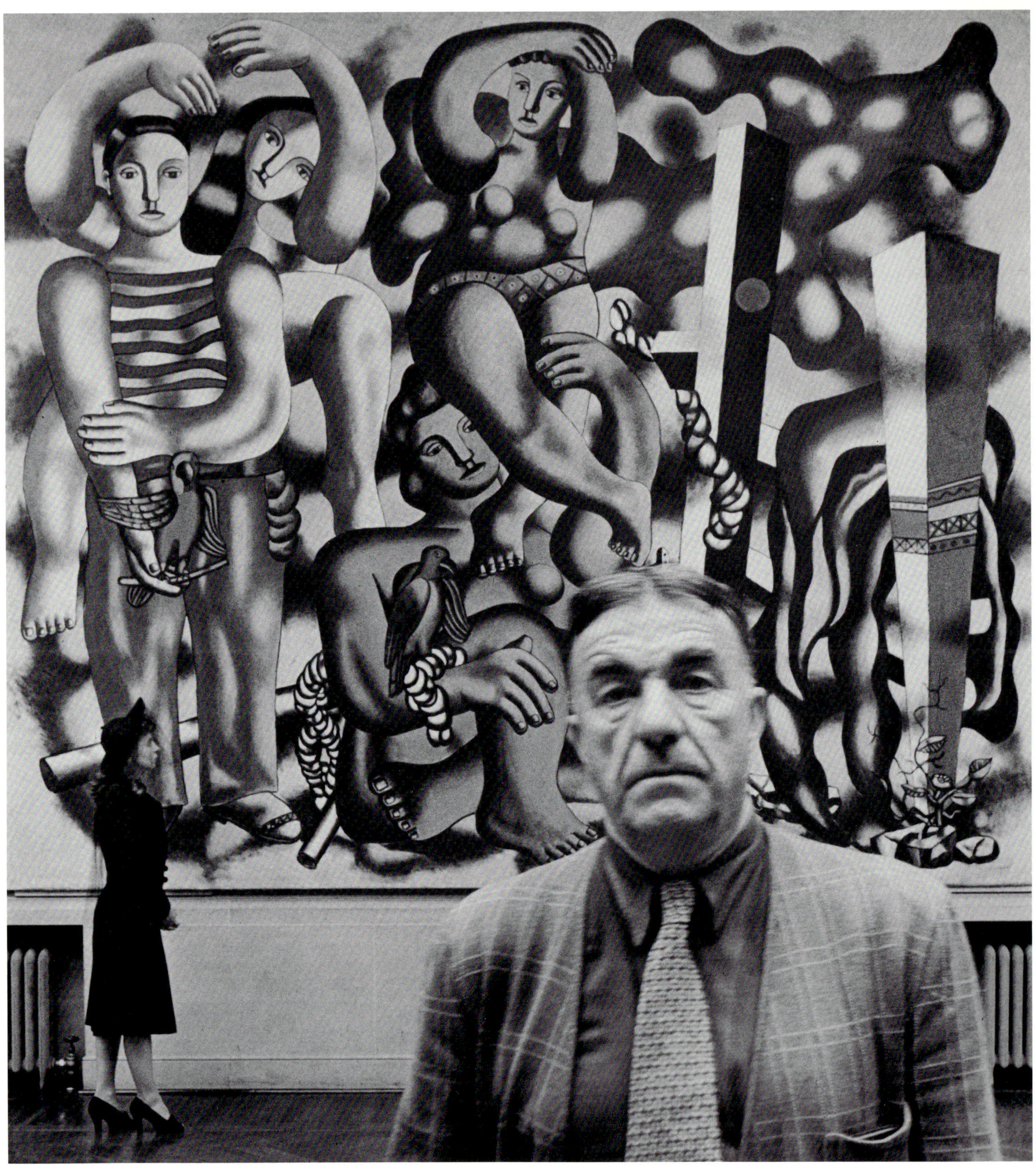

69 *Fernand Léger with Irene and "Composition with Parrots"*. 1940.

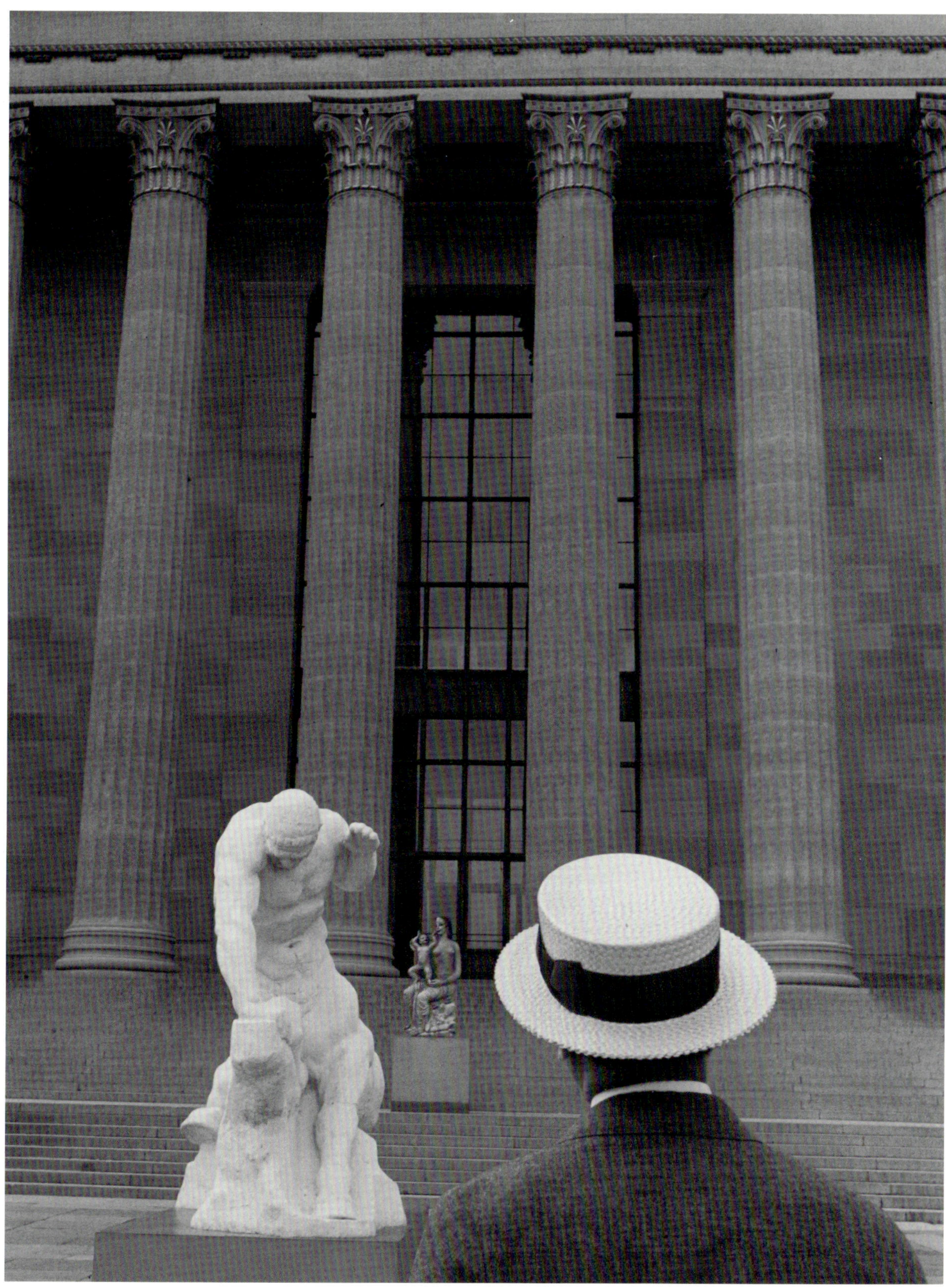

62 *Back and Up and Around.* Philadelphia, 1939.

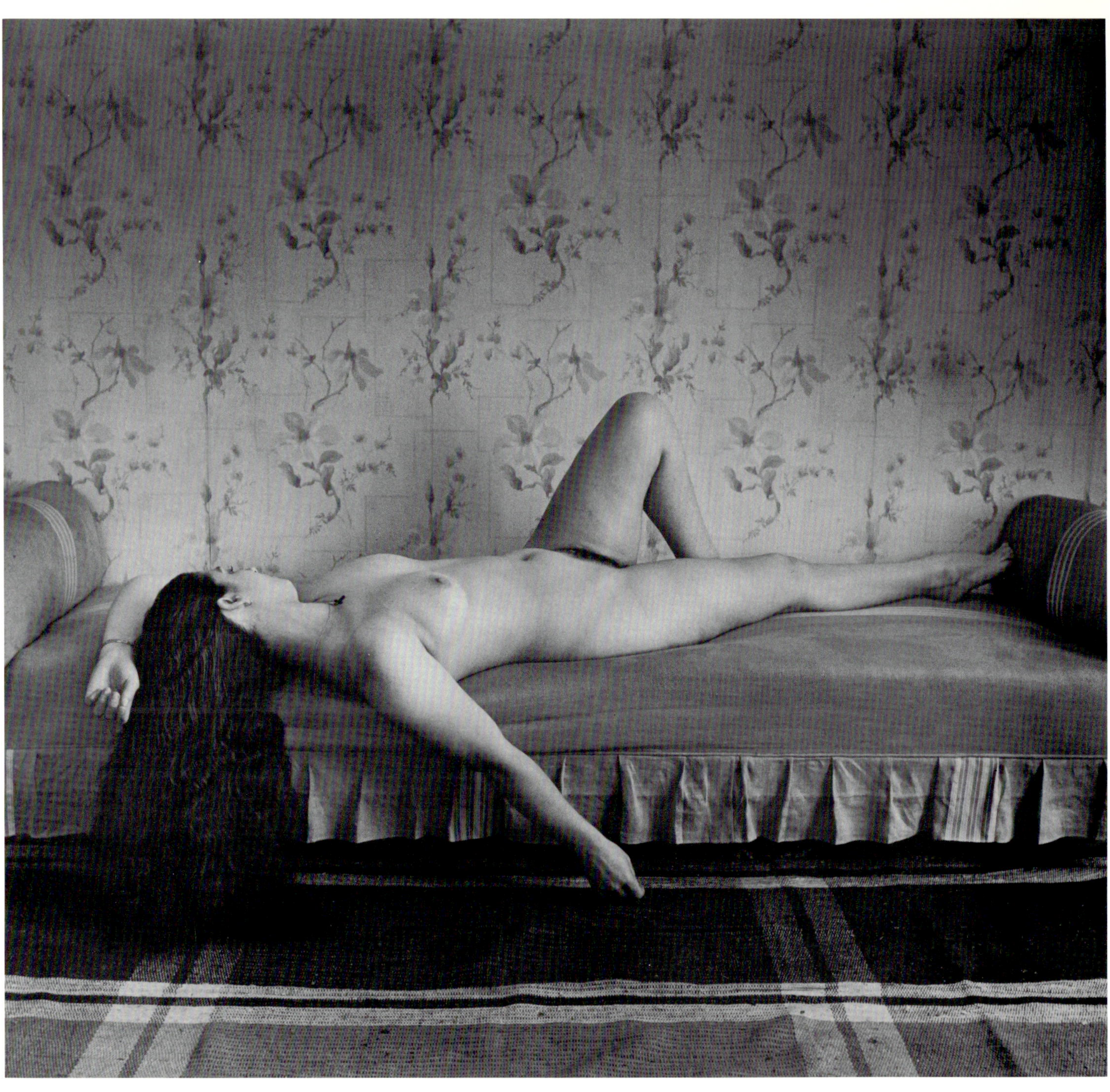

49 *Nude on Couch*. 1937.

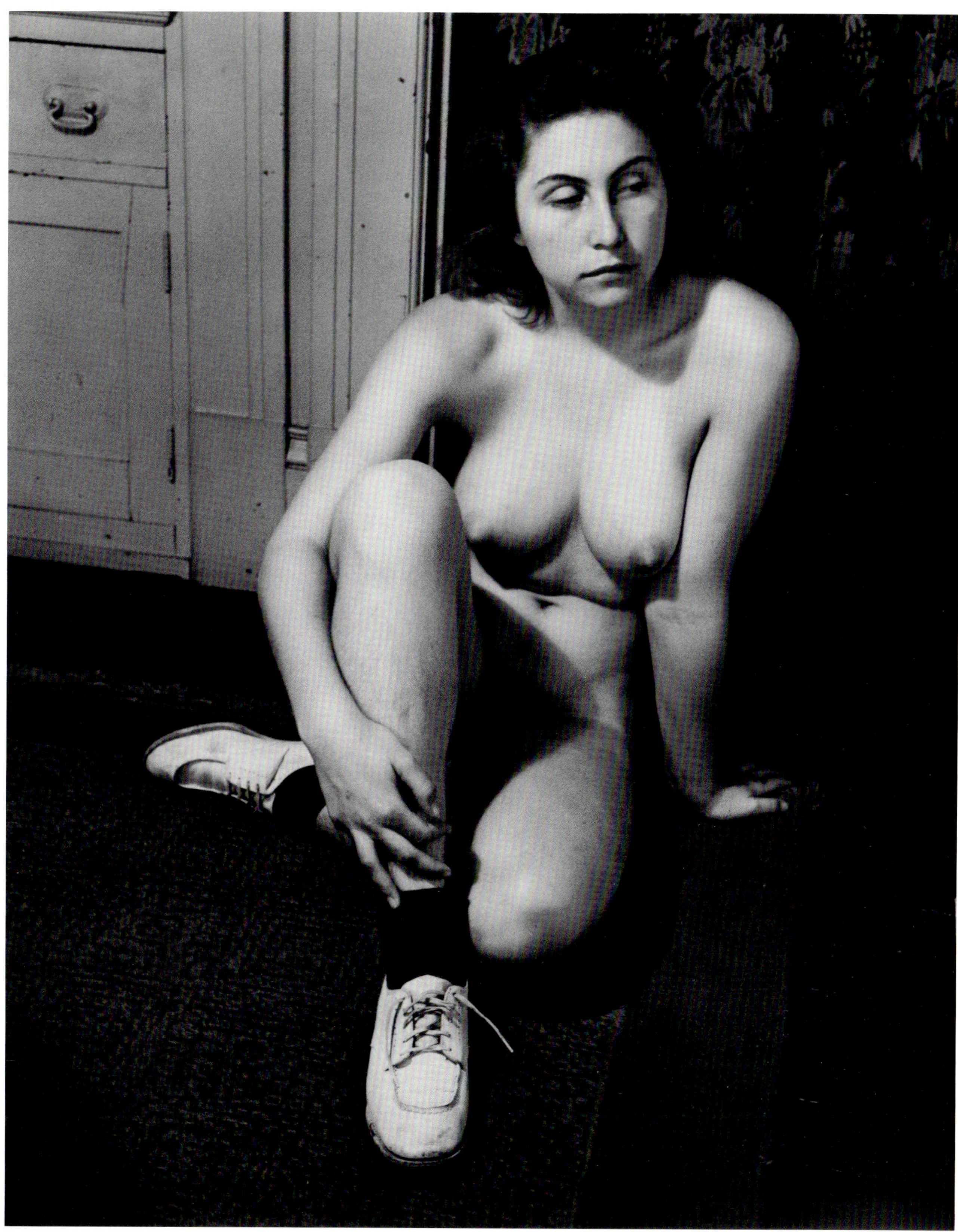

22 *Wanda*. 1935.

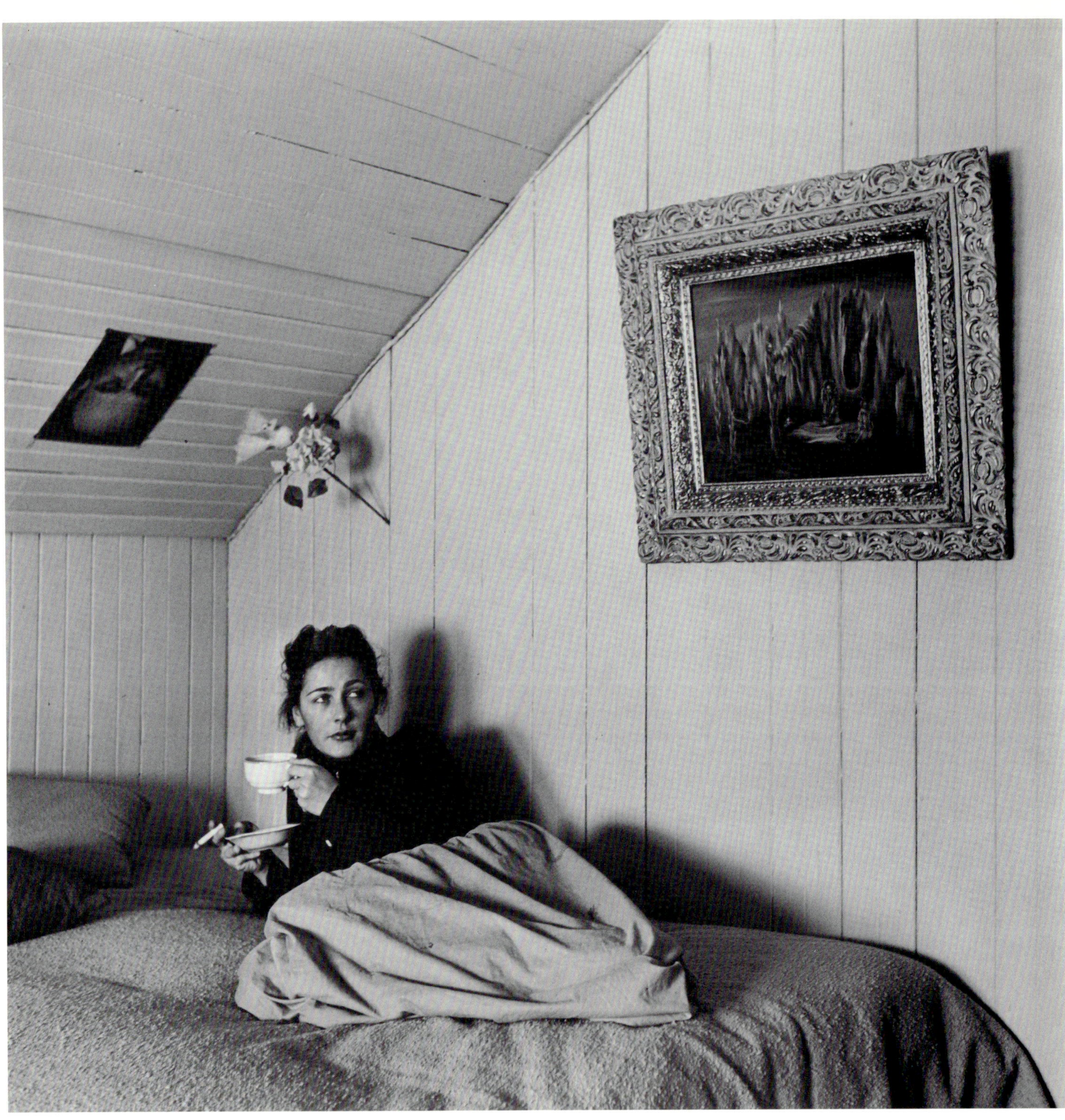

103 *Cup of Coffee and Cigarette*. 1950.

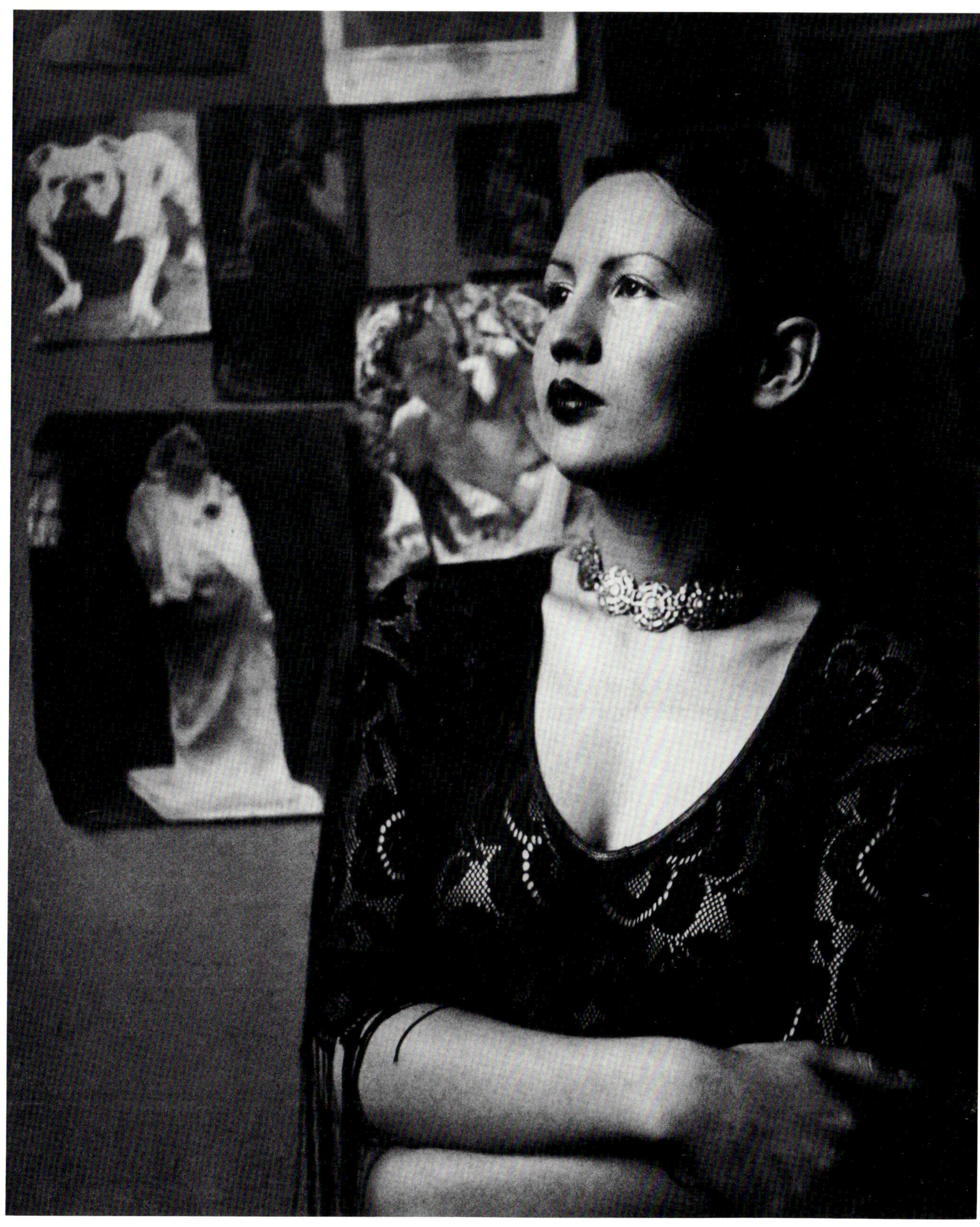

4 *Memory of Friedel*. Berlin, 1933.

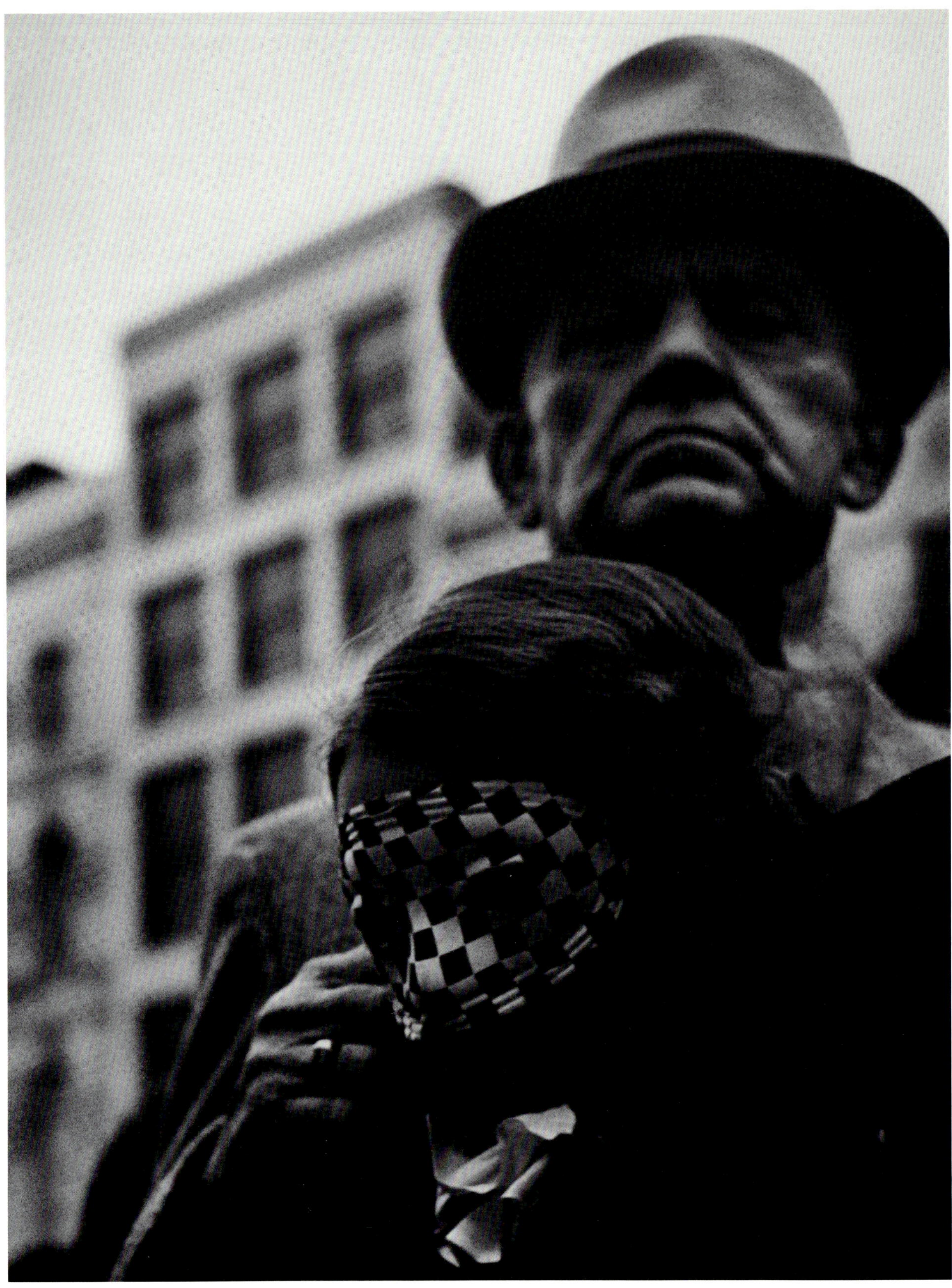

39 *The Father*. New Orleans, 1937.

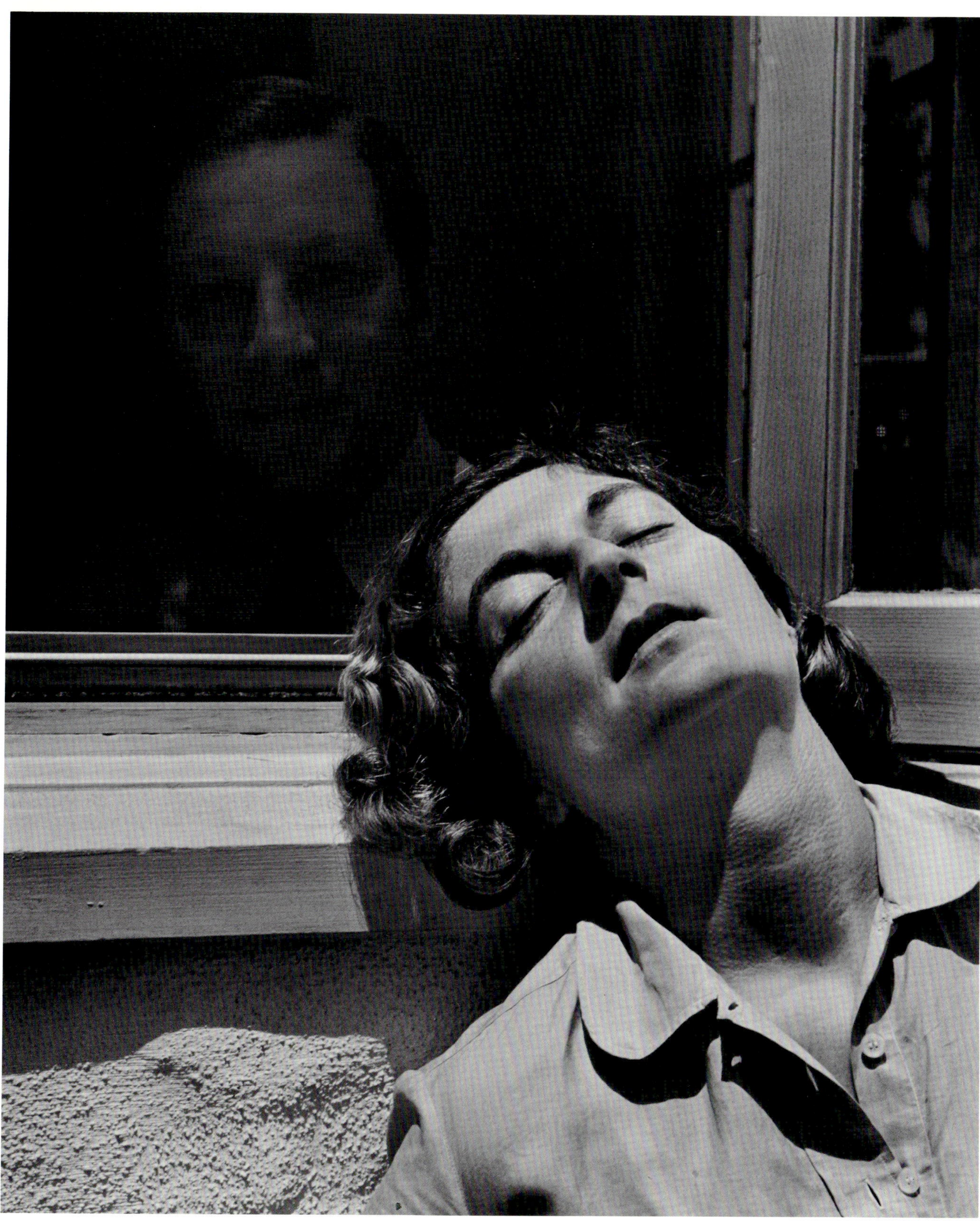

21 *Portrait of a Marriage.* 1935.

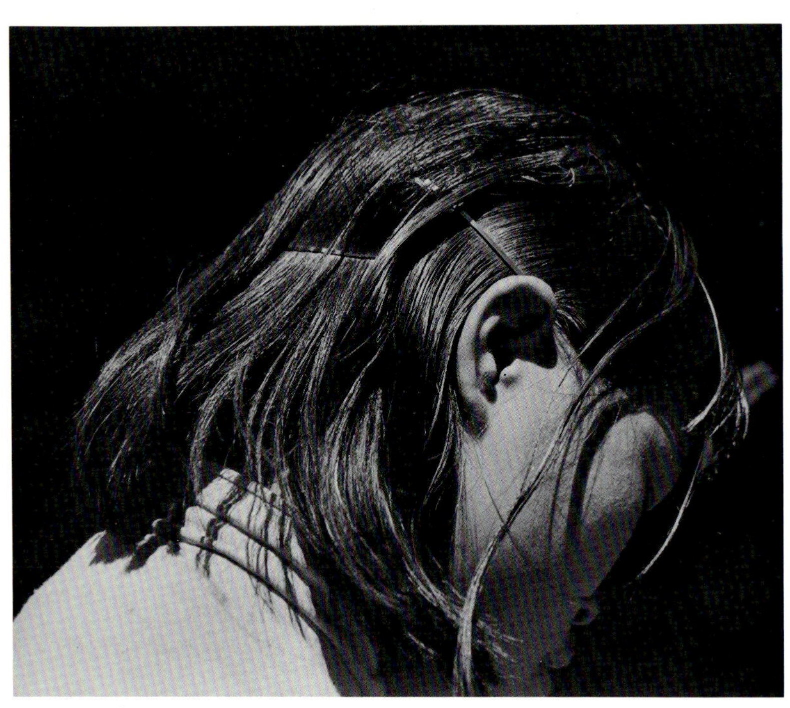

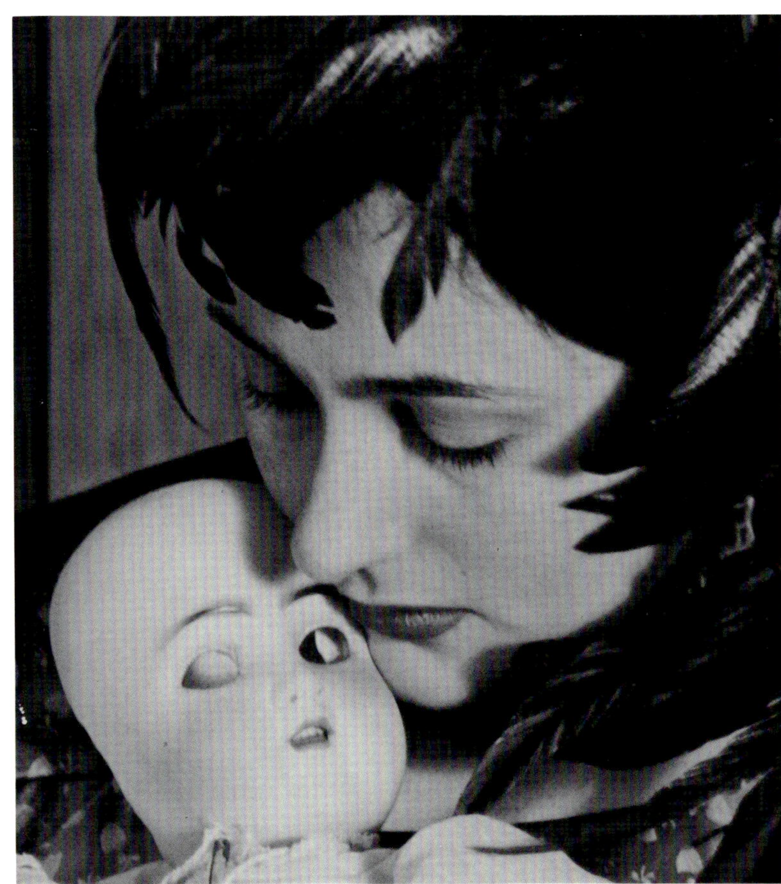

75 *Oiled Hair to Make it Shine.* Yunnan, China, 1944.

105 *Father Doll.* 1951.

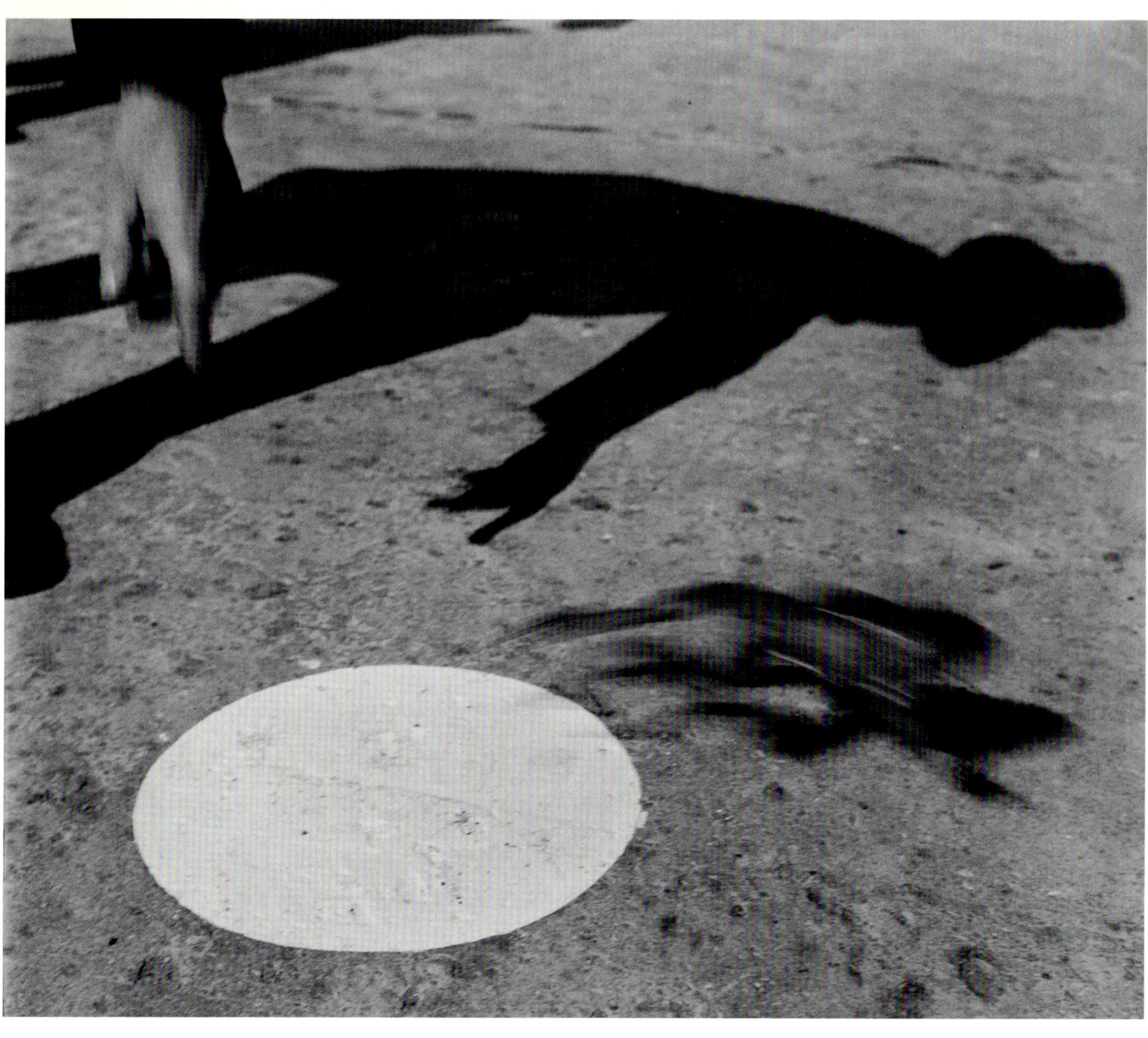

64 *The Jump.* 1939.

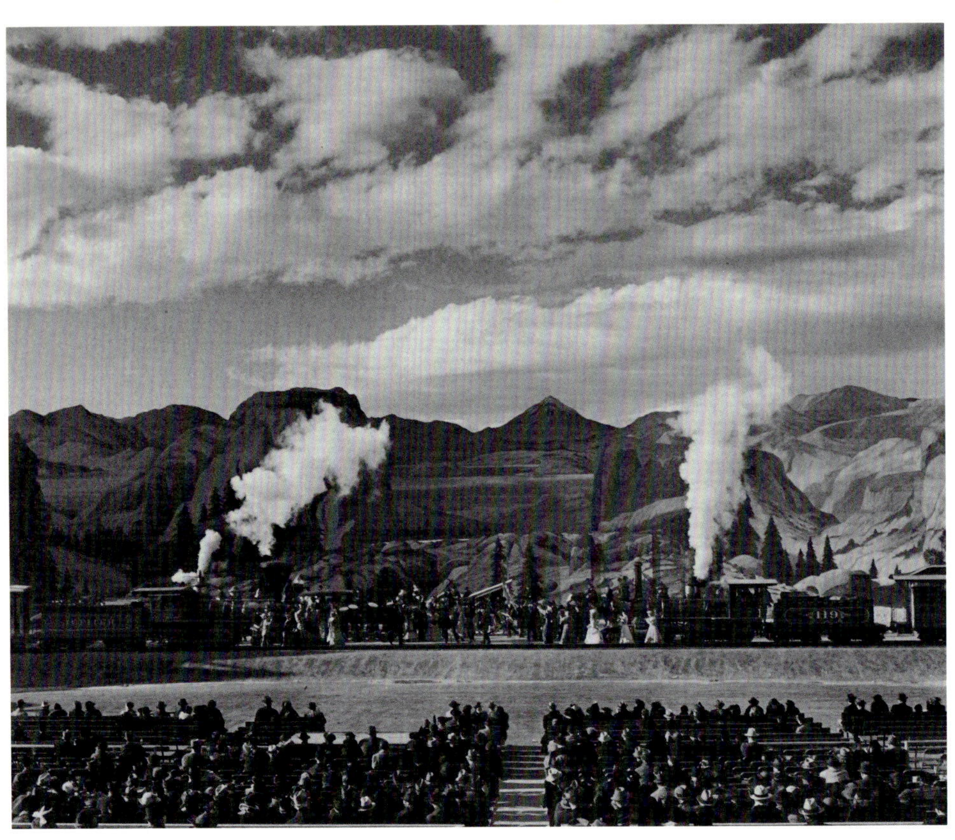

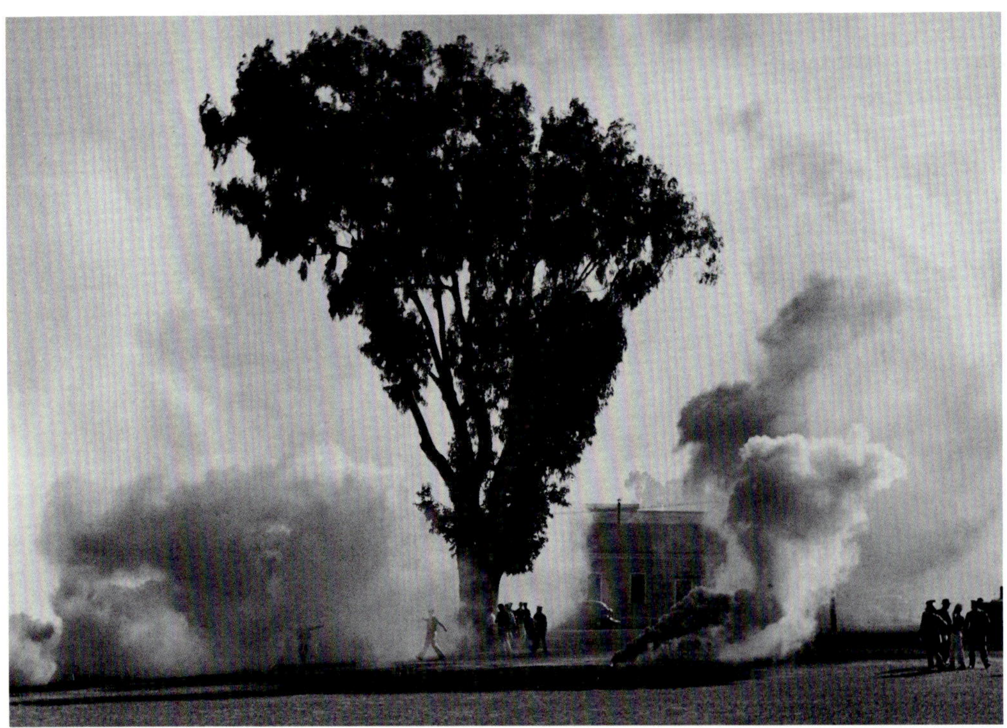

58 *"Cavalcade of the West"*. San Francisco, 1939.

55 *Ultimate Rehearsal*. 1938.

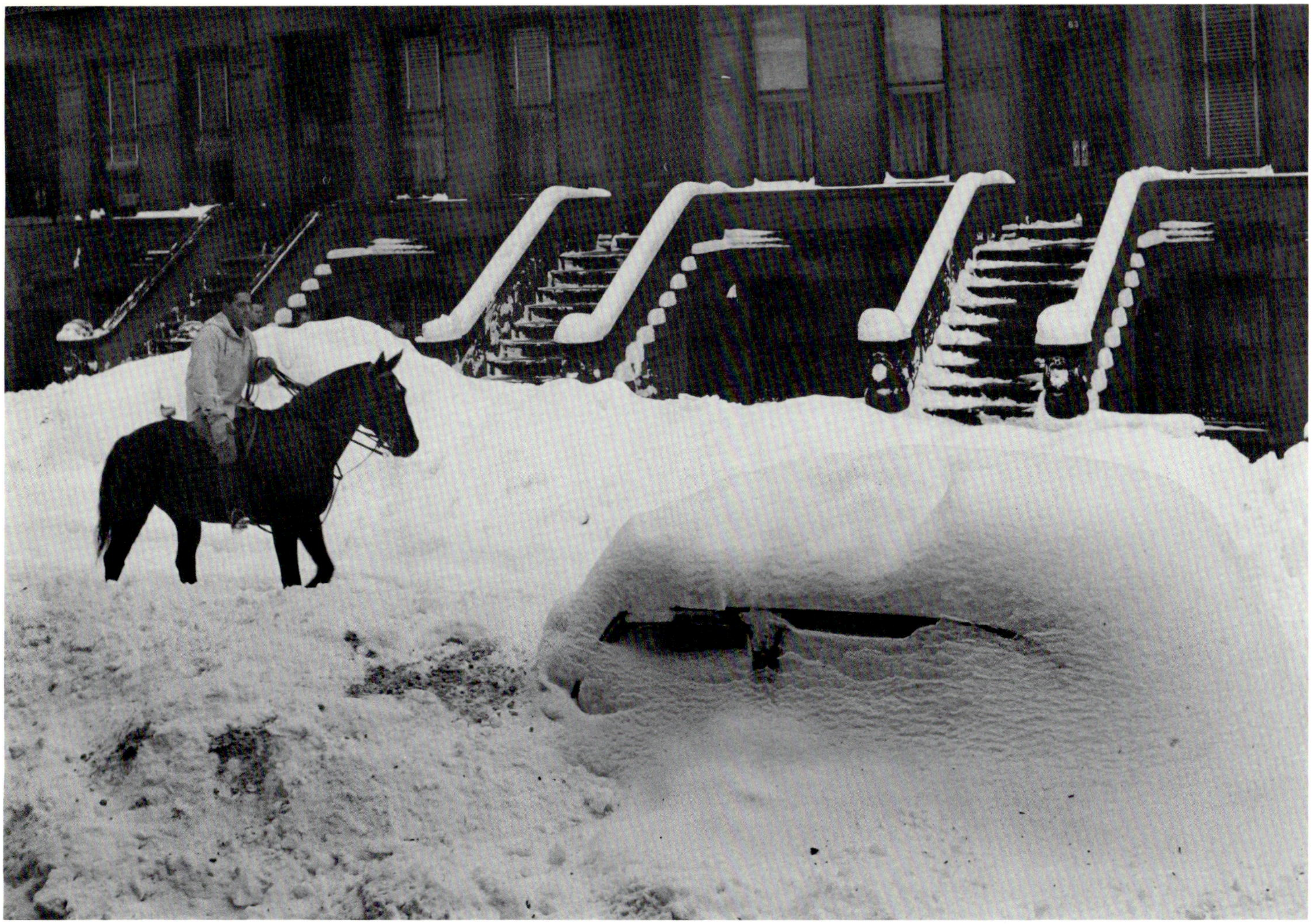

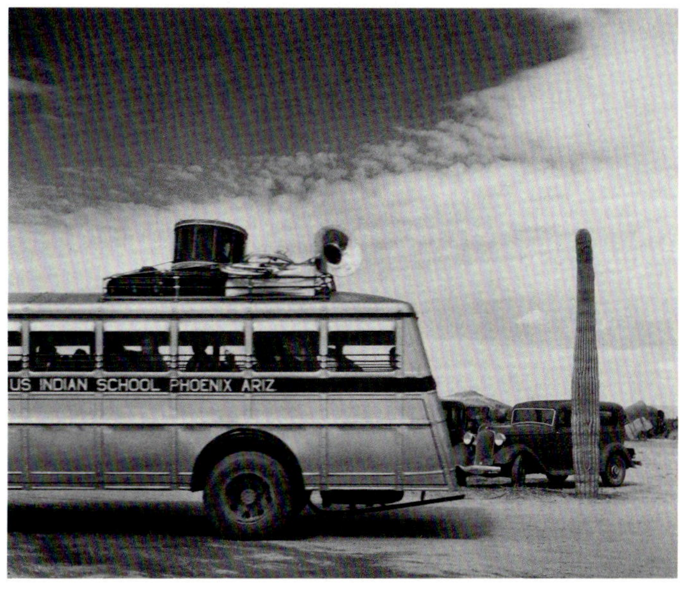

93 *Horseback Rider Passing by Snowed-in Cars on a Manhattan Street.* 1947.

47 *Indian High School Band Travelling Through Desert.* Arizona, 1937.

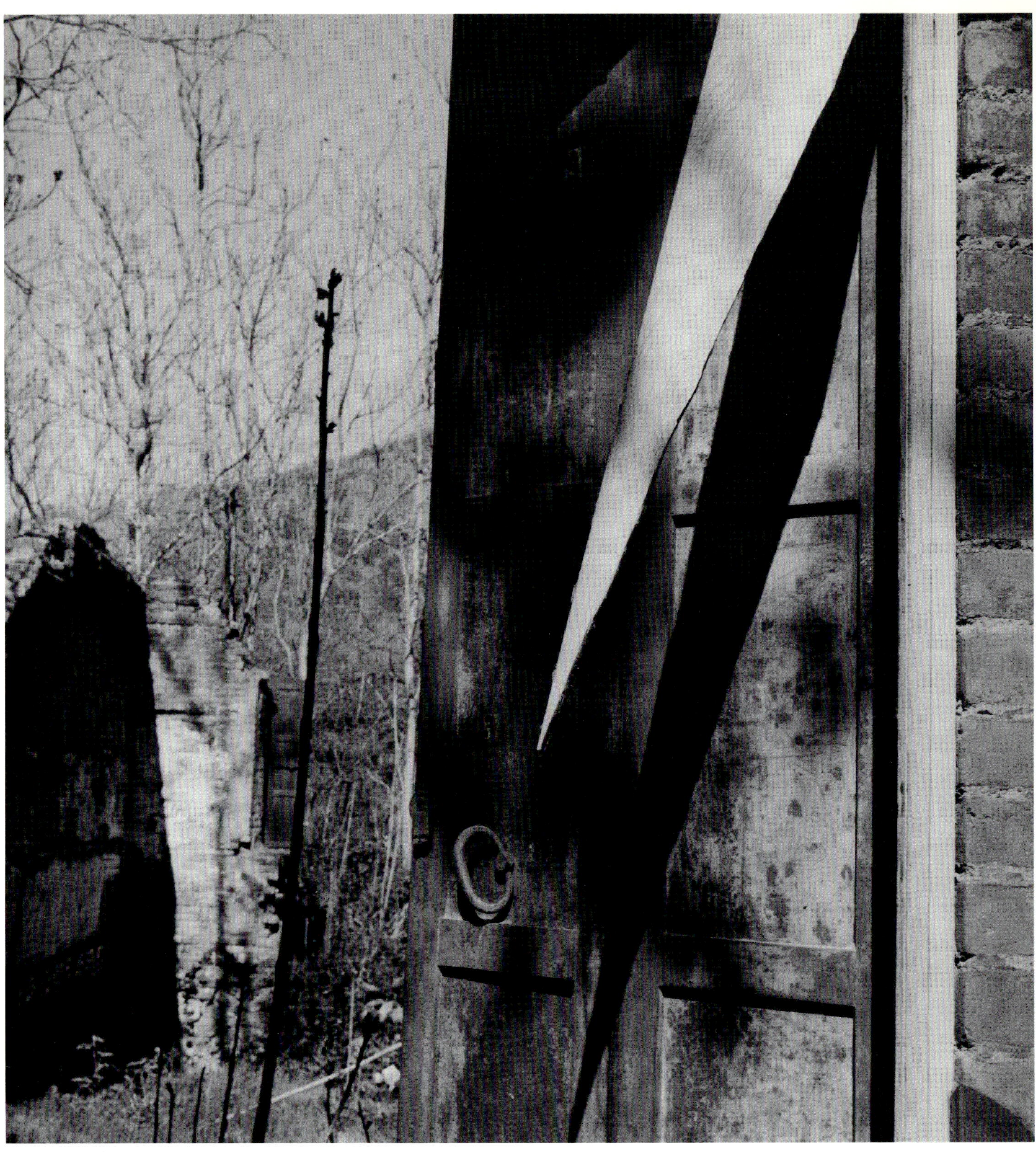

118 *Dagger from the Door.* Gold Country, California, 1961.

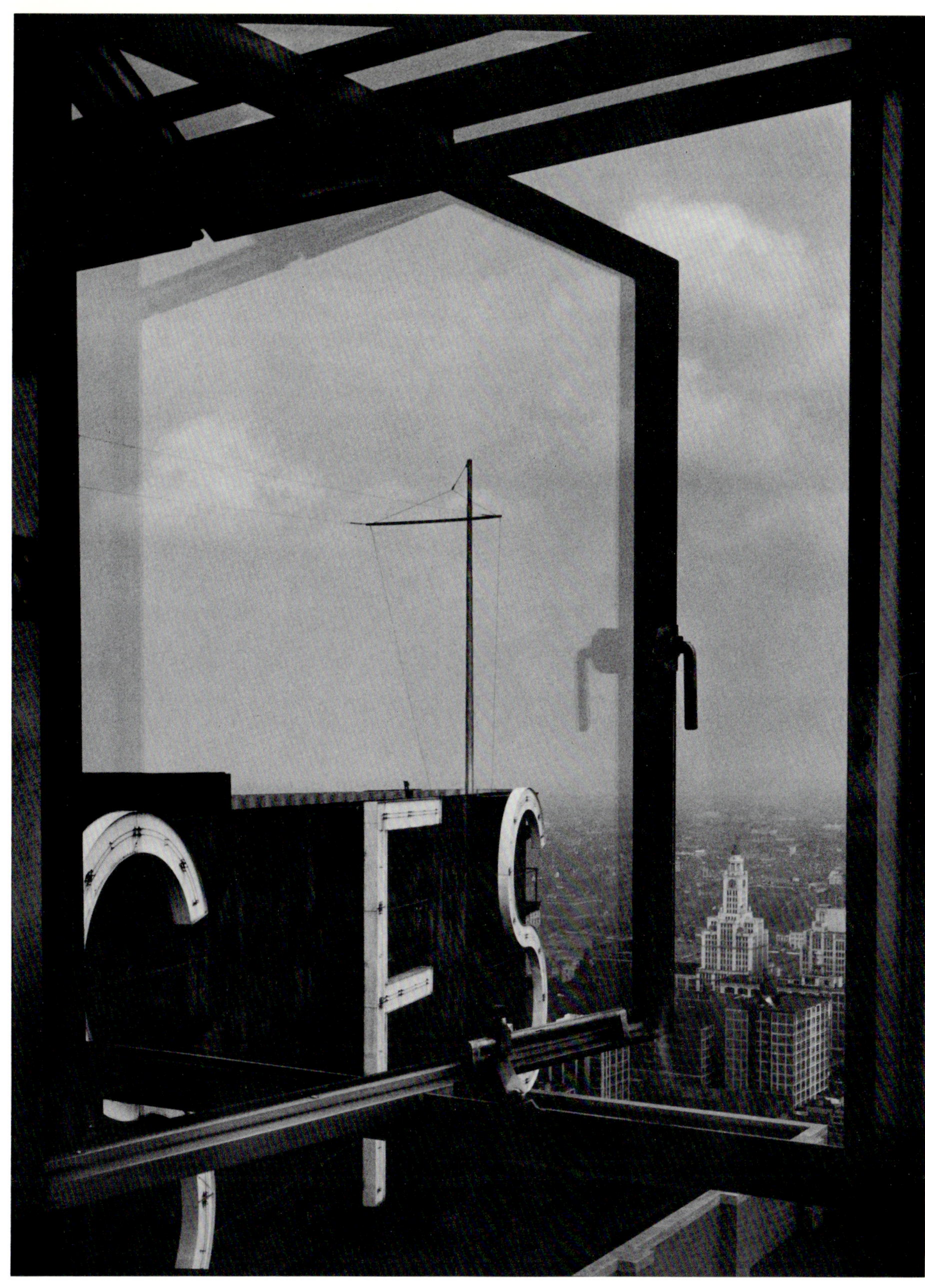

61 *The Open Window*. Philadelphia, 1939.

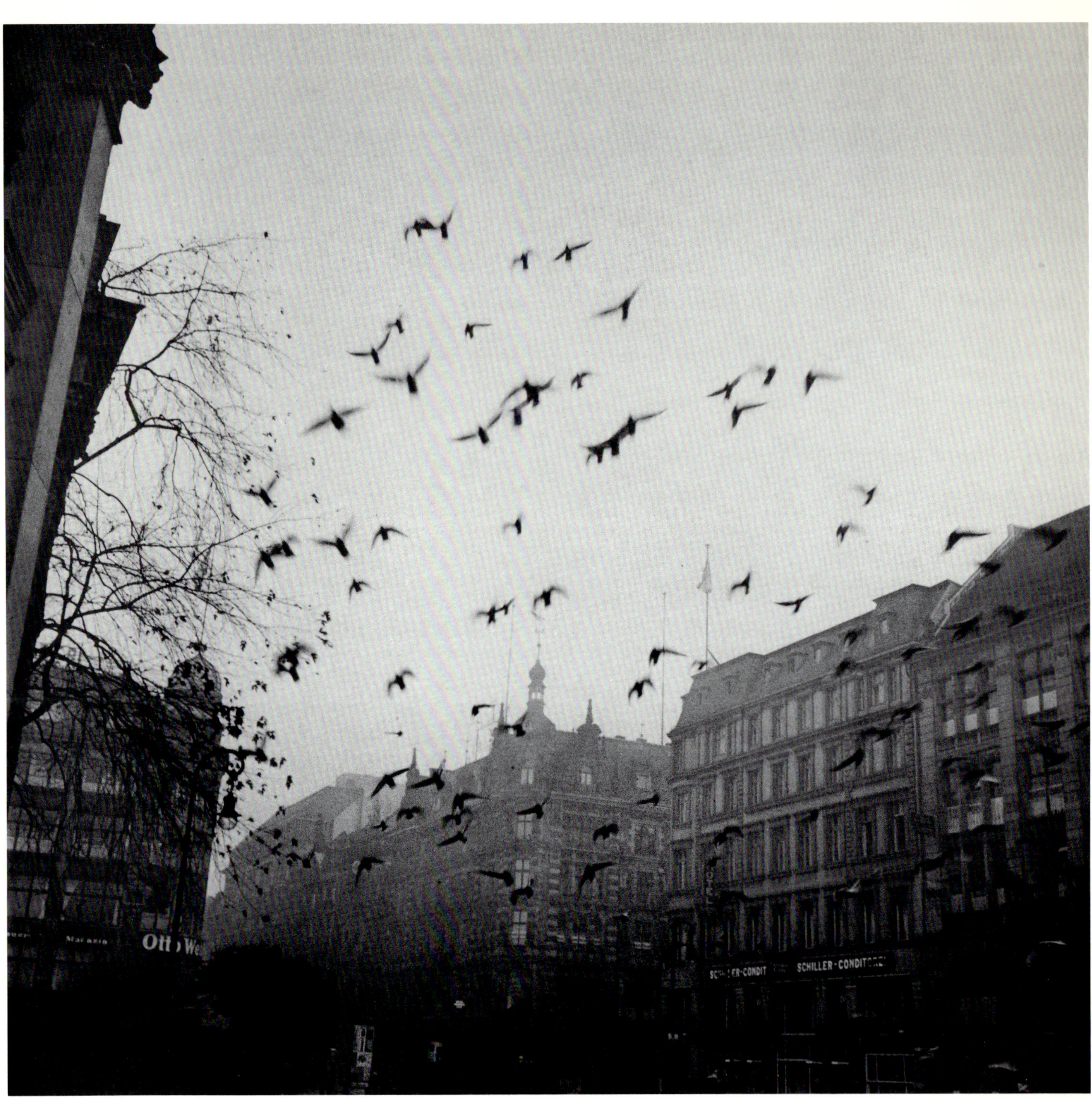

3 *Goodbye Berlin.* 1933.

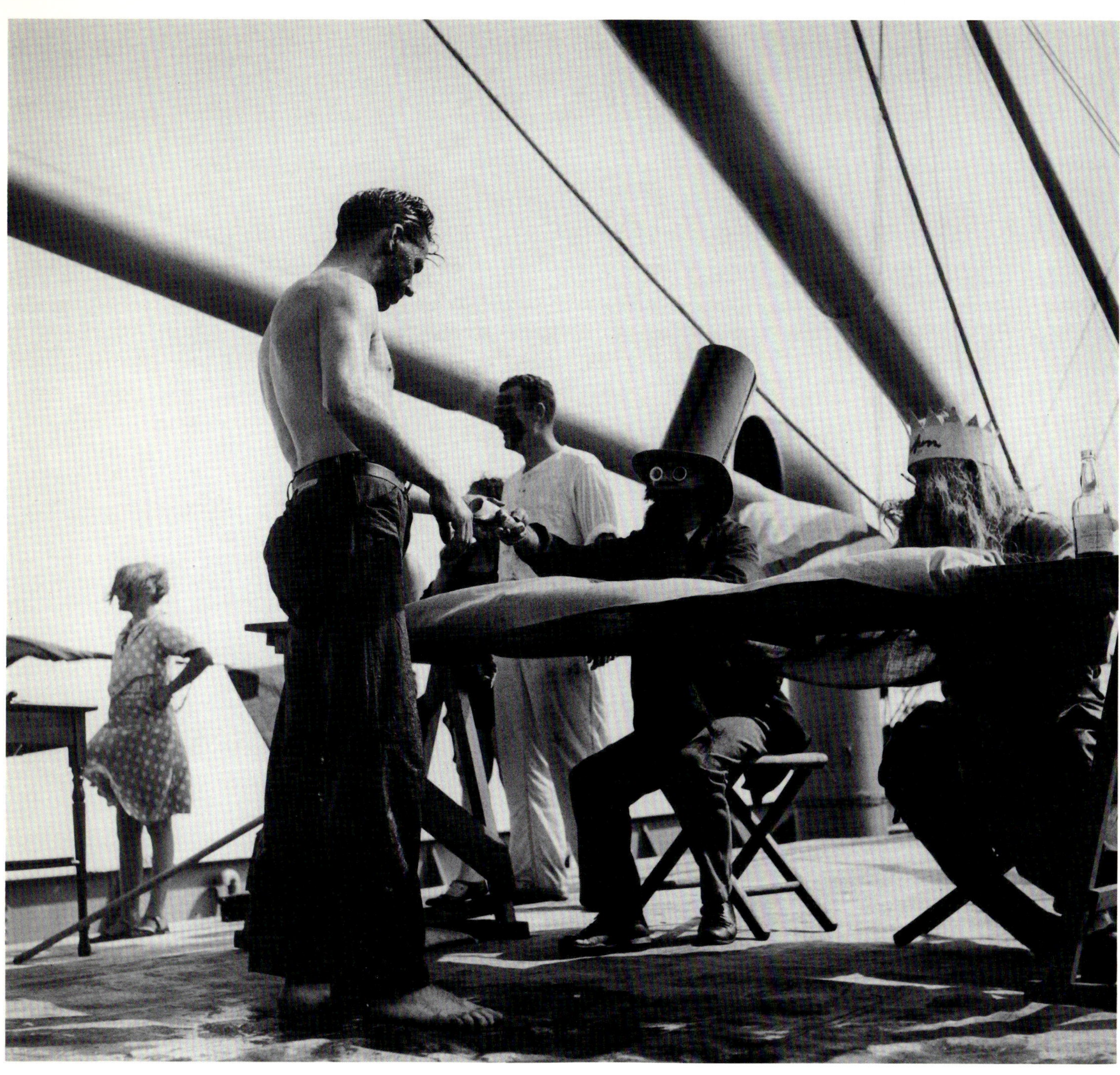

6 *The Initiation*. 1933.

CATALOGUE OF THE EXHIBITION

All works are from the collection of the artist, courtesy the Fraenkel Gallery, San Francisco. All prints are gelatin silver. Prints noted with an asterisk (*) are vintage; all others are modern prints. Measurements are for image size only. Height precedes width.

1 *Autumn in Charlottenburg.* Berlin, 1933.
31.4 x 26.0 cm

2 *October.* Berlin, 1933.
33.3 x 26.5 cm

3 *Goodbye Berlin.* 1933.
25.9 x 26.0 cm

4 *Memory of Friedel.* Berlin, 1933.
23.5 x 19.1 cm

5 *Man with a Dog in an Empty Square.* Rotterdam, 1933.
22.2 x 19.1 cm

6 *The Initiation.* 1933.
25.4 x 27.2 cm

7 *Out of the Pool.* San Francisco, 1934.
31.6 x 25.9 cm

8 *Towards the Pool.* San Francisco, 1934.
30.3 x 25.9 cm

9 *"Vanishing Gangsters".* San Francisco, 1934.
25.2 x 27.3 cm

10 *National Guard on Truck Patrolling Waterfront.* General Strike, San Francisco, 1934.
25.1 x 27.6 cm

11 *Black Man Alone. Union Members in the Funeral Procession for Killed Worker.* General Strike, San Francisco, 1934.
28.6 x 25.7 cm

12 *Night News.* Chinatown, San Francisco, 1934.
22.2 x 18.9 cm

13 *U.C. Cheerleader at Big Game.* Berkeley, 1934.
28.6 x 25.7 cm

14 *Akiko at Door.* 1934.
33.3 x 24.3 cm

15 *Traffic Patrol Boys with Cartoons Painted on their Jackets.* San Francisco, 1935.
20.6 x 19.1 cm

16 *"Auto Loans".* San Francisco, 1935.
25.4 x 32.4 cm

17 *German Gymnasts in America.* San Francisco, 1935.
22.2 x 19.1 cm

18 *The News Photographer.* San Francisco City Hall, 1935.
21.9 x 19.1 cm

19 *Inside the First Drive-In Theatre.* Los Angeles, 1935.
23.7 x 33.3 cm

20 *Turning to Look.* 1935.
25.9 x 27.5 cm

21 *Portrait of a Marriage.* 1935.
31.9 x 25.9 cm

22 *Wanda.* 1935.
33.7 x 26.4 cm

23 *Sex and Crime.* 1935.
28.9 x 25.6 cm

24 *Cord in Harlem.* New York, 1936.
26.0 x 33.7 cm

25 *The Sharpshooters.* Harlem, 1936.
25.7 x 33.2 cm

26 *"We Stand by the American Flag".* Maritime Strike, New York, 1936.
20.8 x 19.1 cm

27 *Automobile Transport.* Chicago, 1936.
26.7 x 34.3 cm

28 *American Landscape I.* Cleveland, 1936.
29.4 x 26.0 cm

29 *"We're not Talking".* Lovelock, Nevada, 1936.
25.9 x 26.4 cm

30 *Blackjack in Reno at Election Time.* Nevada, 1936.
21.4 x 19.1 cm

31 *Leap-Year Parade.* Berkeley, 1936.
25.7 x 31.4 cm

32 *Simulated Street Front of Early San Francisco.* Portsmouth Square, S.F., 1937.
25.7 x 31.0 cm

33 *The Landlady Graffiti.* San Francisco, 1937.
16.8 x 24.5 cm

34 *Mardi Gras Crowd on Canal Street.* New Orleans, 1937.
22.2 x 34.0 cm

35 *Freckle Face.* Mardi Gras, New Orleans, 1937.
33.0 x 25.9 cm

36 *Man Placing Hat Over Mask.* Mardi Gras, New Orleans, 1937.
25.9 x 31.1 cm

37 *Making a Movie in New Orleans.* 1937.
19.1 x 21.0 cm

38 *Member of the Band.* New Orleans, 1937.
24.3 x 18.1 cm

39 *The Father.* New Orleans, 1937.
24.3 x 18.1 cm

40 *Jitterbug.* New Orleans, 1937.
21.0 x 19.1 cm

41 *Nurses of the All-Black Flint-Goodridge Hospital.* New Orleans, 1937.
20.5 x 19.4 cm

42 *"Notary Public Here".* Alabama, 1937.
28.6 x 26.0 cm

43 *Bicycling by the Old Village Church.* Georgia, 1937.
30.3 x 26.2 cm

44 *The Soap Box Brothers.* Georgia, 1937.
29.4 x 26.2 cm

45 *Small-town Railroad Water Stop.* Texas, 1937.
18.9 x 21.3 cm

46 *Child's Grave.* Mexican Cemetery, El Paso, Texas, 1937.
21.3 x 19.4 cm

47 *Indian High School Band Travelling Through Desert.* Arizona, 1937.
25.9 x 30.8 cm

48 *Papagos Indian Race.* Tucson, 1937.
20.6 x 19.1 cm

49 *Nude on Couch.* 1937.
25.9 x 27.0 cm

50 *Funny Face.* 1938.
32.7 x 25.9 cm

51 *Longshoreman's Poem.* Waterfront, San Francisco, 1938.
28.7 x 26.0 cm

52 *The Artist Lives Dangerously.* San Francisco, 1938.
27.8 x 26.7 cm

53 *Nob Hill.* San Francisco, 1938.
25.7 x 32.7 cm

54 *Breathless Lesson.* 1938.
25.9 x 26.7 cm

55 *Ultimate Rehearsal.* 1938.
23.8 x 33.3 cm

56 *San Francisco Celebrates Opening of World's Fair.* 1939.
26.7 x 30.8 cm

57 *"God is Love".* San Francisco, 1939.
17.3 x 23.8 cm

58 *"Cavalcade of the West".* San Francisco, 1939.
25.9 x 30.5 cm

59 *Portrait of Count Basie.* San Francisco, 1939.
31.4 x 26.0 cm

60 *Voyeur Alarmed.* California, 1939.
32.4 x 25.9 cm

61 *The Open Window.* Philadelphia, 1939.
33.0 x 24.5 cm

62 *Back and Up and Around.* Philadelphia, 1939.
33.3 x 24.6 cm

63 *American Landscape V.* Chicago, 1939.
24.1 x 19.1 cm

64 *The Jump.* 1939.
25.7 x 29.5 cm

65 *H.B. Passing by Pickle Puss Billboard.* San Francisco, 1940.
19.1 x 23.0 cm

66 *The Beautiful Clown.* 1940.
26.2 x 28.6 cm

67 *Between Acts.* 1940.
26.4 x 31.0 cm

68 *Two Aerialists Between Shows.* 1940.
33.7 x 26.0 cm

69 *Fernand Léger with Irene and "Composition with Parrots".* 1940.
29.2 x 25.9 cm

70 *Rajput Bearers.* Madras, India, 1943.
27.0 x 26.4 cm*

71 *Two Moslem Women on Monsoon Swept Calcutta Street.* India, 1943.
33.7 x 26.2 cm*

72 *Country Market at Cheng-Kiang.* Yunnan, China, 1944.
26.0 x 32.5 cm*

73 *From the Temple of the Blue Mountain a View of the Picnic Place and arriving Pilgrims.* Yunnan, China, 1944.
33.0 x 25.9 cm*

74 *Peasant Girl Selling Hemp in Kunming.* Yunnan, China, 1944..
25.9 x 32.7 cm*

75 *Oiled Hair to Make it Shine.* Yunnan, China, 1944.
25.7 x 29.2 cm*

76 *Single File of Chinese Soldiers in Maneuver.* Yunnan, China, 1944.
18.1 x 23.8 cm*

77 *European-Trained Troops of the Chinese Nationalist Army at Parade.* Kunming, China, 1944.
19.2 x 24.0 cm*

78 *Small Boy with Embroidered Tiger-cap, Symbol of Courage.* Kunming, China, 1944.
28.6 x 26.0 cm*

79 *Peasants Repair Dams across Yuan River for Irrigation of near-by Rice Fields.* Hunan, China, 1944.
25.9 x 33.3 cm*

80 *Aerial View of Intricate Irrigation System on Terraced Mountains.* Hunan, China, 1944.
32.7 x 25.9 cm*

81 *Hysterical Mourners in Funeral Procession through Mountainous Miao Country.* Kweichow, China, 1944.
31.4 x 25.9 cm*

82 *Dead Hindu Girl Awaiting Burning at the Pyres of the Nimtolla Ghat.* Calcutta, India, 1945.
26.4 x 30.5 cm*

83 *Huge Posters Advertising Anything from a Hindu Movie Epic to a Chinese Dentist, Cover Buildings on Bowbazaar Street.* Calcutta, India, 1945.
32.9 x 26.0 cm*

84 *Advertisement of a Sex Specialist for the Treatment of "World Famous Diseases".* Calcutta, India, 1945.
33.8 x 26.5 cm*

85 *A Load of Army Nurses.* 1945.
33.8 x 25.2 cm

86 *Ben's Barber Shop Window.* San Francisco, 1946.
27.3 x 26.2 cm

87 *Day and Night Branch.* Bank of America, San Francisco, 1947.
21.1 x 18.4 cm

88 *The Lady is Getting a Loan.* Bank of America, San Francisco, 1947.
21.3 x 18.3 cm

89 *Hamilton Field Branch of the Bank of America.* San Francisco, 1947.
18.4 x 21.6 cm

90 *Maintenance Worker Moving Down on Main Cable of the Golden Gate Bridge.* San Francisco, 1947.
25.9 x 25.9 cm

91 *From the North Tower of the Golden Gate Bridge.* San Francisco, 1947.
31.0 x 26.2 cm

92 *Huge Class in Final Exam.* U.C. Berkeley, 1947.
27.8 x 26.2 cm

93 *Horseback Rider Passing by Snowed-in Cars on a Manhattan Street.* 1947.
23.3 x 33.2 cm

94 *A Tree at Hunter's Point.* San Francisco, 1948.
22.9 x 33.3 cm

95 *Moving into Row House.* Hunter's Point, San Francisco, 1948.
10.1 x 29.4 cm

96 *"Business Opportunities".* Fontana, California, 1948.
23.5 x 33.2 cm

97 *Shrub in the Desert.* Southern California, 1948.
26.4 x 25.1 cm

98 *Three Crossings.* The American Canal, California near the Arizona Border. 1948.
24.1 x 33.2 cm

99 *"Betty Love Ben".* 1948.
33.2 x 25.6 cm

100 *The Killer.* 1948.
25.7 x 32.4 cm

101 *Machine Gunners.* San Francisco, 1950.
27.2 x 25.9 cm

102 *Modoc Petroglyphs with X in Circle.* California, 1950.
25.7 x 28.3 cm

103 *Cup of Coffee and Cigarette.* 1950.
27.0 x 25.9 cm

104 *Very Beautiful in Feather Hat.* 1951.
31.6 x 26.4 cm

105 *Father Doll.* 1951.
29.5 x 25.9 cm

106 *Stanley Hiller up in the "Hornet".* California, 1952.
25.7 x 29.7 cm

107 *Gamblers in the Window.* Portland, Oregon, 1954.
29.9 x 25.9 cm

108 *Visiting Nuns passing through a Galleria of the Camposanto di Staglieno.* Genoa, Italy, 1957.
30.5 x 25.4 cm

109 *Holy Week Crowd in Prayer.* Granada, Spain, 1957.
30.3 x 25.4 cm

110 *All the Cave Dwellings in the Hills of Puerto Lumbrera.* Spain, 1957.
25.7 x 30.8 cm

111 *Chairs in Portugal.* 1957.
33.5 x 24.8 cm

112 *Woman Hurrying through Alley.* Tetuan, Morocco, 1957.
32.1 x 25.6 cm

113 *The Sisters.* Mexico, 1960.
24.3 x 19.2 cm*

114 *The Victims.* Guanajuato, Mexico, 1960.
25.9 x 28.9 cm

115 *The Confessional.* Mexico, 1960.
25.6 x 32.4 cm

116 *Carson Mansion with Parked Automobile Seen through Cross-barred Window.* Eureka, California, 1960.
30.3 x 25.9 cm

117 *"Ain't Mad at Nobody"*. Oregon, 1960.
24.9 x 25.9 cm

118 *Dagger from the Door.* Gold Country, California, 1961.
28.6 x 25.9 cm

119 *Ghost-town Ruins.* California, 1961.
31.1 x 25.9 cm

120 *White Car Away from Lumber Tunnel.* New York City, 1965.
26.2 x 26.0 cm

121 *Metal and Wood.* 1965.
26.5 x 25.9 cm

122 *Fancy Eyes.* London, 1970.
24.5 x 17.5 cm*

123 *Elevated Parking.* New York City, 1978.
27.8 x 26.5 cm

124 *Rolls Royce with Charred Garbage.* New York City, 1978.
26.7 x 29.4 cm

125 *Three Star Building and Fence with Jasper Johns Posters.* New York City, 1978.
26.0 x 32.4 cm

126 *Anti-Marcos Demonstration.* 5th Avenue, New York City, 1978.
34.1 x 23.2 cm

127 *Pooper-Scooper and Dumpster.* New York City, 1978.
31.1 x 26.4 cm

128 *Facade with Sign, "Old Jewelery Bought".* W. 47th Street, New York City, 1979.
34.0 x 25.9 cm

129 *Russian Antiques.* New York City, 1979.
26.4 x 29.9 cm

130 *The More the Better.* W. 47th Street, New York City, 1979.
34.0 x 26.2 cm

131 *"Diamond Horseshoe 29".* W. 47th Street, New York City, 1979.
32.1 x 26.7 cm

132 *A Funny Conversation.* W. 47th Street, New York City, 1979.
27.0 x 26.4 cm

133 *View Camera on W. 47th Street.* New York City, 1979.
18.7 x 18.7 cm

134 *Dance Macabre.* New York City, 1979.
22.7 x 24.0 cm

135 *The Garbage Cache.* New York City, 1979.
28.7 x 26.4 cm

136 *"Gold and Silver Coins Bought Here".* W. 47th Street, New York City, 1981.
25.9 x 26.5 cm

137 *Soho Mural.* New York City, 1981.
25.7 x 27.0 cm

CHRONOLOGY

This chronology includes exhibitions of paintings, drawings, and only the major exhibitions of photography. See page 93 for a complete listing of all photography exhibitions.

1905 Born in Breslau, Germany

1914–1923 Attends Johannes Gymnasium, Breslau, Germany. Abiturium.

1923–1927 Receives B.A., Staatliche Akademie für Kunst und Kunstgewerbe zu Breslau, Germany. Studies with Otto Mueller as a master student.

1926 Meets Erich Heckel. Travels to London.

1926–1927 Studies art and philosophy at Schlesische Friedrich Wilhelms Universität zu Breslau.

1927 Exhibits paintings at Schlesischer Künstlerbund and in *Junge Talente*, Museum der Bildenden Künste, Breslau, Germany. Moves to Berlin.

1928 Receives M.A., Preussisches Schulkollegium fur Höhere Erziehung, Berlin.

1928–1931 Travels in Europe.

1929–1930 Post-graduate studies at Humboldt Universität zu Berlin and Berliner Akademie der Bildenden Künste.

1929–1932 One-man exhibition of paintings and drawings, Gurlitt Gallery, Berlin (1931). Included in exhibition of Berliner Secession and Preussische Akademie der Künste. Teaches art at various schools in Berlin.

1933 Plans to leave Germany; purchases Rolleiflex camera and begins to photograph. Signs contract as photojournalist with Presse-Foto, Berlin. Journey to San Francisco, California, via Panama Canal, Ecuador.

1934 Joins California Camera Club, San Francisco, to use their darkroom facilities and meets many members, mostly of the Pictorialist school. Travels through U.S. West Coast to British Columbia.

1935 One-man exhibition of drawings, Paul Elder Gallery, San Francisco, California.

1936 Begins teaching art, San Francisco State College, part-time. Travels across the United States from San Francisco to New York. Four months' stay in New York. Stops include Reno, Salt Lake City, Chicago, Detroit, Cleveland, Baltimore, Philadelphia, Atlanta, New Orleans, Birmingham, San Antonio, Tucson, San Diego, and Los Angeles before returning to San Francisco. Ceases affiliation with Presse-Foto and begins work for Pix, Inc., New York. Works on numerous magazine assignments until 1963. Meets George Grosz during stay in New York.

1937 Returns to San Francisco. Continues teaching art, San Francisco State College, part-time. One-man exhibition of drawings, San Francisco Museum of Art, California. One-man exhibition of drawings and paintings, Delphic Studios, New York, N.Y.

1938 Appointed Assistant Professor of Art, San Francisco State College. Establishes studio courses and a comprehensive scholarly course on history of modern art. One-man exhibition of photographs, *Colorful America*, M.H. de Young Memorial Museum, San Francisco, California; circulated nationally. One-man exhibition of watercolours and drawings, Wayne State University, Detroit, Michigan.

1939 Exhibited in "Contemporary Art", Golden Gate International Exposition, San Francisco, Ca. Meets with László Moholy-Nagy.

1940 Meets with and photographs Fernand Léger.

1940–1962 Photographs published in *Saturday Evening Post*, *Life*, *Time*, *Look*, *Picture Post*, *National Geographic*, *Pictorial Press*, *Coronet*, *Asia*, *The Geographic Magazine*, *U.S. Camera Annuals*, and other magazines and periodicals.

1941 One-man exhibition of photographs, *Wondrous World*, M.H. de Young Memorial Museum, San Francisco, California. Exhibited in *Image of Freedom*, The Museum of Modern Art, New York, N.Y.

1942 Two-man exhibition, *Paintings by John Gutmann and Karl Baumann*, San Francisco Museum of Art, California.

1942–1943 Staff photographer for *The Dispatch*, Camp Roberts, California. Graduates from the Signal Corps Motion Picture School, Astoria, New York. Serves with U.S. Army Signal Corps as still and motion picture cameraman.

1943–1945 Serves overseas in the China-Burma-India Theatre, U.S. Office of War Information with the Psychological Warfare Team.

1946 Returns to teaching. Establishes a creative photography program at San Francisco State College.

1947 One-man exhibition of photographs, *The Face of the Orient*, M.H. de Young Memorial Museum, San Francisco, California.

1949 Appointed Associate Professor of Art, San Francisco State College. Produces documentary films, *The Chinese Peasant Goes to Market* and *Journey to Kunming*. Marries artist Gerrie von Pribosic.

1949–1963 Founder of international film program, "Art Movies," San Francisco State College. Directs programs of experimental, documentary, art, and early classic films.

1950 Travels to Mexico; post-graduate work at the University of Mexico.

1951–1960 Several visits to New York City.

1955 Appointed full Professor of Art, San Francisco State College.

1956 Meets with Wynn Bullock.

1957 Seven months travelling through Portugal, Spain, Morocco, France, Italy, Germany, Holland, Belgium, and England. Extensive still photography and motion picture footage on modern architecture.

1960 Travels to Mexico.

1960–1982 Repeated visits to New York City.

1962–1972 Little work in photography due to prolonged illness, but continues teaching 1965–1973.

1968 Honored for Distinguished Teaching by the California State Colleges.

1970 Visits Berlin for the first time since 1933. Visits Oslo (Edvard Munch Museum), Norway, and northern European capitals.

1972 Starts to reprint early negatives.

1973 Retires from full-time teaching; Professor Emeritus at San Francisco State University (formerly San Francisco State College).

1974 One-man exhibition of photographs, *John Gutmann*, Light Gallery, New York City.

1976 Two-man exhibition, *John Gutmann and Walker Evans, Vintage Photographs of the 1930s*, Phoenix Gallery, San Francisco, California. One-man exhibition of photographs, *as i saw it*, San Francisco Museum of Modern Art, California.

1977 Receives Guggenheim Fellowship for proposed series of photographic images dealing with the visual use of language and popular emblems in American life during the 1930s and 1940s.

1979 to present Active in exhibiting, nationally and internationally. Production of documentary film, *Le Palais Idéal* (1983). Involved in the production of major book, *The Restless Decade: John Gutmann's Photographs of the Thirties* (1984). Lives in San Francisco.

LIST OF PHOTOGRAPHY EXHIBITIONS

One-Man Exhibitions

1938 San Francisco, Ca. *Colorful America.* M.H. de Young Memorial Museum.

1941 San Francisco, Ca. *Wondrous World.* M.H. de Young Memorial Museum.

1947 San Francisco, Ca. *The Face of the Orient.* M.H. de Young Memorial Museum.

1974 New York, N.Y. *John Gutmann.* Light Gallery.

1976 San Francisco, Ca. *as i saw it.* San Francisco Museum of Modern Art.

1979 New York, N.Y. *The Fourth Decade.* Castelli Graphics.

1980 San Francisco, Ca. *San Francisco 1934–1939.* Fraenkel Gallery.
Birmingham, Michigan. *John Gutmann Photographs.* Halsted Gallery.

1981 New Orleans, Louisiana. *John Gutmann Photographs of San Francisco and New Orleans, ca. 1937.* A Gallery for Fine Photography.
New York, N.Y. *Women.* Castelli Graphics.

1983 San Francisco, Ca. *Ten Photographs.* Fraenkel Gallery.
New York, N.Y. *John Gutmann: A Portfolio of Photographs.* Robert Freidus Gallery.
San Francisco, Ca. *Women.* Fraenkel Gallery.
San Francisco, Ca. *American Images 1930s–40s.* Bank of America, Giannini Gallery.

1985 New York, N.Y. *by my choice.* Castelli Uptown.

Two-Man Exhibitions

1976 San Francisco, Ca. *John Gutmann and Walker Evans, Vintage Photographs of the 1930s.* Phoenix Gallery.

1984 San Diego, Ca. *John Gutmann/Berenice Abbott.* Museum of Photographic Arts.

Group Exhibitions

1941 New York, N.Y. *Image of Freedom.* The Museum of Modern Art.
Oakland, Ca. *New Possibilities in Photography.* Invitational Western Camera Conclave.

1976 San Francisco, Ca. *Photography and Language.* LaMamelle and Camerawork.

1978 San Francisco, Ca. *Aesthetics of Grafitti.* San Francisco Museum of Modern Art.
San Francisco, Ca. *Work.* The Fine Arts Museums of San Francisco (Downtown Center).
San Francisco, Ca. *Photographs from the Permanent Collection.* San Francisco Museum of Modern Art.

1979 New Orleans, Louisiana. *Photography in Louisiana.* New Orleans Museum of Art.
Zurich, Switzerland. *Amerika Fotografie 1920–1940.* Kunsthaus. (circulated in Europe)

1980 San Francisco, Ca. *Photography and Architecture.* Fraenkel Gallery.
Sacramento, Ca. *Forty American Photographers.* Crocker Art Museum. (travelled to Kestnergestellschaft, Hannover, West Germany, and internationally)
New York, N.Y. *Amalgam.* Castelli Graphics.
San Francisco, Ca. *Avant-Garde Photography in Germany, 1919–1939.* San Francisco Museum of Modern Art. (travelled internationally)
San Francisco, Ca. *Curator's Choice.* San Francisco Museum of Modern Art.
New York, N.Y. *When Words Fail.* International Center of Photography.
Paris, France. *Creatis Exposition: Nu.* Galerie Ufficio Dell'Arte.

1981 New York, N.Y. *Fleeting Gestures: Treasures of Dance Photography.* International Center of Photography. (travelled internationally)
New York, N.Y. *American Children.* Museum of Modern Art.
Vienna, Austria. *Erweiterte Fotografie.* 5th International Biennale Wien.
San Francisco, Ca. *Germany: The New Vision.* Fraenkel Gallery.
Chicago, Ill. *Avant-Garde Photography in Germany, 1919–1939.* Edwynn Houk Gallery.

1982 Stockholm, Sweden. *New York Panorama.* Stockholm International Art Expo.
San Francisco, Ca. *New Aspects of San Francisco and Los Angeles.* San Francisco Airport Gallery.
New York, N.Y. *Sports.* (General Electric, Fairfield, Connecticut and Freeport-McMoran, Conn.) Museum of Modern Art.
San Francisco, Ca. *Motor Trends.* Grapestake Gallery.
Cambridge, Mass. *Space Framed I: Work by Contemporary Photographers.* Gund Hall Gallery.
San Francisco, Ca. *Cityscapes.* The Fine Arts Museum of San Francisco (Downtown Center).
San Francisco, Ca. *Cancelled Prints.* San Francisco Photo Group.
Fort Worth, Texas. *Masterworks from the Photography Collection.* Amon Carter Museum.

1983 Hartford, Conn. *American Bathing Styles: 1900–1940.* Wadsworth Athaneum.
Tampa, Fla. *Photography in America, 1910–Present.* The Tampa Museum.
New York, N.Y. *People in an Urban Environment.* Seagram Collection.

1984 New York, N.Y. *Fifteenth Anniversary Exhibition.* Castelli Graphics.
San Francisco, Ca. *Photography in California, 1945–1980.* San Francisco Museum of Modern Art.
New York, N.Y. *Signs of the Times: Storefronts and Billboards.* Seagram Collection.
Stamford, Conn. *Autoscape: The Automobile in the American Landscape.* WMAA Fairfield County Branch.
Los Angeles, Ca. *Automobile and Culture.* The Museum of Contemporary Art.
San Francisco, Ca. *Fifth Anniversary Exhibition.* Fraenkel Gallery.
San Francisco, Ca. *Highlights: Selections from the Bank America Corporation Art Collection.* Bank of America World Headquarters.
New York, N.Y. *Selections from the Bank America Corporation Art Collection.* Bank of America Plaza.

1985 London, England. *American Images – American Photography 1945–1980.* Barbican Centre.
Lausanne, Switzerland. *L'Autoportrait à l'âge de la Photographie: Peintres et Photographes en Dialogue avec leur Propre Image.* Musée Cantonal des Beaux-Arts. (travelled to Württembergischer Kunstverein Stuttgart)

BIBLIOGRAPHY

Books and Catalogues on John Gutmann

Humphrey, John. *as i saw it: Photographs by John Gutmann.* San Francisco: San Francisco Museum of Modern Art, 1976.

Kozloff, Max. *The Restless Decade: John Gutmann's Photographs of the Thirties.* Edited by Lew Thomas. New York: Harry N. Abrams Inc., 1984.

References to John Gutmann

Appel, Alfred Jr. *Signs of Life*, 32, 33. New York: Alfred A. Knopf, 1983.

Clisby, Roger, and Harvey Himelfarb, 22, 48. *Forty American Photographers.* Sacramento: E.B. Crocker Art Gallery Press, 1978.

Coke, Van Deren. *Photography 1919–1939*, 23, 48, illust. no. 32. New York: Pantheon Books, 1982.

Fondiller, Harvey V., ed. *The Best of Popular Photography*, illust. "Before Pearl Harbor", plate section, unnumbered. New York: Ziff-Davis Publishing Co., 1979.

Freeman, Tina. *Diverse Images* (from the New Orleans Museum of Art), 63. New York: Amphoto, 1979.

Katzman, Louise. *Photography in California 1945–1980*, 14, 18, 28, 29, 47, 184, 191. New York: Hudson Hills Press/San Francisco Museum of Modern Art, 1984.

Kismaric, Susan. *American Children*, 60. New York: Museum of Modern Art Press, 1980.

MacLeish, Archibald. *Land of the Free*, plate 78. New York: Harcourt, Brace & Co., 1978.

Maloney, T.J., ed. *U.S. Camera 1941.* Vol. 2, 117. New York: Duell, Sloan & Pearce.
U.S. Camera 1942. Vol. 1, 174.
U.S. Camera 1943. Vol. 1, 116.
U.S. Camera 1944. Vol. 1, 71, 73.
U.S. Camera 1947. Vol. 1, 223.

Nash, Graham, Susan Nash, and Graham Howe, eds. *The Graham Nash Collection*, 29, 58. Los Angeles: Nash Press, 1978.

Sandweiss, Martha A. *Masterworks of American Photography*, 144, plate 88. Burmingham: Oxmoor House Inc., 1982.

Thomas, Lew. *Photography and Language*, 0–3. San Francisco: NFS Press, 1976.

Thomas, Lew. *Structural(ism) and Photography*, 7–8. San Francisco: NFS Press, 1978.

Thomas, Lew, and Peter D'Agostino, eds. *Still Photography: The Problematic Model*, 42–45. San Francisco: NFS Press, 1981.

Articles and Reviews on John Gutmann

Albright, Thomas. "A Fresh Look through the Camera Lens." *San Francisco Chronicle*, 12 April 1980.

Albright, Thomas. "Photographs That Suggest: 'As John Gutmann Saw It'." *San Francisco Chronicle*, 19 August 1976.

Ansen, David. "California by Strobe Light." *Newsweek*, 5 March 1984, p. 80.

Atkins, Robert. "John Gutmann: San Francisco 1934–1939." *San Francisco Guardian*, 24 April 1980.

Burnside, Madeline. "John Gutmann/Castelli Graphics." *Arts Magazine*, February 1980, p. 43.

Carroll, Jerry. "John Gutmann, Revisited." *San Francisco Chronicle*, 26 February 1985, pp. 16–17.

Chahroudi, Martha. "Talking Pictures." *Afterimage*, vol. 4, no. 10 (April 1977), pp. 16–17.

Damsker, Matt. "Chronicler of 'The Restless Decade'." *Los Angeles Times*, January 1985.

Fischer, Hal. "Photographers Using Language." *Artweek*, 6 November 1976, p. 1.

Fischer, Hal. "What's What: 'An Outsider's View of the 30s'." *Modern Photography*, February 1977, p. 62.

Frankenstein, Alfred. "The Circus Exhibition." *San Francisco Chronicle*, 1942.

Frankenstein, Alfred. "Face of the Orient." *San Francisco Chronicle*, 1947.

Frankenstein, Alfred. "Wondrous World Exhibition." *San Francisco Chronicle*, 14 May 1941.

Fried, Alexander. "Fine Focus of Feeling." *San Francisco Examiner*, 12 August 1976.

Goin, Peter. "Looking at the Thirties." *Artweek*, 16 June 1984, pp. 11, 12.

Green, Roger. "Strange and Exotic Scenes: 'John Gutmann Photographs'." *The Time – Picayune*, 16 August 1981.

Grundberg, Andy. "Photography: Off Beaten Path," *New York Times*, 10 May 1985.

Handy, Ellen. "John Gutmann/Robert Freidus." *Arts Magazine*, June 1983, p. 34.

Hedgreth, Ted. "San Francisco and Los Angeles." *Scene*, November 1981, p. 54.

Hugunin, James R. "Metropolis." *Afterimage*, December 1984, p. 19.

Jeffrey, Ian. "Current Comment." *Creative Camera*, October 1984, p. 1543.

Kozloff, Max. "The Extravagant Depression: John Gutmann's Photographs of the Thirties." *Art Forum*, November 1982, pp. 34–41.

Krause, Rosalind. "When Words Fail." *October*, November 1981, pp. 100–101.

Linker, Kate. "John Gutmann 'Woman'." *Art Forum*, March 1982, p. 67.

MacDonald, Robert. "Manifestations of Grafitti." *Artweek*, 3 June 1978, p. 20.

Mitchell, Margaretta K. "Profile: 'John Gutmann, American Icons'." *35mm Photography*, Winter 1977, pp. 30–39, 105–106.

Murray, Joan. "As John Gutmann Saw It." *Artweek*, 4 September 1976, p. 5.

Murray, Joan. "The Art of Recording History." *Artweek*, 26 April 1980, p. 11.

Novak, Ralph. "Picks and Pans 'The Restless Decade'." *People Weekly*, 4 June 1984, p. 23.

Paltridge, Blair. "Photos by a Documentary Master." *San Francisco Bay Guardian*, August 1976.

Reynolds, Lisa. "Photos Show Depression's Positive Side." *Daily Aztec*, 12 December 1984.

Scully, Julia. "Seeing Pictures." *Modern Photography*, August 1978, p. 11.

Shiflett, David. "Photos Worth a Million Words." *The Washington Times*, 1984.

Simmons, Charles. "Hello Columbus." *New York Times*, 1 April 1984.

Squiers, Carol. "John Gutmann: A Transported Vision." *Art Forum*, January 1980, pp. 31–35.

Stevens, Nancy. "Question and Answer: John Gutmann." *American Photographer*, May 1981, pp. 48–55.

Tarshis, Jerome. "John Gutmann at Fraenkel and Bank of America." *Art in America*, April 1984, pp. 194, 199.

Thornton, Gene. "Three Ways of Seeing America." *New York Times*, 4 November 1979, pp. 33, 34.

Weber, Jeffrey. "History through the Camera's Eye." *Phoenix* (S.F. State University), 5 May 1977.

Workman, John. "Berenice Abbott/John Gutmann." *Gourmet Guide*, January 1985, pp. 18, 19.

San Francisco Chronicle. "The Old and the New." 14 May 1941.

San Francisco Chronicle. "A Professor Speaks." 7 September 1947.

San Francisco Chronicle (Call Bulletin). Exhibition review, Paul Elder Gallery, San Francisco. (?) 1935.

San Francisco Examiner. Exhibition review, "Colorful America," De Young Museum, San Francisco. (?) 1938.

San Francisco Examiner. Exhibition review, "Gutmann Exhibits Far East Photos," De Young Museum, San Francisco. (?) 1947.

Saturday Evening Post. "Inside Information: 'A Camera is an Unwinking Proctor'." 30 August 1947.

This World. Chronicle Publications Co., San Francisco. 29 August 1976.

Tempo. Exhibition review, Akademie of Arts, Berlin. 12 October 1931.

Transaction: Social Science and Modern Society (Gutmann). July/August 1978.

Articles and Reviews by Unattributed Authors

Specific dates were not available for all articles and reviews. Unverified dates are indicated with a question mark.

Archetype Magazine. "A Portfolio of 5 Photographs." Vol. 3 (1983).

Bay Area Lifestyle. "Exhibition of Gutmann Photography." (?) September 1976.

Berliner Boersen-Courier. (Exhibition review, Gurlitt Galerie, Berlin). 15 April 1931.

Berliner Boersen-Courier. (Exhibition review, Akademie of Arts, Berlin) 11 October 1931.

Berliner Lokal-Anzeiger. (Exhibition review, Akademie of Arts, Berlin). 10 October 1931.

California Living, Magazine of the San Francisco Examiner/Chronicle. "Fresh Eyes in a New Land." 6 April 1980.

Forwaerts. (Exhibition review, Gurlitt Galerie, Berlin). October 1931.

Golden Gator, SFU Campus Newspaper. "Face of the Orient at the De Young Museum." 6 December 1946.

Golden Gator, SFU Campus Newspaper. "San Francisco Cultural Crisis?" (?)

Interview. "Photography at the New York, Paris and Barcelona Galleries." November 1981.

Los Angeles Herald Examiner. "Chilling Images from Pre-War Germany." 5 September 1982.

Manhattan Inc. "Gallery Guide: Noteworthy Shows for Collectors of Contemporary Art." April 1985.

MOPA: 4 (Museum of Photographic Arts, San Diego). "The Restless Decade." 1984.

New Herald Tribune. (Exhibition review, Delphic Studios, New York). 21 February 1937.

Neue Revue. (Exhibition review, Gurlitt Galerie, Berlin). 10 October 1931.

Oakland Tribune. Exhibition review, "Face of the Orient," De Young Museum, San Francisco. (?) 1947.

Oregonian. "Judges in Photo Contest Give Views on Qualities." 19 December 1953.

Print Collectors Newsletter. "John Gutmann: Ten Photographs." March/April 1983.

Assignments and Magazine Illustrations

This comprises a partial listing of photographs issued by Gutmann's agencies, Presse-Foto, Berlin, and Pix, New York. Specific dates were not available for all issues. Unverified dates are indicated with a question mark.

Asia Magazine. "Japanese Sailors." (Cover) November 1939.

Asia Magazine. "Soviet Sailors." (Cover) October 1941.

Beatrys. "Vrouwen in Bengalen." (8 illust.) 12 December 1947.

Beatrys. "Kloosterzusters." (4 illust.) Vol. 6, no. 26.

Berliner Illustrirte Zeitung. "Bufano's Sunyat-sen Statue." (3 illust.) (?)

Billed-Bladet. "Crown Princess Ingrid of Denmark." (Cover; 3 illust.) 16 May 1939.

The Bystander. "Arnold Schoenberg." (1 illust.) 6 January 1937.

Capper's Farmer Magazine. (Cover) April 1943.

CBI Round Up. (Various illust.) 1944–45.

Coast. "Arnold Schoenberg." (1 illust.) July 1938.

Coast. "Egg Basket." (9 illust.) 1938 (?)

Coast. "Cavalcade of the Golden West." (7 illust.) May 1939.

Coast. "Czechoslovakian Day." (9 illust.) August 1939.

Coast. "Pageant of the Pacific." (6 illust.) August 1939.

Coronet. "Chinese Country Market." (1 illust.) November 1949.

Coronet. "Cancer Research." (3 illust.) October 1953.

Coronet. "Ernie Nevers." (4 illust.) December 1954.

Coronet. "Erle Stanley Gardner." (2 illust.) May 1955.

Coronet. (total 24 illust.). 1940, March, April, May, September, November, December; 1941, January, April, June, August, October.

Das Illustrierte Blatt. "Hostile Street Cars." (5 illust.). No. 26.

Der Ring. "General Strike in San Francisco." (6 illust.) (?) 1934.

Der Welt-Spiegel. "Die 'Karlsruhe' in San Francisco." (8 illust.) (?) 1935.

The Detroit News Pictorial. "Chinese in U.S. Raise Money to Fight Japs." (4 illust.) 12 December 1937.

Die Woche. (Berlin) "Olympic Fencing Champion" and "Chinese Cemetery." 18 August 1934.

The Dispatch. Camp Robert, California. (various illustrations) September 1942 to January 1943.

Dresdner Neueste Nachrichten. "Wild West Romance." (5 illust.) (?) 1934.

Enterprise. (Paris) "La Banque de Babitt." (1 illust.) (?) 1948.

The Geographical Magazine. (London) "Market Day in Cheng Kiang." (notes; 8 illust.) (?) 1948.

Hamburger Woche. "Strassenbahnen Rasen um die Wette." (9 illust.) 16 February 1934.

Heute. (Munich) Title unknown. (1 illust.) (?) 1946.

KL Illustratie. "Negrinnen op de Universitett." (Cover; 10 illust.) 13 January 1938.

Ken Magazine. Title unknown. (4 illust.) Vol. 2, no. 1 and no. 10.

Laender Voelker. "Aequator Uberquert." (6 illust.) (?)

The Leader. "Negro Girls Go to College." (5 illust.) 7 June 1941.

Life. "Bufano's Sunyat-sen Statue." (1 illust.) 29 November 1947.

Life. "Pageant of the Pacific." (6 illust.) 6 March 1939.

Life. "Picture of the Week." (1 illust.) 14 December 1942.

Look. "Dorothy Dix." (4 illust.) 28 September 1937.

Mademoiselle. "They Mind Their Own Business." (1 illust.) September 1946.

Mademoiselle. "California Builders." (1 illust.) February 1947.

Mademoiselle. "Industrial Design." (1 illust.) June 1961.

McCall's Magazine. "Chinese Women." (6 illust.) (?)

The National Geographic. "John Gutmann: Kunming Pilgrimage." (20 illust.) February 1950.

The National Geographic. "Mexico City's Multi Familial Houses." (2 illust.) December 1951.

The National Geographic. "Irrigation." (1 illust.) August 1952.

The National Geographic. "Check Up in Bangalore." (1 illust.) (?)

The National Geographic. "Land Route to China." (1 illust.) (?)

Newsweek. "Rookie Bad Dreams." (3 illust.) 18 January 1943.

Newsweek. "Reno Gambling." (2 illust.) (?)

Panorama. "Pilgrimage Der Chinezen." (8 illust.) 19 May 1950.

Parade. "Jap Sailors." (Cover) 7 November 1943.

Parents Magazine. "Heaven at Our Doorstep." (8 illust.) June 1953.

Parents Magazine. "How Our Daughter Spends Her Allowance." (9 illust.) April 1954.

Pix. "Colored Nuns." (8 illust.) 2 September 1939.

Pix. "Frog Jumpers Grand National." (7 illust.) 23 September 1939.

PM Daily. "Ski Jump Champ." (1 illust.) 13 November 1942.

PM Magazine. (New York) "The Old and New in Changing Kunming." (4 illust.) 3 December 1944.

Pour Tous. (France) "Paris, Les Pèlerins Chinois se Rendent à leurs Temples." (6 illust.) (?) 1951.

Redbook. "Mexican Architecture." (1 illust.) (?)

Rotogravure Magazine. (The Detroit Free Press) "New Orleans." (3 illust.) (?)

Rotogravure Magazine. (The Detroit Free Press) "Senorita, California." (5 illust.) (?)

San Francisco Museum of Modern Art Artist's Soap Box Derby. "1936 Soap Box Derby." (text and 6 illust.) 21 May 1978.

The Saturday Evening Post. "Jack Foisie." (1 illust.) 11 May 1946.
"The Impossible Peak." (2 illust.) 28 June 1947.
"Is Education Getting Too Big?" (2 illust.) 6 September 1947.
"Big Bull of the West." (5 illust.) 4 October 1947.
"E.M. Forinki." (1 illust.) 6 March 1948.
"Sandy Pratt." (1 illust.) 10 April 1948.
"Diplomats with Handcuffs." (2 illust.) 10 April 1948.
"California's Biggest Headache." (2 illust.) 14 August 1948.
"I Took Off My White Collar." (3 illust.) 4 September 1948.
"Real Estate's Mighty Atom." (1 illust.) 12 February 1949.
"So You are Going to Retire." (1 illust.) 9 April 1949.
"He Works at 459 Below." (1 illust.) 10 December 1949.
"Mystery of the Deadly Dust." (1 illust.) 17 December 1949.
"Herbert Hoover, International Detective." (3 illust.) 11 March 1950.
"They Want to Rebuild San Francisco Bay." (1 illust.) 18 November 1950.
"Trouble Shooter of the Big House." (4 illust.) 12 May 1951.
"Are You Letting Your Trees Die?" (2 illust.) 12 May 1951.
"Broken Leg Mended Quick." (1 illust.) 2 June 1951.

"Railroad Car Saves Lives." (2 illust.) 4 August 1951.
"To the Stratosphere in a Glider." (3 illust.) 25 August 1951.
"Adventures for Hire." (4 illust.) 6 October 1951.
"Does Lichty Really Hate People?" (1 illust.) 16 February 1952.
"The Easy Way to Get Rich." (1 illust.) 29 March 1952.
"Trucks in the Air." (2 illust.) 28 June 1952.
"The Daring Young Men of Transocean." (5 illust.) 2 August 1952.
"Does Your Town Need a Hospital?" (4 illust.) 13 September 1952.
"Boss of the Sailors Union." (3 illust.) 18 April 1953.
"Retire and Take up Farming." (4 illust.) 23 May 1953.
"He's a Sucker for Nasty Jobs." (4 illust.) 28 November 1953.
"They Escaped from Civilization." (5 illust.) 14 August 1954.
"Your Voice Reveals Your Secrets." (2 illust.) 28 August 1954.
"The Doctor was a Fake." (1 illust.) 13 November 1954.
"I am Glad I went to Washington." (1 illust.) 27 November 1954.
"The Army's Tower of Babel." (4 illust.) 4 December 1954.
"Doctors Crack Down on Doctors." (4 illust.) 12 February 1955.
"I Lost my Voice to Cancer." (3 illust.) 1 September 1956.

Schweizerische Allgemeine Volks-Zeitung. "Auf Einem Chinesischen Markt." (2 illust.) (?)

SE. (Denmark) "Kina Grater och Arbeter." (Cover; 9 illust.) August 1947.

SE. (Denmark) "Ond ande Ger ris at Kina." (9 illust.) 4 September 1949.

Sie Und Er. "Dorothy Dix." (4 illust.) (?)

The Sign. "All the Rice in China." (6 illust.) (?)

Sirene. (Berlin) "Soldaten in USA." (4 illust.) 1 August 1935.

Society. Rutgers, the State University, New Brunswick, N.J. "American Women in the 1930s." (text; 11 illust.) July/August 1978.

The Star Weekly. (Toronto) "On the Eve of Independence for Polyglot India." (3 illust.) 29 December 1945.

The Star Weekly. (Toronto) "The Irrigation of China's Good Earth." (4 illust.) 22 February 1947.

The Star Weekly. (Toronto) "Little Change in Chiang's Land." (3 illust.) 17 January 1948.

The Star Weekly. (Toronto) "Chinese Pilgrimage." (5 illust.) 1 April 1950.

The Star Weekly. (Toronto) "How the Mexican Government Fights Illiteracy." (4 illust.) 20 January 1951.

This Week Magazine. "We'll Lose the Next War." (1 illust.) 11 January 1948.

Time Magazine. "Foreign News, 'Chinese Cave Arsenal'." (1 illust.) 18 December 1944.

Travel Magazine. Title unknown. (2 illust.) January 1939.

U.S. Camera. "Gutmann's Circus." (6 illust.) 1940 (?)

U.S. Camera. Title unknown. (1 illust.) April 1942.

U.S. Camera. Title unknown. (1 illust.) May 1942.

U.S. Camera. "Photo 'Face' China Style." (1 illust.) 1948 (?)

U.S. Camera. "Coeds of the University of California." (1 illust.) January 1949.

U.S. Camera. Title unknown. (1 illust.) February 1949.

Vecko-Journalen. "Kronprinsessan Ingrid." (Cover) 1939.

Weekly Illustrated. "Japan Fleet Enters the Golden Gate." (4 illust.) 29 August 1936.

Welt Im Bild. "Mission School." (8 illust.) no. 45.

Yank Magazine (The Army Weekly). (various illust.) 1944 (?)

General Bibliography

Baltz, Lewis, ed. *Contemporary American Photographic Works.* Houston: The Museum of Fine Arts, 1977.

Baltz, Lewis. *Nevada.* New York: Castelli Graphics, 1978.

Coke, Van Deren. *Avant Garde Photography in Germany 1919–1939.* New York: Pantheon Books, 1982.

Elliott, George P., intro. *Dorothea Lange.* New York: The Museum of Modern Art, 1966.

Frank, Robert. *The Americans.* Introductory essay by Jack Kerouac. New York: Grove Press, 1959. Revised eds. Millerton, New York: Aperture, 1969, 1978.

Green, Jonathan. *American Photography: A Critical History 1945 to the Present.* New York: Harry N. Abrams Inc., 1984.

Hurley, Jack. *Portrait of a Decade: Roy Stryker and the Development of Documentary Photography in the Thirties.* New York: Da Capo Press, 1977.

Kirstein, Lincoln. *Walker Evans: American Photographs.* New York: The Museum of Modern Art, 1938.

Lyons, Nathan, ed. and intro. *Aaron Siskind: Photographer.* Essays by Henry Holmes Smith and Thomas B. Hess. Rochester: George Eastman House, 1965.

Meltzer, Milton. *Dorothea Lange: A Photographer's Life.* New York: Farrar, Straus & Giroux, 1978.

Newhall, Beaumont. *The History of Photography from 1839 to the Present.* rev.ed. New York: The Museum of Modern Art, 1964.

O'Neal, Hank. *Berenice Abbott: American Photographer.* New York: McGraw-Hill Book Co., An Artpress Book, 1982.

O'Neal, Hank, ed. *A Vision Shared: A Classic Portrait of America and Its People, 1935–1943.* New York: St. Martin's Press, 1976.

Tucker, Anne. *Photographic Crossroads: The Photo League.* Ottawa: National Gallery of Canada, 1978. (Special supplement to *Afterimage*)

Willett, John. *Art and Politics in the Weimar Period: The New Sobriety, 1917–1933.* New York: Pantheon Books, 1979.